The INDOOR PLANT & FLOWER EXPERT
Dr. D. G. Hessayon

Published by Expert Books
a division of Transworld Publishers

Copyright © Expert Publications Ltd 2013

The right of Dr. D. G. Hessayon to be identified
as author of this work has been asserted in accordance with sections
77 and 78 of the Copyright Designs and Patents Act 1988.

A catalogue record for this book is available from the British Library

TRANSWORLD PUBLISHERS
61-63 Uxbridge Road, London W5 5SA
a division of the Random House Group Ltd

Contents

The Random House Group Limited supports the Forest Stewardship Council® (FSC®), the leading international forest certification organisation. Our books carrying the FSC label are printed on FSC® certified paper. FSC is the only forest certification scheme supported by the leading environmental organisations, including Greenpeace. Our paper procurement policy can be found at www.randomhouse.co.uk/environment

Reproduction by Spot On Digital Imaging Ltd, Gomm Road, High Wycombe, Bucks HP13 7DJ
Printed and bound in Great Britain by Butler Tanner & Dennis Ltd, Frome

MIX
Paper from responsible sources
FSC® C016897

ISBN 978 1909 663 008

© Expert Publications Ltd 2013

Chapter 1

DECORATING WITH PLANTS AND FLOWERS

According to government figures we spend 2000 million pounds each year on indoor plants and cut flowers. Everywhere you go you will find pots standing on windowsills and sideboards — in countless homes there are vases filled with bunches of flowers.

This is not surprising. We have an inborn desire to have living leaves and flowers close to us, but for a fifth of us there is no garden to satisfy this need. For the rest of us there is a plant-filled garden outside for us to enjoy, but even here there are the long winter months when the garden is asleep.

So for most of us plants in pots and cut flowers in vases are an integral part of our life indoors, but they can do so much more to add to the beauty of our rooms and to satisfy our desire to be creative. Isolated pots of varied but unexciting plants can be turned into an eye-catching focal point by being grouped together. With a little time and some guidance a selection of cut flowers can be turned into an artistic arrangement.

It's up to you. A new world of how to decorate your rooms with living plants and flowers awaits you. The purpose of this book is to show you what is available, the way to take care of your plants and how to prepare your cut flowers, and then provides an insight into the methods and rules followed by the experts to create professional-looking displays.

Chapter 2

INDOOR PLANTS A–Z

You need two separate skills in order to create an outdoor garden which people will admire. The first one is how to choose and care for attractive plants which will succeed in your situation. The second skill you will need is a knowledge of the basic principles of garden design in order to have attractive plant-filled beds and borders. And so it is with roomscaping — the art of using indoor plants and cut flowers to produce professional-style arrangements and displays. As with the outdoor garden the first step is to learn about the living material which is available.

The purpose of this chapter is to show you the range of indoor plants. Included here are all the ones you can expect to find at garden centres, supermarkets, DIY stores and florists. In addition there are many unusual ones which may be worth searching for. The Latin name rather than the common one has been used as the heading for each plant in nearly all cases in this A–Z list. But with a few the well-established popular name (e.g Cineraria, Croton, Geranium) has been used instead and the Latin name included in the index. Some of these plants are very easy to care for, others are very fussy. Don't guess — with every plant on the following pages you will find the Secrets of Success. Following this A–Z list is the Special Groups section — plants listed together as they belong to the same family or share similar characteristics.

Indoor plants are divided into two basic groups. **Pot Plants** which have only a limited display life, and **House Plants** which under the right conditions can be expected to be permanent residents indoors.

So on to the first step to becoming a roomscaper — getting to know the plants which are available.

HOUSE PLANT

A variety which can be expected to live permanently under room conditions, provided that its particular needs are met. The foliage remains alive all year round, but with some flowering types the leaves may not be attractive. The plant may need to be overwintered in an unheated room and in a few cases it may benefit from spending part of the summer outdoors.

POT PLANT

A variety which provides a temporary floral display under room conditions and is removed when the display is over. It may be bought as a plant in bud and/or flower, or as a dormant bulb ready for planting. Most pot plants are discarded after flowering, but some can be stored indoors as leafless plants or dry bulbs, while others can be put in the greenhouse or planted in the garden.

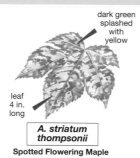

dark green splashed with yellow

leaf 4 in. long

A. striatum thompsonii

Spotted Flowering Maple

TYPES

Abutilon striatum thompsonii is the best-known foliage type — **A. megapotamicum** is a climber grown for its lantern flowers. For bell-like blooms choose a colourful **A. hybridum** variety.

Abutilon megapotamicum

ABUTILON
HOUSE PLANT (see page 5)

The typical Abutilon is a vigorous shrub with large Sycamore-shaped leaves and pendant flowers between early summer and autumn. The blooms are lantern- or bell-shaped. The leaves are often variegated — two varieties are grown for their foliage rather than floral display. This shrub needs room to spread — in late autumn cut back to about half its size.

SECRETS OF SUCCESS

Temperature: Average warmth. Keep cool in winter.
Light: Choose a well-lit spot — a few hours sunlight is beneficial.
Water: Water liberally from spring to late autumn — water sparingly in winter.
Air Humidity: Mist leaves occasionally.
Repotting: Repot in spring every year.
Propagation: Take stem cuttings in spring, or sow seeds for green-leaved varieties.

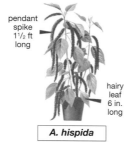

pendant spike 1½ ft long

hairy leaf 6 in. long

A. hispida

Red-hot Catstail

TYPES

The Red-hot Catstail (**Acalypha hispida**) is the usual flowering one — the red or white tails appear in late summer. **A. wilkesiana** (Copperleaf) is a large shrub which bears 2 in. (5 cm) long leaves.

Acalypha wilkesiana

ACALYPHA
HOUSE PLANT (see page 5)

There are two distinct groups. The more popular type bears long tassels of tiny flowers among plain leaves — the other type has colourful foliage with insignificant blooms. All varieties are woody shrubs — remove dead tassels and cut back to half size in late summer. Quick growing, but unfortunately the dryness of the air makes it difficult to overwinter in the average room.

SECRETS OF SUCCESS

Temperature: Warmth is essential — a minimum of 60°F (16°C) at night is necessary.
Light: Bright light with little or no direct sun.
Water: Keep compost moist at all times.
Air Humidity: Moist air is vital. Stand pot on a pebble tray — see page 115.
Repotting: Repot in spring every year.
Propagation: Take stem cuttings in spring.

---

stems 6–12 in. high

leaf 1–1½ in. across — heart-shaped, serrated and velvety

trumpet-like flared flower

A. hybrida

Cupid's Bower

TYPES

Named varieties of **Achimenes hybrida** are easy to find. The species are more difficult to locate — **A. erecta** and **A. longiflora** are both trailers, the tallest species is **A. grandiflora**.

Achimenes hybrida English Waltz

ACHIMENES
POT PLANT (see page 5)

Modern varieties of Achimenes bear masses of large flowers amid glistening hairy leaves. White, blue, purple, pink and yellow ones are available. Each bloom is short-lived, but the flowering season extends from June to October. The stems are weak, making this plant an excellent subject for a hanging basket. For a bushy plant stake stems and pinch out young tips.

SECRETS OF SUCCESS

Temperature: Average warmth — minimum 55°F (13°C).
Light: Brightly lit spot away from summer sun.
Water: Keep compost moist at all times.
Air Humidity: Mist occasionally around but not on leaves.
Care After Flowering: Stop watering once flowering has finished. Water in spring to bring back into growth.
Propagation: Separate rhizomes in early spring and plant several in a compost-filled pot.

Aglaonema Silver Queen

leathery leaf attached to a long stalk

short, bare stem may form when plant is mature

A. modestum

Chinese Evergreen

AGLAONEMA

HOUSE PLANT
(see page 5)

Large, spear-shaped leaves on long stalks are the decorative feature of Aglaonema. The all-green ones will thrive in poorly-lit conditions but the variegated types need brighter light. Young specimens are virtually stemless, but older ones have a short trunk. They are not easy plants to grow — they must be kept well away from draughts and the leaf tips turn brown if the air is too dry.

TYPES

Aglaonema modestum is an all-green variety with 6 in. (15 cm) long leaves. One of the variegated types is usually chosen — these range from **A. commutatum** (nearly all-green) to **A. Silver Queen** (nearly all-white).

SECRETS OF SUCCESS

Temperature: Warm in summer — minimum 60°F (16°C) in winter.
Light: Semi-shade or bright light. Keep away from direct sunlight.
Water: Water thoroughly — sparingly in winter.
Air Humidity: Moist air is necessary — mist regularly.
Repotting: In spring every 3 years.
Propagation: Basal shoots in spring or summer.

ALOE — 88 • AMARYLLIS: see Hippeastrum — 70 • ANANAS — 63

Anigozanthos flavidus

green tubular flower segment

A. manglesii

Kangaroo Paw

ANIGOZANTHOS

HOUSE PLANT
(see page 5)

An Australian plant grown for its unusual flowers. In late spring the long flower stalks appear above the grassy foliage and each one bears woolly blooms with segments which have some resemblance to the paws of a Kangaroo. Despite its exotic appearance it does not need warm conditions — it should do well in a bright airy room.

SECRETS OF SUCCESS

Temperature: Cool or average warmth — at least 40°F (5°C) in winter.
Light: Bright light with little or no direct sun.
Water: Water regularly from spring to autumn. Water more sparingly in winter. Do not use hard water.
Air Humidity: Misting is not necessary.
Repotting: Repot, if necessary, in early summer.
Propagation: Divide plant at repotting time.

TYPES

Anigozanthos flavidus has 1½ in. (4 cm) long flowers on 2 ft (60 cm) high stalks. **A. manglesii** has 3 in. (8 cm) long blooms which are bright red at the base.

Anthurium scherzerianum

glossy, puckered 'flower' 4 in. long

heart-shaped leaf 9 in. long

A. andreanum

Oilcloth Flower

ANTHURIUM

HOUSE PLANT
(see page 5)

Anthuriums are neither cheap nor easy, but they do have an exotic air — large waxy palettes with a colourful tail at the centre. The blooms last for many weeks and the flowering season stretches from spring to autumn. There are two species available for decorating your room. The Crystal Anthurium is one of the most eye-catching of all foliage plants, but it belongs in a conservatory.

SECRETS OF SUCCESS

Temperature: Average warmth — minimum 60°F (16°C) in winter.
Light: Bright in winter — protect from summer sun.
Water: Give a little water every few days to keep compost moist at all times.
Air Humidity: Mist leaves very frequently.
Repotting: Repot in spring every 2 years.
Propagation: Divide plants at repotting time.

TYPES

Anthurium scherzerianum (Flamingo Flower) has 8 in. (20 cm) lance-shaped leaves — the orange tail is curly. **A. andreanum** (Oilcloth Flower) is harder to grow — the tail is straight or arched.

Aphelandra squarrosa Dania

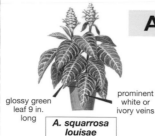

glossy green leaf 9 in. long

prominent white or ivory veins

A. squarrosa louisae

Zebra Plant

TYPES

Aphelandra squarrosa louisae grows about 1½–2 ft (45–60 cm) high with 4–6 in. (10–15 cm) heads of red-tipped yellow flowers. Dwarf varieties include **A. s. Brockfeld** and **Dania**.

APHELANDRA

HOUSE PLANT
(see page 5)

Aphelandra is a dual-purpose plant — there is all-year-round colour from its silvery-veined large leaves, and golden flower cones for about 6 weeks in autumn. It is not surprising that it has been a popular house plant, but it is not easy to keep an Aphelandra under ordinary conditions for more than a few months. Success depends on following the care rules below — use soft, tepid water to keep compost moist.

SECRETS OF SUCCESS

Temperature: Average warmth — minimum 55°F (13°C) in winter.
Light: Brightly lit spot away from direct sun in summer.
Water: Keep compost moist at all times. Reduce watering in winter.
Air Humidity: Mist leaves frequently.
Repotting: Repot in spring every year.
Propagation: Take stem cuttings in spring.

APOROCACTUS — 73

Araucaria heterophylla

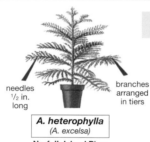

needles ½ in. long

branches arranged in tiers

A. heterophylla
(A. excelsa)

Norfolk Island Pine

TYPE

Araucaria heterophylla is the only species sold as a house plant. It is a slow-growing tree bearing stiff branches covered with prickly needles. Best grown as a specimen plant to ensure symmetrical growth.

ARAUCARIA

HOUSE PLANT
(see page 5)

A handsome and easy-to-grow conifer with many uses — seedlings for the terrarium, small plants for table display and tall trees as bold specimens in halls or large rooms. It flourishes in cool and light conditions, and will grow to about 5 ft (1.5 m). Keep it pot-bound to restrict growth. The major problem is leaf drop and loss of lower branches — the main cause is either hot, dry air or drying out of the compost.

SECRETS OF SUCCESS

Temperature: Average warmth. Keep cool in winter.
Light: Bright light or semi-shade — avoid summer sun.
Water: Water regularly from spring to autumn. Water sparingly in winter.
Air Humidity: Mist leaves occasionally, especially if room is heated in winter. Ventilate in summer.
Repotting: Repot in spring every 3–4 years.
Propagation: Difficult — best to buy plants.

Asparagus plumosus

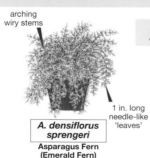

arching wiry stems

A. densiflorus sprengeri

1 in. long needle-like 'leaves'

Asparagus Fern (Emerald Fern)

TYPES

Asparagus plumosus is a compact plant with spreading branches — **A. p. nanus** is a dwarf variety. **A. densiflorus sprengeri** has trailing stems. The Plume Asparagus is **A. meyeri**.

ASPARAGUS

HOUSE PLANT
(see page 5)

The most popular types are the Asparagus Ferns — spreading plants with graceful feathery foliage. Despite their appearance they are not ferns and they are much easier to grow as they are able to adapt to a wide range of light, heat and frequency of watering. The sole representative of the Plume Asparagus group is A. meyeri — its stiff 'bottle brush' stems providing contrast in house plant arrangements.

SECRETS OF SUCCESS

Temperature: Average warmth — minimum 50°F (10°C).
Light: Bright or semi-shady conditions. Keep away from direct sunlight.
Water: Water regularly from spring to autumn — occasionally water from below. Water sparingly in winter.
Air Humidity: Mist occasionally, especially in winter.
Repotting: Repot in spring every year.
Propagation: Divide plants at any time of the year.

Aspidistra elatior variegata

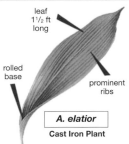

leaf
1½ ft
long

rolled
base

prominent
ribs

A. elatior

Cast Iron Plant

TYPES

The dark green leaves of **Aspidistra elatior** withstand both air pollution and neglect but are scorched by sunlight. A cream-striped variety (**A. elatior variegata**) is available — it is more attractive but less hardy.

ASPIDISTRA
HOUSE PLANT
(see page 5)

An old favourite, once maligned but now regaining some of its former popularity. The common name of Cast Iron Plant indicates its tolerance of neglect. It can withstand periods of dryness at the roots if the temperature is not too high, but it does have two strong dislikes. It will die if the soil is constantly saturated and it will be harmed by frequent repotting.

SECRETS OF SUCCESS

Temperature: Average warmth. Keep cool but frost-free in winter.
Light: Extremely tolerant, but not of direct sun.
Water: Water regularly from spring to autumn. Water sparingly in winter.
Air Humidity: Can stand dry air but wash leaves occasionally.
Repotting: Repot in spring every 4–5 years.
Propagation: Divide plants at repotting time.

ASPLENIUM — 77

Aucuba japonica variegata

serrated
leaves

leaf
5 in.
long

A. japonica variegata

Spotted Laurel

TYPES

Aucuba japonica is an outdoor shrub with leathery, glossy foliage. Only the variegated types are used indoors. **Variegata** is the most popular — **goldiana** (almost all-yellow) is the most colourful.

AUCUBA
HOUSE PLANT
(see page 5)

A useful plant for a shady spot which is not heated in winter. It is not suitable for hot and dry locations as serious leaf fall will occur. Brown edges in summer mean that you are not watering frequently enough. When small, the Spotted Laurel can be stood on a windowsill or table. It will reach 5 ft (1.5 m) or more, but it can be kept in check by pruning in the spring.

SECRETS OF SUCCESS

Temperature: Average warmth. Keep cool in winter — minimum temperature 40°F (4°C).
Light: Bright light or shade — avoid direct sun in summer.
Water: Water regularly from spring to autumn. Water sparingly in winter.
Air Humidity: Mist plant frequently, especially in winter.
Repotting: Repot in spring every year.
Propagation: Take stem cuttings in late summer.

HANDLE WITH CARE

Very few house plants pose any problems, but it is useful to know which ones can have undesirable effects if eaten or handled.

CACTI .... Hooked spines
DATURA .... All parts poisonous
DIEFFENBACHIA .... Poisonous sap
NERIUM .... All parts poisonous
POINSETTIA .... Irritating sap
PRIMULA OBCONICA .... Irritating leaves
SOLANUM CAPSICASTRUM .... Poisonous berries
YUCCA ALOIFOLIA .... Sword-like leaves

Begonia tuberhybrida
Sugar Candy

flower
2 in.
across

glossy,
round
leaf
3 in.
across

red
stems

B. Fireglow

BEGONIA POT PLANT VARIETIES — POT PLANT (see page 5)

There are three groups of Begonias which are grown for their temporary floral display. The most spectacular are the Tuberous Begonias and Basket Begonias which are raised from tubers for summer flowers. The Lorraine Hybrids were once popular — these weak-stemmed varieties bloom in winter. The Elatior Hybrids are the usual choice and are available in flower all year round.

TYPES

Begonia tuberhybrida varieties have 1 ft (30 cm) blooms — **B. t. Multiflora** types have 2 in. (5 cm) flowers. Elatior Hybrids also have 2 in. (5 cm) flowers — **B. Fireglow** is bright red.

SECRETS OF SUCCESS

Temperature: Average warmth — minimum 55°F (13°C) in winter.
Light: A bright spot away from direct sunlight.
Water: Water freely when plant is in flower, but do not keep compost constantly moist.
Air Humidity: Moist air is necessary — mist leaves occasionally.
Care After Flowering: Keep tubers — discard other types.

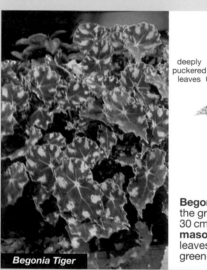

Begonia Tiger

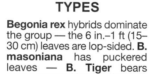

deeply
puckered
leaves

leaf
6 in.
long

B. masoniana

Iron Cross Begonia

BEGONIA FOLIAGE VARIETIES — HOUSE PLANT (see page 5)

These Begonias are grown for their decorative foliage — any flowers which appear are insignificant. The off-centre heart-shaped leaves of the colourful B. rex varieties are easy to recognise, but there are many other shapes and colours. Compact varieties are available as well as tall-growing ones. These foliage types are usually short lived.

TYPES

Begonia rex hybrids dominate the group — the 6 in.–1 ft (15–30 cm) leaves are lop-sided. **B. masoniana** has puckered leaves — **B. Tiger** bears green-spotted bronze foliage.

SECRETS OF SUCCESS

Temperature: Average warmth — minimum 60°F (16°C) in winter.
Light: A bright spot away from direct sunlight.
Water: Keep compost moist from spring to autumn — water sparingly in winter.
Air Humidity: Moist air is necessary — mist air around but not on the leaves.
Repotting: Repot in spring to retain leaf colour.
Propagation: Divide plants at repotting time.

Begonia fuchsioides

single or
double
flower
1 in.
across

round, waxy
leaf 2 in.
across

B. semperflorens

Wax Begonia

BEGONIA EVERGREEN VARIETIES — HOUSE PLANT (see page 5)

The species in this group are less spectacular when in bloom than the large-flowered tuberous ones, but they keep their leaves all year round. The height range is enormous — varying from 6 in. (15 cm) bushes to 10 ft (3 m) climbers. By far the most popular one is the Wax Begonia which blooms freely for several months. Avoid exposure to really cold nights, too much water and too much sun.

TYPES

Bushy varieties include **Begonia semperflorens** (Wax Begonia) with 1 in. (2.5 cm) wide blooms, and the more difficult **B. fuchsioides**. There are also trailing types and tall-growing cane-stemmed varieties.

SECRETS OF SUCCESS

Temperature: Average warmth — minimum 60°F (16°C) in winter.
Light: A bright spot away from direct sunlight.
Water: Keep compost moist between spring and autumn — water sparingly in winter.
Air Humidity: Moist air — mist around but not on the leaves.
Repotting: Repot, if necessary, in spring.
Propagation: Take stem cuttings in spring or summer.

Beloperone guttata

curved
flower-head
4 in. long

oval
leaf
2 in.
long

B. guttata

Shrimp Plant

BELOPERONE
HOUSE PLANT
(see page 5)

An easy-to-grow shrubby plant which bears salmon-coloured, prawn-shaped flower-heads at the end of arching stems. The blooms appear nearly all year round, and the simple requirements are warm days, cool nights and a sunny windowsill. When young, remove some of the first flowers to make sure that a vigorous bush is formed. Cut the plant back to half size each spring.

TYPE

Beloperone guttata is the only species grown. Stems and leaves are downy, and each flower-head is made up of bracts through which small white flowers protrude.

SECRETS OF SUCCESS

Temperature: Average warmth. Keep cool in winter.
Light: Some direct sun is essential.
Water: Water liberally from spring to late autumn. Water sparingly in winter.
Air Humidity: Mist leaves occasionally.
Repotting: Repot, if necessary, in spring.
Propagation: Stem cuttings root easily.

BILLBERGIA — 63 • BLECHNUM — 77

**Bougainvillea buttiana
Mrs Butt**

pink or
purple
flower
1 in.
across

leaf
narrow
and
smooth

stems
woody
and
spiny

B. glabra

Paper Flower

BOUGAINVILLEA
HOUSE PLANT
(see page 5)

It is difficult to grow Bougainvillea under ordinary room conditions. A well-grown plant brought indoors will bloom profusely in spring and summer on the windowsill, after which you have the challenge of trying to make it bloom next season. Prune in autumn and reduce watering. Keep the plant cool throughout the winter and then increase temperature and watering once spring arrives.

TYPES

The basic species is **Bougainvillea glabra**, but its hybrids are more popular. Top of the list is the large-leaved large-flowered **B. buttiana Mrs Butt** (rose-crimson).

SECRETS OF SUCCESS

Temperature: Warm in summer. Keep cool in winter.
Light: Choose sunniest spot available.
Water: Keep compost moist in spring and summer — almost dry in winter.
Air Humidity: Mist leaves if room is heated.
Repotting: Repot, if necessary, in spring.
Propagation: Take stem cuttings in summer. Use a rooting hormone and provide bottom heat.

BRASSIA — 80

Browallia major

drooping
leaf 2 in.
long

star-shaped
tubular flower
2 in. across

B. speciosa

Bush Violet

BROWALLIA
POT PLANT
(see page 5)

The Bush Violet is a tender annual which is usually bought in flower, but it can be easily raised from seed. Sow in early spring for summer flowers or delay sowing until summer for winter flowering. It branches very close to compost-level — pinch out the growing tips occasionally to promote bushiness. With proper care the flowering period will last for many weeks — keep the pot in a cool room. Feed regularly and pick off the flowers as they fade.

TYPES

Browallia speciosa bears violet flowers with white throats. The stems are weak — stake to maintain bushy shape. Varieties **major** (large, blue-violet) and **alba** (white) are available.

SECRETS OF SUCCESS

Temperature: Cool during the flowering season.
Light: Bright light with some direct sun.
Water: Keep compost moist at all times.
Air Humidity: Mist leaves occasionally.
Care After Flowering: Plant should be discarded.
Propagation: Sow seeds in spring or summer.

BRUGMANSIA: see Datura — 22

Brunfelsia calycina

fragrant white-eyed flower 2 in. across

leathery leaf 3 in. long

B. calycina

Yesterday, Today and Tomorrow

TYPE

Brunfelsia calycina is an evergreen which bears clusters of flowers. These blooms are borne nearly all year round. Place outdoors occasionally during the day in summer.

BRUNFELSIA
HOUSE PLANT (see page 5)

A slow-growing evergreen shrub with an unusual common name — Yesterday, Today and Tomorrow. It describes the changing flower colours — yesterday's purple, today's pale violet and tomorrow's white. Success depends on putting the plant in a room where there will be no sudden changes in temperature. With care it will grow to 2 ft (60 cm).

SECRETS OF SUCCESS

Temperature: Average warmth — minimum 50°F (10°C) in winter.
Light: Semi-shade in summer — a well-lit spot in winter with a little direct sunlight.
Water: Water freely from spring to autumn — sparingly in winter. Use soft water.
Air Humidity: Mist leaves in summer.
Repotting: Repot, if necessary, in spring.
Propagation: Take stem cuttings in summer.

Caladium hortulanum candidum

paper-thin decorative leaves

C. hortulanum

Angel's Wings (Elephant's Ears)

TYPES

Caladium hortulanum Rosebud is a typical example of the many red/green varieties — for green/white foliage choose **candidum** or **Seagull**. **C. picturatum** has narrow leaves.

CALADIUM
POT PLANT (see page 5)

The striking arrow-shaped leaves are spectacular — paper thin and beautifully marked and coloured. This attractive foliage, however, is not permanent and lasts only from late spring to early autumn. Caladiums can be raised by planting tubers in spring but it is more usual to buy a Caladium plant. Protect it from cold on the way home. There are scores of varieties but they are usually sold unnamed.

SECRETS OF SUCCESS

Temperature: Warm — minimum 60°F (16°C).
Light: A moderately well-lit spot away from direct sunlight.
Water: Water freely during the growing season.
Air Humidity: Mist leaves frequently, especially in spring.
After Care: Stop watering when foliage dies. Keep dry and replant tubers in spring. Small 'daughter' tubers can be potted up separately.

Calathea crocata

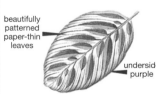

beautifully patterned paper-thin leaves

underside purple

C. makoyana
(Maranta makoyana)

Peacock Plant

TYPES

Calathea makoyana is the showiest and most popular foliage species — the 1 ft (30 cm) long leaves are borne erect. **C. crocata** bears heads of long-lasting flowers in spring.

CALATHEA
HOUSE PLANT (see page 5)

The Calatheas are grown for their ornately patterned leaves which have coloured veins or prominent blotches on a background ranging from white to dark green. There is an exception — C. crocata is grown for its flowers. Calatheas are not easy to grow. Protection against direct sunlight is essential, and both high air humidity and winter warmth are required. Cold draughts can be fatal.

SECRETS OF SUCCESS

Temperature: Average warmth — minimum 60°F (16°C).
Light: Partial shade — move to a well-lit spot in winter.
Water: Keep compost moist — reduce watering in winter. Use soft water.
Air Humidity: Mist leaves regularly.
Repotting: Repot in spring every 2 years.
Propagation: Divide plants at repotting time.

Calceolaria herbeohybrida

hairy leaf 4–6 in. across

pouch-like flower 1–2 in. across

C. herbeohybrida

Slipper Flower

TYPES

Calceolaria herbeohybrida is the only popular species. The plants grow about 1¹/₂ ft (45 cm) high and the pouch-shaped flowers are available in several colours — yellow, orange, red or white with dark-coloured blotches.

CALCEOLARIA
POT PLANT (see page 5)

The Slipper Flower is a springtime favourite. The soft leaves are large and hairy and the flowers are curious and colourful. The plant is bought in flower (propagation is a skilled job best left to the nurseryman) and should last about a month. Provide moist conditions, keep away from draughts and keep careful watch for aphids.

SECRETS OF SUCCESS

Temperature: Cool — 50°–60°F (10°–16°C) is ideal.
Light: Bright light away from direct sunlight.
Water: Keep compost moist at all times.
Air Humidity: Stand the pot on a pebble tray (see page 115) or surround with moist peat. Mist occasionally but do not wet the leaves.
Care After Flowering: Plant should be discarded.
Propagation: Difficult — sow seeds in summer in a cool greenhouse for flowering next year.

Callisia elegans

leaf 1–1¹/₂ in. long

underside purple

C. elegans

Striped Inch Plant

TYPES

Callisia elegans has small leaves and long stems — the upper surface of the foliage is dull and boldly striped with white lines. **C. fragrans** turns pink in bright light.

CALLISIA
HOUSE PLANT (see page 5)

Callisia is a member of the Tradescantia family — one of the Wandering Jews which are a popular choice for clothing the sides of hanging baskets. The leaves clasp the creeping or trailing stems — the flowers which occasionally appear are of little decorative value. Pinch out tips regularly to encourage bushiness.

SECRETS OF SUCCESS

Temperature: Average warmth — minimum 45°–50°F (7°–10°C) in winter.
Light: Bright light is essential.
Water: Water thoroughly from spring to autumn. Water sparingly in winter.
Air Humidity: Mist leaves occasionally.
Repotting: Repot, if necessary, in spring.
Propagation: Take stem cuttings between spring and autumn.

CAMBRIA — 80

Camellia japonica Florentine

glossy leaf 4 in. long

single or double flower 3–5 in. across

C. japonica

Camellia

TYPES

Camellia japonica is the basic species. Well-known varieties include **Adolphe Audusson** (red, semi-double), **Alba Simplex** (white, single) and **Pink Perfection** (pink, double).

CAMELLIA
HOUSE PLANT (see page 5)

It is a waste of time and money to try to grow this temperamental shrub if the conditions are not right. The room must be cool and airy. Buds appear in profusion in early spring, but they will rapidly drop if the plant is moved or if there is a sudden change in temperature or soil moisture. Stand the pot out-doors during summer.

SECRETS OF SUCCESS

Temperature: Cool — keep in the 45°–60°F (7°–16°C) range.
Light: Brightly lit spot away from direct sun in summer.
Water: Keep compost moist at all times but never waterlogged. Use soft water.
Air Humidity: Mist leaves frequently.
Repotting: Repot in spring — do not repot unless root bound.
Propagation: Take stem cuttings in summer. Use a rooting hormone and provide bottom heat.

grey-green
hairy stems

star-shaped
flower
1½ in.
wide

C. isophylla

Italian Bellflower

TYPES

Campanula isophylla is the favourite species. The stems grow about 1 ft (30 cm) long and the pale blue or mauve flowers are 1½ in. (4 cm) wide. A white variety (**alba**) is available.

Campanula isophylla alba

CAMPANULA
HOUSE PLANT (see page 5)

The grey-green stems tumble down the sides of the pot and during summer they bear a profusion of small star-shaped flowers. For generations it has been grown on windowsills and sideboards. Remove the flowers once they have faded in order to prolong the flowering season. It is an easy plant to care for — once flowering is over cut back the stems and keep the pots cool and fairly dry during the winter rest period.

SECRETS OF SUCCESS

Temperature: Cool or average warmth — minimum 45°F (7°C).
Light: A bright spot away from direct sun in summer.
Water: Keep compost moist at all times — reduce watering in winter.
Air Humidity: Mist leaves occasionally.
Repotting: Repot, if necessary, in spring.
Propagation: Take stem cuttings or sow seeds in spring.

CANNA — 67

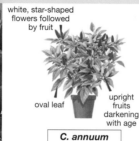

white, star-shaped
flowers followed
by fruit

oval leaf

upright
fruits
darkening
with age

C. annuum

Christmas Pepper

TYPES

Capsicum annuum grows about 1 ft (30 cm) tall with oval 1½ in. (4 cm) long leaves. The variety **Christmas Greeting** has 1 in. (2.5 cm) long fruits — **Red Missile** fruits are twice as long.

Capsicum annuum Red Missile

CAPSICUM
POT PLANT (see page 5)

One of the common names for this plant is Christmas Pepper as large quantities are sold in December to provide festive colour. It is grown for its decorative fruits rather than its leaves or flowers. These oval or pointed fruits are green at first and turn to yellow, orange or red. With care they should remain attractive for 2 or 3 months. Some direct sunlight is essential, and so is regular misting.

SECRETS OF SUCCESS

Temperature: Cool or average warmth — minimum 55°F (13°C).
Light: Brightly lit spot with morning or afternoon sun.
Water: Keep compost moist at all times. Water occasionally by the immersion method.
Air Humidity: Mist leaves frequently.
Care After Fruiting: Plant should be discarded.
Propagation: Difficult — sow seeds in early spring.

CARYOTA — 86

LIME HATERS

Most house plants prefer water which is lime-free but in general they will tolerate reasonably hard water and a compost which contains lime. However, there are a few types which cannot tolerate lime and so it is necessary to use an ericaceous compost when transplanting and soft water when watering. These lime haters are listed below.

APHELANDRA
AZALEA
BRUNFELSIA
CAMELLIA
CITRUS MITIS

ERICA
GARDENIA
HYDRANGEA (blue)
PLATYCERIUM
STEPHANOTIS

Catharanthus roseus

star-shaped
flower 1–1½ in.
across

oval
leaf
2 in.
long

C. roseus
(Vinca rosea)

Madagascar Periwinkle

TYPES

Catharanthus roseus bears white, lavender or rose flowers with a darker-coloured throat. It is compact and the leaves have a pale midrib.

CATHARANTHUS

**POT PLANT
(see page 5)**

You will probably have to raise this uncommon house plant from seed if you want to see what it looks like — few nurserymen offer it for sale. Seed sown in late winter will produce plants which start to flower in late spring and you can expect them to stay in bloom until the autumn. The Periwinkle-like flowers form at the stem tips and may cover much of the shiny foliage. Catharanthus is an easy plant to grow — it should be more popular.

SECRETS OF SUCCESS

Temperature: Average warmth — minimum 50°F (10°C).
Light: Bright light with some sun.
Water: Keep compost moist at all times.
Air Humidity: Mist leaves occasionally.
Care After Flowering: Plant should be discarded.
Propagation: Sow seeds in late winter or early spring.

CATTLEYA — 80

Celosia cristata

conical
flower-head
6–9 in. long

lance-shaped
leaf 4 in.
long

C. plumosa

Plume Flower

TYPES

Celosia plumosa bears its red or yellow plumes in summer — dwarfs (8–12 in./20–30 cm) such as **Golden Plume** and **Kewpie** are available. **C. cristata** has a convoluted flower-head.

CELOSIA

**POT PLANT
(see page 5)**

There are two distinct types. Celosia plumosa has feathery plumes — C. cristata has a curious velvety 'cockscomb'. Celosia is sometimes sold for bedding outdoors, but it can be kept in full flower for many weeks indoors. Some direct sunlight is essential, and regular feeding is necessary. It needs cool, airy conditions to prolong the flowering season. The usual height is 1½–2 ft (45–60 cm). Celosia can be raised from seed, but it is usually more satisfactory to buy nursery-grown plants.

SECRETS OF SUCCESS

Temperature: Cool — 50°–60°F (10°–16°C) is ideal.
Light: As much light as possible. Shade from hot sun.
Water: Keep compost moist at all times.
Air Humidity: Mist leaves occasionally.
Care After Flowering: Plant should be discarded.
Propagation: Sow seeds in spring at 60°–65°F (16°–18°C).

CEREUS — 73 • CEROPEGIA — 88 • CHAMAECEREUS — 73 • CHAMAEDOREA — 84 • CHAMAEROPS — 84 • CHIONODOXA — 61

**Chlorophytum comosum
vittatum**

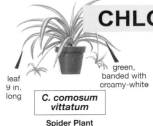

leaf
9 in.
long

green,
banded with
creamy-white

**C. comosum
vittatum**

**Spider Plant
(St. Bernard's Lily)**

TYPES

The basic species is **Chlorophytum comosum** which has plain green leaves. There are several varieties. **Vittatum** has green leaves with a central cream band — **variegatum** has white-edged green leaves.

CHLOROPHYTUM

**HOUSE PLANT
(see page 5)**

It is not surprising that the Spider Plant is so popular — it is extremely adaptable, it will grow in hot or cool rooms, in sun or shade and tolerates dry air. The quick-growing wiry stems bear arching leaves. In spring and summer the cascading stems bear small white flowers followed by tiny plantlets. If left to grow these plantlets add to the display — if removed they can be potted up to provide new plants.

SECRETS OF SUCCESS

Temperature: Average warmth — minimum 45°F (7°C) in winter.
Light: A well-lit spot away from direct sun.
Water: Water liberally from spring to autumn. Water sparingly in winter.
Air Humidity: Mist leaves occasionally in summer.
Repotting: Repot, if necessary, in spring.
Propagation: Divide plants at repotting time.

CHRYSALIDOCARPUS — 43

CHRYSANTHEMUM

**POT PLANT
(see page 5)**

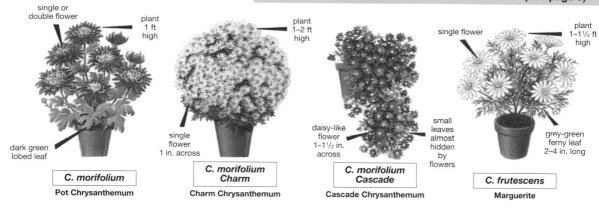

single or double flower — plant 1 ft high

dark green lobed leaf

C. morifolium
Pot Chrysanthemum

plant 1–2 ft high

single flower 1 in. across

C. morifolium Charm
Charm Chrysanthemum

daisy-like flower 1–1½ in. across

C. morifolium Cascade
Cascade Chrysanthemum

single flower

plant 1–1½ ft high

small leaves almost hidden by flowers

grey-green ferny leaf 2–4 in. long

C. frutescens
Marguerite

Chrysanthemum morifolium

TYPES

Chrysanthemum morifolium (Pot Chrysanthemum) bears 4 in. (10 cm) long lobed leaves and single or double blooms which are 2½–4 in. (5–10 cm) wide. Pot Chrysanthemums are bought by colour and not variety — all colours apart from blue are available. **Charm** and **Cascade** Chrysanthemums are not common — they are varieties of C. morifolium which bear masses of small flowers. **C. frutescens** is the summer-flowering Marguerite bearing 2 in. (5 cm) wide blooms. The 1½ ft (45 cm) plants are usually bought in spring. White is the usual colour of the daisy-like flowers, but yellow and pink varieties are available.

Pot Chrysanthemums are popular indoor plants which can be bought at any time of the year. At the nursery chemicals are used to stunt growth, and the flowering date is controlled by keeping them in the dark for part of the day. In this way a plant less than 1 ft (30 cm) high is produced in full flower. Some early morning or evening sun is beneficial — they should stay in flower for 6–8 weeks if bought when there are lots of buds and few open flowers.

SECRETS OF SUCCESS

Temperature: Cool — 50°–60°F (10°–16°C) is ideal.
Light: Bright light is essential, but Pot Chrysanthemums must be shaded from midday sun.
Water: Keep compost moist at all times. It may be necessary to water several times each week.
Air Humidity: Mist leaves occasionally.
Care After Flowering: Most plants are discarded, but Pot Chrysanthemums can be planted out in the garden where they will revert to their natural growth habit.
Propagation: Raising Pot Chrysanthemums is for the professional. Marguerites — take stem cuttings in early summer. Cascade and Charm Chrysanthemums — sow seeds in spring.

Senecio cruentus Spring Glory

daisy-like flower 1–3 in. across

plant 9 in.–2½ ft tall

underside usually purple

heart-shaped leaf up to 8 in. across

Senecio cruentus
(Senecio hybridus)
Cineraria

TYPES

The Grandiflora group of **Senecio cruentus** hybrids (1½ ft/45 cm) bears 8 in. (20 cm) wide clusters of 2–3 in. (5–8 cm) flowers. The Multiflora Nana group produces 1–2 in. (3–5 cm) blooms.

CINERARIA

**POT PLANT
(see page 5)**

Cinerarias (Latin name Senecio cruentus) are bought in winter or early spring, and should last for 4–6 weeks. Buy plants with some open flowers and masses of unopened buds. The Stellata group (2 ft/60 cm) are the tallest, the Grandifloras are the showiest, and the Multiflora Nana group are the most compact. Cineraria can be a disappointing plant — they will collapse in a week or two in a hot room or if watered incorrectly.

SECRETS OF SUCCESS

Temperature: Cool — 45°–55°F (7°–13°C) is ideal.
Light: Bright light away from direct sunlight.
Water: Keep compost moist at all times with tepid water.
Air Humidity: Use a pebble tray (page 115) or surround with damp peat. Mist occasionally.
Care After Flowering: Discard plant.
Propagation: Sow seed — not easy.

Cissus rhombifolia

leaf
4 in.
long

glossy
surface

C. antarctica
Kangaroo Vine

TYPES

Cissus antarctica (Kangaroo Vine) grows about 10 ft (3 m) tall. Use **C. a. minima** where space is limited — **C. striata** is a red-stemmed trailer. **C. rhombifolia** (**Rhoicissus rhomboidea**) is very popular — each leaf is made up of 3 leaflets.

CISSUS
**HOUSE PLANT
(see page 5)**

This climber is a member of the Grape family — a true vine which clings to supports by means of tendrils. Grape Ivy (C. rhombifolia) is one of the most tolerant of all house plants, surviving sun or shade, hot or cold air, and dry or moist surroundings. Kangaroo Vine is a little less tolerant, suffering in bright sun. All vines need good drainage — pinch out stem tips to induce bushiness.

SECRETS OF SUCCESS

Temperature: Cool or average warmth — minimum 45°F (7°C).
Light: Brightly lit spot away from direct sunlight.
Water: Water liberally from spring to autumn. Water sparingly in winter.
Air Humidity: Mist leaves occasionally.
Repotting: Repot, if necessary, in spring.
Propagation: Take stem cuttings in spring or summer.

Citrus mitis

leathery
leaf
3 in.
long

white fragrant
flowers followed
by small fruit —
flowers and fruit
appear all year
round

C. mitis
Calamondin Orange

TYPES

Citrus mitis (**Citrofortunella microcarpa**) is a 4 ft (1.2 m) bush with white fragrant flowers and 2 in. (5 cm) wide bitter oranges. Pollinate the flower by dabbing with cotton wool.

CITRUS
**HOUSE PLANT
(see page 5)**

The dwarf Citrus bush with its flowers and fruit at your garden centre is an obvious temptation, but it will not be a good buy if you cannot provide a sunny window and a draught-free site. Cool but not cold conditions are required in winter. The Calamondin Orange is the popular choice and is also the best one — the flowers and fruit appear nearly all year round.

SECRETS OF SUCCESS

Temperature: Average warmth. Minimum 50°F (10°C) in winter.
Light: Choose the sunniest spot available, but protect from midday summer sun.
Water: Keep compost moist all year round. Use soft water.
Air Humidity: Mist leaves occasionally.
Repotting: Repot, if necessary, in spring.
Propagation: Take stem cuttings in spring. Use a rooting hormone and provide bottom heat.

CLEISTOCACTUS — 73

Clerodendrum thomsoniae

inflated
flower
1 in.
long —
white
with
red tip

leaf
5 in.
long

C. thomsoniae
Glory Bower

TYPES

Clerodendrum thomsoniae has long, weak stems — pinch out tips for room display. Allow stems to trail or to twine around an upright support. The leaves have a quilted look.

CLERODENDRUM
**HOUSE PLANT
(see page 5)**

The Glory Bower is usually regarded as a greenhouse plant, its climbing stems reaching 8 ft (2.5 m) or more. By pruning in winter, however, it can be trained as a bush or hanging basket plant. The flowers appear in summer among the heart-shaped leaves. In summer it requires high air humidity, good light and warmth — in winter it must be given a rest with infrequent watering and cool conditions.

SECRETS OF SUCCESS

Temperature: Warm or average warmth. Keep cool (55°–60°F/13°–16°C) in winter.
Light: Brightly lit spot away from direct sunlight.
Water: Keep compost moist at all times throughout spring and summer — water very sparingly in winter.
Air Humidity: Mist leaves frequently.
Repotting: Repot in spring every year.
Propagation: Take stem cuttings in spring.

Clivia miniata

bell-shaped flower 3 in. across

strap-like leaf 1½ ft long

C. miniata

Kaffir Lily

TYPES

Clivia miniata bears clusters of 10–20 flowers in early spring on top of a tall stalk. Orange, red, yellow and cream varieties are available.

CLIVIA
HOUSE PLANT (see page 5)

An old favourite which will fail to bloom year after year if it is left in a heated room in winter or if the watering rules are not followed. It needs space. It needs winter rest — an unheated room, no fertilizer and just enough water to prevent wilting. And it needs to be undisturbed — don't move the pot when in bud or flower.

SECRETS OF SUCCESS

Temperature: Cool or average warmth. Keep cool (40°–50°F/5°–10°C) in winter.
Light: Bright light — avoid direct sun in summer.
Water: Water moderately from spring to autumn. Water sparingly from late autumn until stalk is 4–6 in. (10–15 cm) high.
Air Humidity: Sponge leaves occasionally.
Repotting: Repot, if necessary, after flowering.
Propagation: Divide plants at repotting time.

COCOS — 85 • CODIAEUM: see Croton — 19

Coleus Salmon Lace

saw-edged leaves

stems square in cross section

C. blumei

Flame Nettle

TYPES

There is a wide choice of **Solenostemon blumei** hybrids. There are varieties with ruffled, frilly or the standard nettle-like leaves, dwarf types (e.g **Sabre**) and both single-coloured and multicoloured ones.

COLEUS
POT PLANT (see page 5)

Coleus (Latin name Solenostemon blumei) provides the easiest and cheapest way to add brightly-coloured foliage to a house plant collection — raise the plants from cuttings or seeds, or buy from the bedding plants bench. The bushy 1 ft (30 cm) plants need pinching regularly to stop them becoming leggy. They can be overwintered but it is much better to treat them as pot plants and renew the stock each spring.

SECRETS OF SUCCESS

Temperature: Average warmth — minimum 50°F (10°C).
Light: Give as much light as possible, but shade from summer midday sun.
Water: Keep compost moist at all times — reduce in winter.
Air Humidity: Mist leaves frequently.
Repotting: Cut back and repot in spring.
Propagation: Take cuttings or sow seeds.

Columnea gloriosa

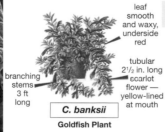

leaf smooth and waxy, underside red

tubular 2½ in. long scarlet flower — yellow-lined at mouth

branching stems 3 ft long

C. banksii

Goldfish Plant

TYPES

Columnea banksii has smooth leaves — the hybrid **C. Stavanger** has larger flowers. The hairy-leaved types are more difficult — **C. gloriosa** bears Gloriosa-like (p.29) flowers. **C. microphylla** has tiny leaves.

COLUMNEA
HOUSE PLANT (see page 5)

This trailing plant bears abundant yellow, orange or red flowers in winter and early spring — it belongs in a hanging basket or on a shelf where its stems can hang freely. It is not an easy plant to grow — a moist atmosphere and cool winter nights are essential. Columnea banksii is the most popular species and is also the easiest to grow. Trim stems back once flowering is over.

SECRETS OF SUCCESS

Temperature: Average warmth — minimum 55°F (13°C).
Light: Bright light — avoid direct sunshine.
Water: Keep compost moist at all times — water sparingly in winter.
Air Humidity: Mist leaves frequently.
Repotting: Repot in late spring every 2 years.
Propagation: Take stem cuttings after flowering. Use a rooting hormone and provide bottom heat.

Cordyline terminalis Kiwi

3–4 ft high

arching leaves

C. australis
(Draceana indivisa)
**Cabbage Tree
(Grass Palm)**

TYPES

Cordyline terminalis (Ti Plant) grows about 2 ft (60 cm) high — the leaves are long and lance-shaped. **C. t. Rededge** (red-streaked green) is the favourite one. **C. australis** is the popular tall species.

CORDYLINE
HOUSE PLANT (see page 5)

The Cordylines are popular specimen plants for living rooms, hallways and public buildings. Most of them are false palms — a crown of arching leaves and a stem which becomes bare and woody with age. C. terminalis is a compact species to use where space is limited — there are also tall types such as C. australis and C. stricta to grow in tubs as focal points where space permits.

SECRETS OF SUCCESS

Temperature: Average warmth — minimum 60°F (16°C) in winter.
Light: Partial shade in summer — bright light in winter.
Water: Water regularly in spring to autumn — water sparingly in winter.
Air Humidity: Mist frequently — wash leaves occasionally.
Repotting: Repot in spring every year.
Propagation: Use pieces of cane as stem cuttings.

Crossandra undulifolia

tubular flower 1½ in. across

glossy leaf 3 in. long

C. undulifolia
Firecracker Flower

TYPES

Crossandra undulifolia (sometimes sold as **C. infundibuliformis**) grows about 1–2 ft (30–60 cm) high. The variety **Mona Wallhed** is reputed to be the best type.

CROSSANDRA
HOUSE PLANT (see page 5)

Crossandra starts to flower when only a few months old and the flowering season lasts from spring to autumn. The blooms are borne on top of green flowering spikes. The disadvantage of the Firecracker Flower is its need for moist air — it will probably not survive unless frequently misted and surrounded by other plants.

SECRETS OF SUCCESS

Temperature: Average warmth — minimum 55°F (13°C) in winter.
Light: Bright light — avoid direct sun in summer.
Water: Keep compost moist at all times. Reduce watering in winter.
Air Humidity: Mist leaves frequently.
Repotting: Repot, if necessary, in spring.
Propagation: Take stem cuttings in summer. Use a rooting hormone and provide bottom heat.

Codiaeum Gold Finger

leathery leaves

stem 1–2 ft, can reach 4 ft

C. variegatum pictum
**Croton
(Joseph's Coat)**

TYPES

There are hundreds of varieties of **Codiaeum pictum**. Most have laurel-like leaves, but there are also forked, lobed, twisted and ribbon-like ones. The colour often changes with age.

CROTON
HOUSE PLANT (see page 5)

Crotons (Latin name Codiaeum variegatum pictum) are popular woody plants with large and colourful foliage. These leaves are usually brightly veined but there are many variations. It is a fussy plant — the lower leaves fall if the conditions are not right. A fairly constant temperature and high air humidity are necessary. Use tepid water and keep away from draughts. Feed regularly during the growing season.

SECRETS OF SUCCESS

Temperature: Warm — minimum 60°F (16°C) in winter.
Light: Good light is necessary.
Water: Water liberally from spring to autumn. Water sparingly in winter.
Air Humidity: Mist leaves frequently — wash occasionally.
Repotting: Repot, if necessary, in spring.
Propagation: Take cuttings in spring. Use a rooting hormone and provide bottom heat.

Ctenanthe oppenheimiana
tricolor

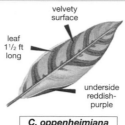

velvety
surface

leaf
1½ ft
long

underside
reddish-
purple

**C. oppenheimiana
tricolor**

Never Never Plant

TYPE

There are several species, but the only one you are likely to find is **Ctenanthe oppenheimiana tricolor**. It grows about 3 ft (1 m) high. The green-banded leaves have pinky-green patches

CTENANTHE
HOUSE PLANT
(see page 5)

Ctenanthe is a member of the Maranta (page 36) group. It is closely related to Calathea — both are eye-catching and difficult to grow. It has a long list of hates — direct sunlight, temperatures below 60°F (16°C), cold or hard water, dry air and cold draughts. With care it can be grown as an uncovered specimen but it is much more suitable for placing in a terrarium (page 132).

SECRETS OF SUCCESS

Temperature: Average warmth — minimum 60°F (16°C).
Light: Partial shade — move to a well-lit spot in winter.
Water: Keep compost moist — reduce watering in winter. Use soft water.
Air Humidity: Mist leaves regularly.
Repotting: Repot in spring every 2 years.
Propagation: Divide plants at repotting time.

Cuphea ignea

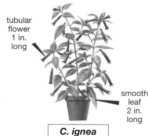

tubular
flower
1 in.
long

smooth
leaf
2 in.
long

C. ignea

Cigar Plant

TYPE

Cuphea ignea is a 1 ft (30 cm) high bush bearing flowers from spring to autumn. Red tubes with white and purple mouths — with a little imagination tiny ash-tipped cigars.

CUPHEA
HOUSE PLANT
(see page 5)

A pretty plant, rather than a spectacular one. It can be used in a mixed display, but it is not bold enough to serve as a specimen plant. It grows quickly, reaching its full height in a single season. Cigar-shaped flowers are borne in profusion among the narrow leaves. Overwinter the plant in a cool room and water sparingly. Cut back the stems in early spring.

SECRETS OF SUCCESS

Temperature: Average warmth — minimum 45°F (7°C) in winter.
Light: Choose a well-lit spot — some direct sunlight is beneficial.
Water: Keep compost moist at all times. Reduce watering in winter.
Air Humidity: Misting is not necessary.
Repotting: Repot, if necessary, in spring.
Propagation: Take stem cuttings in spring or summer.

Curcuma alismatifolia

flower-head
6 in.
high

C. roscoeana

Curcuma

TYPES

The bracts of **Curcuma roscoeana** turn from green to orange or orange-red. There are smaller-headed ones — e.g **C. alismatifolia**.

CURCUMA
POT PLANT
(see page 5)

This showy member of the ginger family appeared in the garden centres during the 1990s. The leaves arise directly out of the compost and in summer the flower heads appear. These are made up of overlapping colourful bracts. Watering stops in autumn, and in spring the fleshy rhizome is removed and repotted. Watering starts again when growth appears above the compost.

SECRETS OF SUCCESS

Temperature: Warm or average warmth — at least 60°F (15°C) in winter.
Light: Brightly lit spot but shade from hot summer sun.
Water: Water regularly from spring to late summer. Do not water during resting period.
Air Humidity: Mist leaves frequently.
Repotting: Repot every year in spring.
Propagation: Divide rhizome when repotting.

CYCLAMEN
POT PLANT (see page 5)

C. persicum
Cyclamen

slender flower-stalk 9–12 in. tall

shuttlecock-like flower 1–2 in. long

heart-shaped leaf 2–3 in. across

Cyclamens are usually bought between September and Christmas. They are popular and their charm is obvious — compact growth, swept-back petals and patterned foliage. With care they will bloom for several months and can be kept to provide another display next winter. Buy in autumn and not mid-winter.

TYPES

The varieties of **Cyclamen persicum** offer a wide variety of colours, leaf patterns and sizes. Standard varieties grow 1 ft (30 cm) high — there are also Intermediates (8 in./ 20 cm) and Miniatures (6 in./ 15 cm or less).

SECRETS OF SUCCESS

Temperature: Cool — 50°–60°F (10°–16°C) is ideal.
Light: Bright light away from direct sunlight.
Water: Keep compost moist at all times.
Air Humidity: Stand on a pebble tray (page 115) or surround with damp peat.
Care After Flowering: Usually thrown away, but tubers with care can be stored for planting next year.
Propagation: Plant tuber in compost, burying to half its depth.

Cyclamen persicum Decora

CYPERUS
HOUSE PLANT (see page 5)

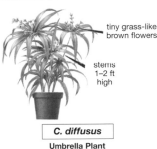

tiny grass-like brown flowers

stems 1–2 ft high

C. diffusus
Umbrella Plant

Grassy leaves radiate from the stiff stalks like the ribs of an umbrella — the tiny flowers are of little decorative value. The roots must be kept constantly wet — place the pot in a saucer or other container which should always contain water. An easy plant to propagate — see below. Wilting, yellow leaves are a sure sign that the plant has been short of water. Choose a dwarf variety if space is limited.

TYPES

Cyperus alternifolius is the popular one — long and narrow leaves are borne on 3 ft (1 m) stalks. **C. papyrus** is a 7 ft (2 m) giant — the best dwarf types are **C. a. gracilis** and **C. diffusus**.

SECRETS OF SUCCESS

Temperature: Not fussy — minimum 50°F (10°C) in winter.
Light: Well-lit or light shade — avoid direct summer sunshine.
Water: Keep compost soaked and restrict drainage.
Air Humidity: Mist leaves frequently.
Repotting: Repot in spring every year.
Propagation: Divide plants at repotting time.

Cyperus alternifolius variegatus

CYTISUS
POT PLANT (see page 5)

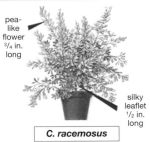

pea-like flower ¾ in. long

silky leaflet ½ in. long

C. racemosus
Genista

Two types of Cytisus are sold for indoor cultivation — C. canariensis and the more attractive C. racemosus. These shrubs must spend their summers outdoors. They are stood out after the shoots which have borne flowers are cut back. In early autumn the plants are brought back indoors and kept in a cool room. In mid-winter move to a bright, warmer spot and water more freely.

TYPES

Cytisus outdoors is called Broom — indoors it is Genista. Long sprays of fragrant yellow flowers appear in spring at the end of arching branches. Choose **Cytisus racemosus** rather than **C. canariensis**.

SECRETS OF SUCCESS

Temperature: Cool — minimum 40°F (5°C) in winter.
Light: Well-lit during the flowering season — light shade in winter.
Water: Water liberally during the flowering season.
Air Humidity: Mist leaves frequently during the flowering season.
Repotting: Repot, if necessary, after flowering.
Propagation: Take stem cuttings in summer.

Cytisus racemosus

Datura suaveolens

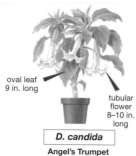

oval leaf 9 in. long

tubular flower 8–10 in. long

D. candida

Angel's Trumpet

TYPES

Two species are sold as house plants — **Datura candida** and **D. suaveolens**. Both bear sweet-smelling white flowers in summer — D. candida is the better choice.

DATURA
HOUSE PLANT (see page 5)

The magnificent 10 in. (25 cm) long flaring trumpets in the photograph may tempt you to rush off and buy a Datura. Before you do, remember that these exotic plants need space and care, and all parts are poisonous. Choose another plant if you have children and/or pets. They are tub plants, spending part of the summer outdoors and the whole of the winter in a cool, well-lit place.

SECRETS OF SUCCESS

Temperature: Average warmth. Keep cool in winter.
Light: A well-lit spot — some direct sunlight is beneficial.
Water: Water regularly from spring to autumn. Water sparingly in winter.
Air Humidity: Mist leaves occasionally.
Repotting: Repot, if necessary, in spring.
Propagation: Take stem cuttings in spring. Use a rooting hormone and provide bottom heat.

DENDROBIUM — 81 • DICKSONIA — 77

Dieffenbachia picta Camilla

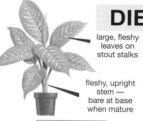

large, fleshy leaves on stout stalks

fleshy, upright stem — bare at base when mature

D. amoena

Dumb Cane (Leopard Lily)

TYPES

Dieffenbachia amoena grows to 5 ft (1.5 m) or more. Leaves are white-banded — very prominent on **D. a. Tropic Snow**. **D. picta** leaves have white blotches or markings.

DIEFFENBACHIA
HOUSE PLANT (see page 5)

The decorative leaves make this plant a favourite with interior decorators — tall specimens are used as focal points. The popular species (D. amoena and D. picta) are reasonably easy to grow in centrally-heated rooms, but most of the others are difficult. These demanding ones require a fairly constant temperature and a draught-free situation. As plants age they may lose their lower leaves.

SECRETS OF SUCCESS

Temperature: Average warmth — minimum 60°F (16°C) in winter.
Light: Partial shade in summer — bright light in winter.
Water: Water frequently from spring to autumn — sparingly in winter.
Air Humidity: Mist frequently — wash leaves occasionally.
Repotting: Repot in spring every year.
Propagation: Remove and repot crown of leaves.

DIPLADENIA: see Mandevilla — 36

DECORATIVE MULCHES

Decorative mulches are a popular finishing touch for some designers — they certainly provide an additional texture and a new colour. It is claimed that they reduce water loss, but this moisture arising from the surface compost increases the air humidity around the leaves.

All sorts of material can be used — glass beads, broken shells, pebbles, polished stones and dried moss. An exciting and attractive new feature or a way of spoiling a display — the choice is yours.

Shell mulch

Glass mulch

Dizygotheca elegantissima

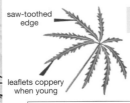

saw-toothed edge

leaflets coppery when young

D. elegantissima
(Aralia elegantissima)

**False Aralia
(Finger Aralia)**

TYPES

Dizygotheca elegantissima is the popular species — delicate in both appearance and constitution. This plant can grow up to 7 ft (2 m) high. **D. veitchii** has wider leaves with wavy (not serrated) edges.

DIZYGOTHECA

**HOUSE PLANT
(see page 5)**

A graceful plant with leaves divided into finger-like serrated leaflets which are dark green or almost black. The bush has a splendid lacy effect when young. It has the usual problems of so many delicate plants — it detests soggy compost but it drops its leaves if the soil ball is allowed to dry out. It does not like sudden changes in temperature and the air must be moist.

SECRETS OF SUCCESS

Temperature: Average warmth — minimum 60°F (16°C) in winter.
Light: Bright light — not direct sun.
Water: Water moderately from spring to autumn. Water sparingly in winter.
Air Humidity: Mist leaves frequently.
Repotting: Repot in spring every 2 years.
Propagation: Difficult. Try stem cuttings in spring — use a rooting hormone and provide bottom heat.

DRACAENA

**HOUSE PLANT
(see page 5)**

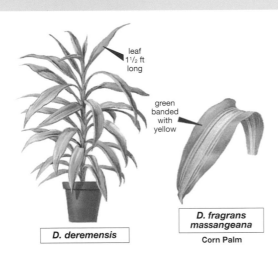

leaf 1½ ft long

green banded with yellow

D. deremensis

D. fragrans massangeana

Corn Palm

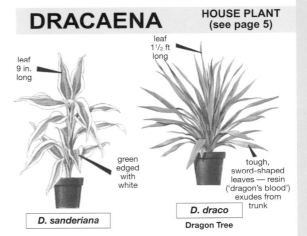

leaf 9 in. long

green edged with white

D. sanderiana

leaf 1½ ft long

tough, sword-shaped leaves — resin ('dragon's blood') exudes from trunk

D. draco

Dragon Tree

Dracaena marginata tricolor

TYPES

Dracaena marginata (10 ft/ 3 m) has red-edged green narrow leaves — the variety **tricolor** is green striped with yellow and red. **D. draco** (4 ft/ 1.2 m) has sword-like leaves. **D. deremensis** is slow growing — the strap-like leaves are usually prominently striped. For wide, yellow-centred foliage pick **D. fragrans massangeana** — for a compact species choose **D. sanderiana** which has cream-edged 8 in. (20 cm) long leaves. The odd one out is **D. godseffiana** — it is a 2 ft/60 cm shrub which has oval rather than strap-shaped leaves. It bears yellow fragrant flowers which are followed by red berries. Variegated types are available.

The Dracaenas and closely-related Cordylines outsell nearly all other large-leaved plants. Most are false palms with woody trunks and a crown of leaves — an excellent choice for an eye-catching focal point. Buy D. marginata or D. draco if you want an easy one which will tolerate shade and some neglect — other Dracaenas are more difficult to grow. Choose D. godseffiana if you want an easy bush rather than a false palm.

SECRETS OF SUCCESS

Temperature: Average warmth — minimum 55°F (13°C) in winter.
Light: Light shade is the best general position — close to an east- or west-facing window is an ideal spot.
Water: Keep compost moist at all times. Reduce watering in winter.
Air Humidity: Mist leaves regularly — only D. draco and D. godseffiana will thrive in dry air.
Repotting: Repot in spring every 2 years.
Propagation: Remove crown from old leggy canes and plant in potting compost — use a rooting hormone and provide bottom heat. Pieces of stem, 2–3 in. (5–8 cm) long, can be used as cane cuttings.

Erica hyemalis

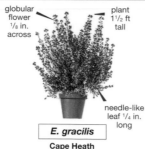

globular flower ¹/₈ in. across

plant 1¹/₂ ft tall

needle-like leaf ¹/₄ in. long

E. gracilis
Cape Heath

TYPES

Erica gracilis is in flower during late autumn and winter — its tiny blooms are pink or pale purple. **E. hyemalis** blooms at the same time — the flowers are larger and white-mouthed pink.

ERICA
POT PLANT
(see page 5)

The small shrubby plants are bought during the winter months when their masses of bell-shaped blooms are open. Attractive, but you cannot expect Ericas to survive for long in the home. The leaves dry very rapidly in a centrally heated room and soft water is necessary, but even with proper care they are not long-lived. The two popular species are E. gracilis and E. hyemalis.

SECRETS OF SUCCESS

Temperature: Cool — 45°–55°F (7°–13°C) when in flower.
Light: Bright light — some direct sun is beneficial.
Water: Keep compost moist at all times — use soft water.
Air Humidity: Mist leaves frequently.
Care After Flowering: Usually discarded, but plants can be trimmed back and pots stood outdoors during summer.
Propagation: Buy new plants.

ESPOSTEA — 74 • EUCOMIS — 7

Euonymus japonica microphyllus

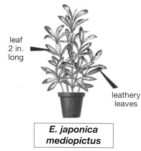

leaf 2 in. long

leathery leaves

E. japonica mediopictus

TYPES

Euonymus japonica is the house plant species. There are several varieties, differing in the distribution of green and yellow (or white) on the leaves. Grow **microphyllus** where space is limited.

EUONYMUS
HOUSE PLANT
(see page 5)

Several variegated types are available — two popular varieties are illustrated here. These shrubby plants have oval, leathery foliage — E. japonica microphyllus leaves are less than 1 in. (2.5 cm) long. Small white flowers may appear in late spring. Euonymus is a useful specimen for a bright unheated room — in a heated place, it will probably shed its leaves in winter. Keep in check by pruning in spring.

SECRETS OF SUCCESS

Temperature: Average warmth. Keep cool in winter.
Light: Bright, indirect light or some sun.
Water: Water regularly from spring to autumn. Water sparingly in winter.
Air Humidity: Mist leaves occasionally.
Repotting: Repot in spring every year.
Propagation: Take stem cuttings in summer.

Euphorbia fulgens

grooved stems covered with sharp thorns

leaf 2 in. long

E. milii
Crown of Thorns

TYPES

Euphorbia milii stems grow about 3 ft (1 m) high and bear tiny flowers which are surrounded by showy bracts. The usual colour is red and the normal flowering season is early spring to midsummer.

EUPHORBIA
HOUSE PLANT
(see page 5)

The Crown of Thorns (Euphorbia milii) is an old favourite which remains a good and undemanding choice for a sunny windowsill. It does not need misting, will withstand some neglect and does not have to be in an unheated room in winter. Some leaves may drop during the resting season, but new leaf buds will appear. Scarlet Plume (E. fulgens) bears arched and thornless stems — it is not often seen.

SECRETS OF SUCCESS

Temperature: Average warmth — minimum 55°F (13°C) in winter.
Light: As much light as possible, but shade from summer sun.
Water: Water moderately between spring and autumn — sparingly in winter.
Air Humidity: Misting not necessary for E. milii.
Repotting: Repot in spring every 2 years.
Propagation: Take stem cuttings in spring or summer.

EUPHORBIA (Succulent) — 89 • EUSTOMIA: see Lisianthus — 35

fragrant gold-centred flower 1/2 in. across

shiny leaf 1 in. long

E. affine

Arabian Violet

TYPE

Raise **Exacum affine** from seed or buy as a pot plant. An easy-to-care-for plant but it does dislike draughts. Remove dead flowers regularly to prolong display.

Exacum affine Starlight Fragrance

EXACUM — POT PLANT (see page 5)

Exacum is a small and neat plant which is only a few inches high when offered for sale. Its flowers, pale purple with a yellow centre, are also small, but this plant still has several points in its favour. The blooms are abundant and fragrant, and the flowering season extends from midsummer to late autumn. Keep reasonably cool and in good light. To ensure the maximum flowering period, pick a plant which is mainly in bud and not in full flower.

SECRETS OF SUCCESS

Temperature: Cool or average warmth — keep at 50°–70°F (10°–21°C).
Light: Bright light — protect from hot summer sun.
Water: Keep compost moist at all times.
Air Humidity: Mist leaves frequently.
Care After Flowering: Plant should be discarded.
Propagation: Sow seeds in late summer.

shiny surface

leaf 7 in. long

F. lizei

Ivy Tree

TYPES

Fatshedera lizei can reach 6 ft (2 m) or more. Support is needed, or you can pinch out the tips and grow it as a bush. The white-blotched form (**variegata**) is more difficult to grow.

Fatshedera lizei variegata

FATSHEDERA — HOUSE PLANT (see page 5)

This easy-to-grow hybrid of Hedera and Fatsia deserves its popularity. It prefers cool conditions, but it can be grown in a heated room as long as the winter temperature is kept below 70°F (21°C) and the light is reasonably bright. It can be grown as a shrub, like its Castor Oil Plant parent — pinch out the growing tips each spring. Or you can grow it as a climber like its Ivy parent — train it to a stake or trellis.

SECRETS OF SUCCESS

Temperature: Average warmth — minimum 35°F (2°C) in winter.
Light: Bright or light shade — keep well-lit in winter.
Water: Water regularly from spring to autumn. Water sparingly in winter.
Air Humidity: Mist leaves frequently.
Repotting: Repot in spring every year.
Propagation: Take stem cuttings in summer.

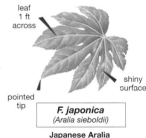

leaf 1 ft across

shiny surface

pointed tip

F. japonica
(Aralia sieboldii)

Japanese Aralia
(Castor Oil Plant)

TYPES

The basic species is **Fatsia japonica** which bears all-green leaves. There are several varieties — **variegata** has cream-edged foliage and **moseri** has a compact growth habit.

Fatsia japonica

FATSIA — HOUSE PLANT (see page 5)

An old favourite which remains a good choice as a specimen plant where conditions are far from perfect. It is an extremely tough plant which grows quickly. Buy a small plant, provide it with a cool and well-lit spot, and it should reach a height of 3 ft (1 m) in a couple of years. Each year cut back the growing tips to maintain the bushy growth habit. Wash the leaves occasionally.

SECRETS OF SUCCESS

Temperature: Cool or average warmth — keep cool in winter.
Light: Bright or light shade — keep well lit in winter.
Water: Water regularly from spring to autumn — sparingly in winter.
Air Humidity: Mist leaves frequently.
Repotting: Repot in spring every year
Propagation: Take stem cuttings in spring or summer.

leaf
1 ft
long

shiny,
leathery
leaves

F. elastica decora
Rubber Plant

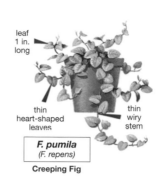

leaf
1 in.
long

thin
heart-shaped
leaves

thin
wiry
stem

F. pumila
(F. repens)
Creeping Fig

FICUS

HOUSE PLANT
(see page 5)

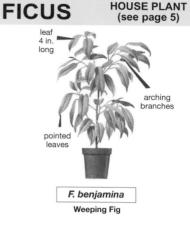

leaf
4 in.
long

arching
branches

pointed
leaves

F. benjamina
Weeping Fig

Ficus benjamina
Starlight

TYPES

Ficus elastica decora is the favourite Tree type — other varieties include **F. e. variegata** (white- and grey-splashed leaves) and **robusta** (large leaves). **F. benjamina** grows about 7 ft (2 m) high — **variegata** (cream-edged leaves) is a popular variety. For the largest leaves grow **F. lyrata**. **F. religiosa** bears heart-shaped leaves with a tail-like tip. **F. triangularis** (triangular) and **F. retusa** (oval) have 3–4 in. (8–10 cm) long leaves. There are two Trailing types — **F. pumila** with small heart-shaped leaves and **F. radicans** which has larger, wavy-edged foliage.

The Tree types are by far the most popular group of Ornamental Figs and have long been great favourites with interior decorators. The upright Rubber Plant (Ficus elastica) and its many varieties are known to everyone, but it is the Weeping Fig (F. benjamina) with its graceful and tree-like form which has greatly increased in popularity. The Trailing types are trailers and climbers which are difficult to grow.

SECRETS OF SUCCESS

Temperature: Average warmth — minimum 55°F (13°C) in winter.

Light: Bright light for Tree types — partial shade for others.

Water: Water with care. With Tree types the compost must dry out to some extent between waterings. The Trailing types need more frequent watering. Cut back watering in winter — use tepid water.

Air Humidity: Mist leaves occasionally in summer — essential for Trailing types.

Repotting: Repot in spring every 2 years until the plant is too large to handle.

Propagation: Take non-woody stem cuttings in summer. Use a rooting hormone and provide bottom heat.

Fittonia argyroneura nana

green,
veined
with
white

leaf
1 in.
long

F. argyroneura nana
Snakeskin Plant

TYPES

Foliage with a network of veins is the distinctive feature — **Fittonia verschaffeltii** has pink veins and **F. argyroneura** has white ones. The Snakeskin Plant (**F. a. nana**) is the easy dwarf.

FITTONIA

HOUSE PLANT
(see page 5)

The standard large-leaved types are very difficult to grow under ordinary room conditions — their need for constant warmth and high moisture around the leaves means that they belong in the glass garden — see page 131. There is a dwarf-leaved variety which is quite easy to grow in the living room. It will thrive in dry air if occasionally misted with water.

SECRETS OF SUCCESS

Care rules for Snakeskin Plant: Average warmth — minimum 60°F (16°C) in winter.

Light: Partial shade — avoid direct sunlight.

Water: Water liberally from spring to autumn — sparingly in winter. Use tepid water.

Air Humidity: Mist leaves occasionally.

Repotting: Repot in spring every year.

Propagation: Divide plants at repotting time. Pot up rooted runners.

Fuchsia Winston Churchill

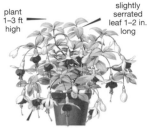

plant 1–3 ft high

slightly serrated leaf 1–2 in. long

F. hybrida

TYPES

Bushes grow 1–3 ft (30 cm–1 m) high. **Fuchsia hybrida** varieties bear single, semi-double or double flowers. **F. triphylla** blooms are pink, orange or red. Trailers (e.g **F. Marinka**) are available.

FUCHSIA
POT PLANT (see page 5)

A Fuchsia collection can provide blooms from spring to autumn — the popular bell-shaped flowers of F. hybrida and the less familiar tube-shaped hybrids of F. triphylla. Most plants are thrown away once flowering is over but you can overwinter them in a cool place — cut back stems in early spring. With young plants pinch out the stem tips to induce bushy growth.

SECRETS OF SUCCESS

Temperature: Cool or average — 50°–60°F (10°–16°C) in winter.
Light: Bright light away from direct sunshine.
Water: Keep compost moist at all times from spring to autumn — water sparingly in winter.
Air Humidity: Mist leaves occasionally during the growing season.
Repotting: Repot in spring every year.
Propagation: Take stem cuttings in spring or summer.

GALANTHUS — 66 • GALTONIA — 67

Gardenia jasminoides

glossy leaf 4 in. long

fragrant flower 3 in. across

G. jasminoides

Gardenia

TYPES

The blooms of **Gardenia jasminoides** are semi-double or double and the petals are waxy. The plant grows about 1½ ft (45 cm) high and several varieties are available.

GARDENIA
HOUSE PLANT (see page 5)

Sadly Gardenia is often a disappointment because it is extremely demanding. For flower buds to form a night temperature of 60°–65°F (16°–18°C) is required, and during the day it should be about 10°F (6°C) higher. An even temperature and careful watering are needed to prevent bud drop.

SECRETS OF SUCCESS

Temperature: Average warmth — minimum 60°F (16°C) in winter.
Light: Bright light is essential, but avoid direct midday sun in summer.
Water: Keep compost moist at all times — reduce watering in winter. Use soft, tepid water.
Air Humidity: Mist leaves frequently.
Repotting: Repot in spring every 2–3 years.
Propagation: Take stem cuttings in spring. Use a rooting hormone and provide bottom heat.

LUCKY BAMBOO

This age-old Oriental novelty appeared in the shops in the late 1990s and now has become a feature of the displays on offer in garden centres, department stores, gift shops etc. Short green stalks with or without small shoots are grouped together in a decorative container with polished stones or pebbles in the bottom. Alternatively you can buy curled or spiralled stalks of Lucky Bamboo.

First of all, it is not a bamboo — it is Dracaena sanderiana, which you will find on page 23. Next, it is grown in water and not compost — the plants should last for years if you change the water every 7–14 days. Do not add fertilizer — use soft water if you want it to last a long time. You can pot up the canes and grow them as ordinary house plants, but the novelty is lost.

Lucky Bamboo makes a great gift for Feng Shui devotees, as these plants like all bamboos are claimed to bring health, wealth and happiness to the owner.

GERANIUM

HOUSE PLANT (see page 5)

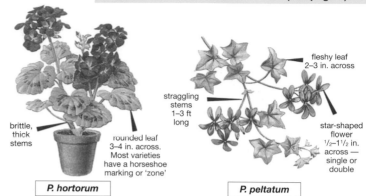

scalloped leaf with serrated edge 3 in. across

brittle, thin stems

P. domesticum

brittle, thick stems

rounded leaf 3–4 in. across. Most varieties have a horseshoe marking or 'zone'

P. hortorum

straggling stems 1–3 ft long

fleshy leaf 2–3 in. across

star-shaped flower ¹/₂–1¹/₂ in. across — single or double

P. peltatum

Pelargonium peltatum roulettii

TYPES

Most varieties of **Pelargonium hortorum** (Common or Zonal Pelargonium) grow 1–2 ft (30–60 cm) high, but the range is 6 in. (15 cm) to 4 ft (1 m). Buy plants which have plenty of buds rather than flowers. Many varieties (e.g **Mrs Henry Cox** and **Mrs Pollock**) have decorative leaves. The **P. domesticum** (Regal or Martha Washington Pelargonium) hybrids are more glamorous but have a shorter flowering season. **P. peltatum** is the Ivy-leaved Geranium with its single or double flowers borne in small clusters, and finally there are the Scented-leaved ones with rose-, mint- and lemon-scented varieties.

Geraniums (Latin name Pelargonium) are one of the world's favourite house plants. The popular ones are easy to grow and propagate, and the colourful blooms are borne in showy clusters. The group is dominated by the Zonal Geraniums which can bloom almost all year round — harder to grow are the more glamorous Regal Pelargoniums. There are also the trailing Ivy-leaved Geraniums for hanging baskets and the Scented-leaved Geraniums which are grown for their aromatic foliage rather than their small flowers.

SECRETS OF SUCCESS

Temperature: Average warmth with cool nights — 45°F (7°C) minimum.
Light: As much light as possible — some sunlight is essential.
Water: Water thoroughly, then leave until compost is moderately dry. Avoid overwatering. Reduce watering in winter.
Air Humidity: Do not mist the leaves.
Repotting: Repot if necessary in spring.
Propagation: Take stem cuttings in summer. Do not use a rooting hormone or cover.

Gerbera jamesonii Happipot

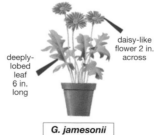

daisy-like flower 2 in. across

deeply-lobed leaf 6 in. long

G. jamesonii

Barbeton Daisy

TYPES

Gerbera jamesonii Happipot is a compact variety — the flower-stalks are 10–12 in. (25–30 cm) high. Home-grown seed produces some tall-stemmed plants — choose the more uniform **Parade**.

GERBERA

POT PLANT (see page 5)

Gerbera jamesonii has been grown as a flowering pot plant for many years, the blooms appearing between May and August. Both single and double forms can be obtained in a range of striking colours — yellow, orange, red, pink and white around a central yellow disc. The flower-stalks can reach 2 ft (60 cm) and give the plant a lanky appearance — recently more compact strains have appeared.

SECRETS OF SUCCESS

Temperature: Average warmth — 50°–70°F (10°–21° C) when flowering.
Light: Brightly lit spot with some direct sun.
Water: Keep compost moist at all times.
Air Humidity: Mist leaves occasionally.
Care After Flowering: Discard or place in a greenhouse.
Propagation: Sow seeds in spring.

GLORIOSA

POT PLANT (see page 5)

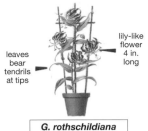

leaves bear tendrils at tips

lily-like flower 4 in. long

G. rothschildiana

Glory Lily

TYPES

Gloriosa rothschildiana grows 3 ft (1 m) or more. Swept-back petals are red with a yellow base — **G. superba** is similar but petals change from green to orange and finally to red.

Gloriosa superba

The Glory Lily bears large flowers in midsummer. The stems are weak and some form of support must be provided. At flowering time keep warm and well-lit. It is either bought in flower or raised at home from a tuber. Plant the tuber upright in a 6 in. (15 cm) pot in spring with the tip 1 in. (2.5 cm) below the surface. Water sparingly at first, then more freely as the stems start to grow.

SECRETS OF SUCCESS

Temperature: Warm or average warmth — minimum 60°F (16°C) in the growing season.
Light: Brightly lit spot, but shade from hot summer sun.
Water: Water liberally during the growing season.
Air Humidity: Mist leaves occasionally.
Care After Flowering: Reduce and then stop watering. Keep the pot at 50°–55°F (10°–13°C). Repot in spring.
Propagation: Remove and plant offsets at repotting time.

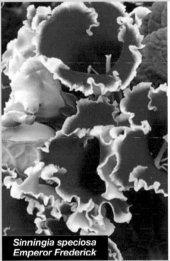

GLOXINIA

POT PLANT (see page 5)

upturned bell-shaped flower 3 in. across

oval, velvety leaf 8 in. long

Sinningia speciosa

Gloxinia

TYPES

The petal edges of **Sinningia speciosa** are plain or ruffled. Multi-lobed (double) varieties are available. For relatively small leaves grow the variety **Brocade**.

Sinningia speciosa Emperor Frederick

Gloxinia (Latin name Sinningia speciosa) is usually bought in flower in summer — it will be in bloom for 2 months or more if you choose a plant with plenty of buds and give it proper care. You can also raise Gloxinias by planting tubers in spring, but this needs careful temperature and water control. Plant tubers level with the compost, hollow side up.

SECRETS OF SUCCESS

Temperature: Average warmth — minimum 60°F (16°C).
Light: Bright light away from direct sunlight.
Water: Keep compost moist at all times — keep water off leaves and flowers.
Air Humidity: Stand pot on a pebble tray (see page 115) or surround with damp peat. Mist around plant occasionally.
Care After Flowering: Pots can be left to dry out and tubers repotted in spring, but this is a difficult procedure.
Propagation: Buy a new plant.

GREVILLEA

HOUSE PLANT (see page 5)

tree-like growth

underside silky

G. robusta

Silk Oak

TYPE

Grevillea robusta is the only type grown. The lacy, Fern-like effect of the foliage tends to disappear with age, so it is usual to cut back or discard plants once they reach 2–3 ft (60 cm–1 m).

Grevillea robusta

Large indoor trees are expensive to buy, but with nearly all suitable varieties buying a seedling will mean a wait of several years before it becomes a specimen tree. Grevillea may be the answer for a cool and bright spot — it can be grown quite easily from seed and will be 1 ft (30 cm) high in the first season. Grevillea is tolerant of a wide temperature range and may reach the ceiling in four or five years.

SECRETS OF SUCCESS

Temperature: Cool or average warmth — minimum 45°F (7°C) in winter.
Light: Brightly lit spot — protect from midday summer sun.
Water: Water liberally from spring to autumn. Water sparingly in winter.
Air Humidity: Mist leaves occasionally.
Repotting: Repot in spring every year.
Propagation: Sow seeds in spring or summer.

Gynura sarmentosa

leaf 3 in. long

dark green, covered with purple hairs

G. sarmentosa

Velvet Plant

TYPES

Gynura sarmentosa is a popular trailer. The foliage has a velvety look — gleaming purple in bright light. **G. aurantiaca** has larger leaves, but it is more upright and less attractive.

GYNURA

HOUSE PLANT
(see page 5)

Gynura grows quickly, it has no special needs and the foliage is covered with shiny purple hairs. This attractive colouring requires good light for development. Gynura produces small Dandelion-like flowers in spring — these should be removed at the bud stage as the aroma is offensive. Pinch out the tips occasionally.

SECRETS OF SUCCESS

Temperature: Average warmth — minimum 50°F (10°C) in winter.
Light: Brightly lit spot — some direct sunlight is beneficial.
Water: Water liberally from spring to autumn. Water sparingly in winter.
Air Humidity: Mist leaves occasionally.
Repotting: Repot, if necessary, in spring.
Propagation: Stem cuttings root very easily.

HAWORTHIA — 89

Hedera canariensis Gloire de Marengo

leaves 3- or 5- lobed

clinging stems

H. helix

Common Ivy

TYPES

Hedera helix (Common Ivy) is the main species — all-green and variegated types are available. Bushy types for trailing include **Eva** and **Glacier**.

HEDERA

HOUSE PLANT
(see page 5)

Ivies have long been a feature of the indoor garden. As climbers they can quickly clothe bare surroundings, provided you choose a vigorous H. helix variety. The stems will cling to woodwork, wallpaper etc, but the slower-growing H. canariensis does not cling, so support is necessary. Excellent climbers, but Ivies are just as useful as trailers. Choose one of the smaller bushy types — see below.

SECRETS OF SUCCESS

Temperature: Cool — ideally unheated in winter.
Light: Bright light — avoid direct sunlight in summer.
Water: Keep compost moist in summer — water sparingly in winter.
Air Humidity: Mist leaves frequently in summer, and in winter if room is heated.
Repotting: Repot in spring every 2 years.
Propagation: Use trimmed shoot tips as cuttings.

Helxine soleirolii argentea

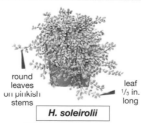

round leaves on pinkish stems

leaf 1/5 in. long

H. soleirolii

Mind Your Own Business (Baby's Tears)

TYPES

The mossy mounds of **Helxine soleirolii (Soleirolia soleirolii)** were used for ground cover in conservatories long before the start of the present boom in house plants. The variety **argentea** has silvery leaves.

HELXINE

HOUSE PLANT
(see page 5)

New pots of Helxine are raised at home rather than on professional nurseries. A small clump is removed from an established plant and placed on the surface of moist compost in a pot — in a short time tiny green leaves cover the surface. Helxine is excellent in hanging baskets or for covering the soil around tall plants.

SECRETS OF SUCCESS

Temperature: Average warmth — minimum 45°F (7°C) in winter.
Light: Bright indirect light is best but will survive almost anywhere.
Water: Keep compost moist at all times.
Air Humidity: Mist leaves frequently.
Repotting: Repot, if necessary, in spring.
Propagation: Very easy — pot up small clumps at any time of the year.

Hemigraphis alternata

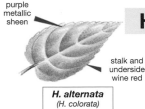
purple metallic sheen

stalk and underside wine red

H. alternata
(H. colorata)

Red Ivy

HEMIGRAPHIS
HOUSE PLANT
(see page 5)

A climbing plant, popular in the U.S for hanging baskets but a rarity in Britain. Red Ivy has coloured leaves — silvery in the shade, metallic purple when exposed to a few hours' sunshine. Hemigraphis is not an easy plant to grow, but it is not quite as difficult as indicated by some textbooks. It needs winter warmth, moist air, and pruning when stems become straggly.

TYPES

Hemigraphis alternata is the usual one offered for sale. Despite its name, this plant is quite different from a True Ivy — growth is limited to 1–1¹⁄₂ ft (30–45 cm) and the 3 in. (8 cm) leaves are oval. **H. exotica** (Waffle Plant) has puckered leaves.

SECRETS OF SUCCESS

Temperature: Average warmth — minimum 55°F (13°C) in winter.
Light: Bright light or semi-shade. Some direct sun will enhance colour.
Water: Water liberally from spring to autumn. Water sparingly in winter.
Air Humidity: Mist leaves regularly.
Repotting: Repot in spring every year.
Propagation: Take stem cuttings in late spring or summer.

Heptapleurum arboricola variegata

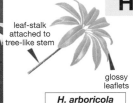
leaf-stalk attached to tree-like stem

glossy leaflets

H. arboricola

Parasol Plant

HEPTAPLEURUM
HOUSE PLANT
(see page 5)

A fast-growing tree-like plant with about ten leaflets radiating from each leaf-stalk. Its main advantage over its close relative Schefflera is that it will happily grow as a bush if the growing point of the main stem is removed. Quite easy to grow if you provide winter warmth, good light and moist air. Leaf fall may occur if there is a sudden change in conditions.

TYPES

Stake **Heptapleurum arboricola** to produce a 6 ft (2 m) unbranched tree. Named varieties are available — **Hayata** (greyish leaves), **Geisha Girl** (rounded leaf tips) and **variegata** (yellow-splashed leaves).

SECRETS OF SUCCESS

Temperature: Average warmth — minimum 60°F (16°C) in winter.
Light: Bright light — not direct sun.
Water: Water liberally from spring to autumn. Water sparingly in winter.
Air Humidity: Mist leaves frequently. Wash leaves occasionally.
Repotting: Repot in spring every year.
Propagation: Take stem cuttings or sow seeds in spring.

Hibiscus rosa-sinensis cooperi

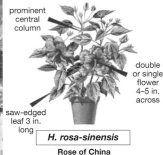
prominent central column

double or single flower 4–5 in. across

saw-edged leaf 3 in. long

H. rosa-sinensis

Rose of China

HIBISCUS
HOUSE PLANT
(see page 5)

Hibiscus is a showy flowering plant for a sunny windowsill. The large papery flowers last for only a day or two, but with proper care there will be a succession of blooms from spring to autumn. Keep it small by regular pruning — cut back stems in late winter to induce bushy growth. Left unpruned a Hibiscus bush can reach 5 ft (1.5 m) or more. It can be trained as a standard — see page 142.

SECRETS OF SUCCESS

Temperature: Average warmth — minimum 55°F (13°C) in winter.
Light: As much light as possible, but shade from full sun.
Water: Keep compost moist at all times — reduce watering in winter.
Air Humidity: Mist leaves occasionally.
Repotting: Repot in spring every year.
Propagation: Take stem cuttings in spring.

TYPES

Hibiscus rosa-sinensis is the basic species with numerous named varieties in white, yellow, orange, pink or red. The variety **cooperi** has variegated foliage.

glossy
leaf
3 in.
long

fragrant pale
pink flower with
red centre —
approximately
20 per cluster

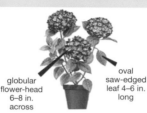

single
flower

H. carnosa variegata

Variegated Wax Plant

TYPES

There are numerous varieties of **Hoya carnosa. H. bella** bears smaller, non-glossy leaves. **H. multiflora** bears pale yellow flowers. Do not remove dead flowers from Hoya stems.

Hoya bella

HOYA

HOUSE PLANT
(see page 5)

The Wax Plant (Hoya carnosa) is an easy-to-grow climber which requires support. The stems can reach 15 ft (4 m) or more, producing clusters of fragrant flowers from May to September. The fleshy leaves are green or variegated. The Miniature Wax Plant (H. bella) is a much more difficult plant to grow under room conditions. It needs more heat and humidity but less light. Grow it in a hanging basket.

SECRETS OF SUCCESS

Temperature: Average warmth. Keep cool (50°–55°F/10°–13°C) in winter.
Light: Bright light — some direct sun is beneficial.
Water: Water liberally from spring to autumn — sparingly in winter.
Air Humidity: Mist regularly when plants are not in flower.
Repotting: Repot, if necessary, in spring.
Propagation: Take mature stem cuttings in spring.

HYACINTHUS — 67

Hydrangea macrophylla

globular
flower-head
6–8 in.
across

oval
saw-edged
leaf 4–6 in.
long

H. macrophylla

**Hydrangea
(Hortensia)**

TYPES

White, pink, purple and blue varieties of **Hydrangea macrophylla** are available — pink varieties can be 'blued' by adding a proprietary blueing compound to the compost before the flowers open.

HYDRANGEA

POT PLANT
(see page 5)

There are the *Mop Heads* (see drawing) with round heads and the *Lacecaps* with an outer ring of open flowers. Hydrangeas have two basic needs — cool conditions and compost which is not allowed to dry out. Brown-edged leaves indicate water shortage. Cut back stems after flowering to half their height.

SECRETS OF SUCCESS

Temperature: Cool — minimum 45°F (7°C) in winter.
Light: Bright light away from direct sunlight.
Water: Keep compost moist at all times from spring to autumn. Use rainwater if tap water is hard.
Air Humidity: Mist leaves occasionally.
Care After Flowering: Repot and continue to water and feed — stand outdoors during summer. Overwinter in a frost-free room. Water sparingly. In mid winter move to a warmer, brighter room and increase watering.
Propagation: Not practical in the home.

HYMENOCALLIS — 70

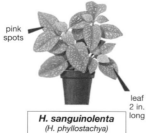

pink
spots

H. sanguinolenta
(H. phyllostachya)

**Freckle Face
(Polka Dot Plant)**

leaf
2 in.
long

TYPES

The leaves of **Hypoestes sanguinolenta** are covered with pale pink spots — they are at their showiest in the variety **Splash**. Pinch out tips to maintain bushiness.

Hypoestes sanguinolenta
.Splash

HYPOESTES

HOUSE PLANT
(see page 5)

Hypoestes is grown for its spotted leaves. In a well-lit place the leaf colouring will be vivid — in a shady site the foliage will be all-green. Young plants make attractive small bushes — prune regularly to keep them 1–2 ft (30–60 cm) high. After flowering, the plant sometimes becomes dormant. Reduce watering until new growth starts.

SECRETS OF SUCCESS

Temperature: Average warmth — minimum 55°F (13°C) in winter.
Light: Bright light — some direct sun will enhance colour.
Water: Keep compost evenly moist. Water liberally from spring to autumn — more sparingly in winter.
Air Humidity: Mist leaves frequently.
Repotting: Repot in spring every year.
Propagation: Sow seeds in spring or take stem cuttings in spring or summer.

IMPATIENS

HOUSE PLANT (see page 5)

leaf 3 in. long

stems brittle and succulent

I. wallerana

Busy Lizzie (Patient Lucy)

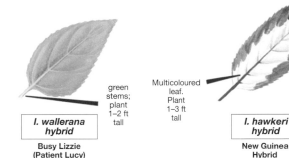

green stems; plant 1–2 ft tall

I. wallerana hybrid

Busy Lizzie (Patient Lucy)

Multicoloured leaf. Plant 1–3 ft tall

I. hawkeri hybrid

New Guinea Hybrid

Impatiens Zig-Zag

TYPES

The range of **Impatiens wallerana** hybrids is extensive. There are dwarfs such as the **Super Elfin** strain and types such as **Blitz** with 2 in. (5 cm) wide blooms. There are bicolours (e.g **Zig-Zag** and **Novette Star**) and doubles (e.g **Rosette** and **Carousel**). Parents of the New Guinea hybrids include **I. hawkeri**, **I. linearifolia** and **I. schlechteri**. These eye-catching plants grow 1–2 ft (30–60 cm) high with long leaves which are nearly always bicoloured or multicoloured — all-red and bronzy leaf types are available. Examples include **Tango**, **Arabesque** and **Fanfare**.

Once only the traditional species led by Impatiens wallerana were available — usually tall with straggly stems. Nowadays the various hybrids have taken over — compact and much more free-flowering. This is the popular Busy Lizzie (Patient Lucy in the U.S) you will find at the garden centre. Pinch out the tips of young plants. For the largest flowers and most colourful leaves choose one of the New Guinea hybrids. Attractive, but the flowering season is limited to summer.

SECRETS OF SUCCESS

Temperature: Average warmth — minimum 55°F (13°C) in winter.

Light: Bright light is necessary, but avoid direct summer sun.

Water: Keep compost moist at all times — reduce watering in winter.

Air Humidity: Mist leaves occasionally — avoid open blooms.

Repotting: The pot must be filled with roots before the plant will flower freely. Repot, if necessary, in spring.

Propagation: Stem cuttings root readily at any time of the year.

IPHEION — 70

IRESINE

HOUSE PLANT (see page 5)

Chicken Gizzard has a most unusual common name and Bloodleaf has remarkable wine red leaves and stems. They are rarities in Britain but are quite widely grown in the U.S. Iresines are sun-lovers — away from a south-facing window the colours tend to fade and growth becomes lank and straggly. Occasionally nip out growing tips.

SECRETS OF SUCCESS

Temperature: Average warmth — minimum 55°F (13°C) in winter.

Light: As much light as possible, but shade from summer noonday sun.

Water: Keep compost moist at all times — reduce watering in winter.

Air Humidity: Mist leaves regularly.

Repotting: Repot, if necessary, in spring.

Propagation: Take stem cuttings in spring or summer.

leaf 3 in. long

wine red leaves

I. herbstii

Bloodleaf

TYPES

Iresine herbstii grows about 2 ft (60 cm) high, its red stems bearing notched leaves. The variety **aureoreticulata** (Chicken Gizzard) is more colourful — red stems, green leaves and yellow veins.

Iresine herbstii aureoreticulata

5-7 leaflets per leaf

twining stems

fragrant star-shaped flower 1 in. across

J. polyanthum

Pink Jasmine

Jasminum primulinum

JASMINUM

HOUSE PLANT
(see page 5)

Most Jasmines are climbers with white fragrant flowers borne in clusters. All need some support for the stems and a cool room for the winter. The favourite one is the Pink Jasmine (Jasminum polyanthum) — pink buds opening into white flowers. It is the easiest one to grow. White Jasmine (J. officinale) also bears white fragrant flowers. Yellow Jasmine (J. primulinum) has yellow scentless flowers.

TYPES

Jasminum polyanthum produces spring flowers on its 8 ft (2.5 m) long twining stems — **J. officinale** flowers in summer to early autumn. **J. primulinum** blooms in spring on its non-twining stems.

SECRETS OF SUCCESS

Temperature: Average warmth — minimum 45°F (7°C) in winter.
Light: Bright light with some direct sun.
Water: Keep compost moist at all times.
Air Humidity: Mist leaves frequently.
Repotting: Repot, if necessary, in spring.
Propagation: Take stem cuttings in spring — use a rooting hormone.

JUSTICIA: see Beloperone — 11

tubular flower ¼ in. across

flower-head of 20–50 blooms

fleshy leaf 2 in. long

K. blossfeldiana

Flaming Katy

Kalanchoe manginii Wendy

KALANCHOE

HOUSE PLANT
(see page 5)

Most Kalanchoes are grown for their flowers rather than their foliage. You can buy pots in bud and flower at any time of the year and the large flower-heads should last for many weeks. You can keep them to bloom again next year — prune, place on a shady windowsill and reduce watering. Keep almost dry for a month before moving to a well-lit spot.

SECRETS OF SUCCESS

Temperature: Average warmth — minimum 50°F (10°C) in winter.
Light: East- or west-facing window from spring to autumn — a south-facing window in winter.
Water: Water thoroughly — let surface dry between waterings.
Air Humidity: Misting is not necessary for K. blossfeldiana.
Repotting: Repot every year in spring after rest period.
Propagation: See Propagation of Succulents page 87.

TYPES

Kalanchoe blossfeldiana (1–1½ ft/30–45 cm) is the most popular species and there are many varieties. **K. manginii** bears pendant flowers.

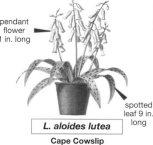

pendant flower 1 in. long

L. aloides lutea

spotted leaf 9 in. long

Cape Cowslip

Lachenalia aloides

LACHENALIA

POT PLANT
(see page 5)

An attractive plant, providing a host of tubular flowers in winter. Despite its novel appearance, Lachenalia has never been popular because of its inability to live in a heated room. In late summer plant 6–8 bulbs in a 6 in. (15 cm) pot with the tips just below the surface. Keep in a cool bright room, water once then leave until shoots appear. At this stage water and feed regularly.

SECRETS OF SUCCESS

Temperature: Cool — minimum 40°F (4°C) in winter.
Light: Bright light with some direct sun.
Water: Keep compost moist at all times during the flowering season.
Air Humidity: Mist leaves occasionally.
Care After Flowering: Continue watering for several weeks, then reduce and stop. Keep dry — repot in autumn.
Propagation: Remove and plant offsets at repotting time.

TYPES

The blooms of **Lachenalia aloides** are yellow tinged with green and red. They are borne on 1 ft (30 cm) stalks which bear brown or purple blotches. The variety **lutea** has all-yellow flowers.

Leea coccinea Burgundy

leaf
1–2 ft long,
leaflets
2–4 in. long

**L. coccinea
Burgundy**

TYPES

A single variety (**Leea coccinea**) is grown as a house plant — sometimes sold as **L. guineensis**. The variety **Burgundy** maintains the red foliage colour in good light.

LEEA
HOUSE PLANT (see page 5)

Leea is not in many textbooks but it can be found in garden centres and large stores. It is a shrubby plant bearing large leaves — each leaf being divided into numerous pointed leaflets. This foliage is bronzy red when young but usually turns green when mature. Feed regularly during the growing season and keep away from draughts. Try this one as an alternative specimen plant to Fatsia japonica (page 25).

SECRETS OF SUCCESS

Temperature: Average warmth — if possible keep cool in winter.
Light: Bright or light shade. Keep well-lit in winter.
Water: Water regularly from spring to autumn. Water sparingly in winter.
Air Humidity: Mist leaves frequently.
Repotting: Repot in spring every year.
Propagation: Take stem cuttings in summer.

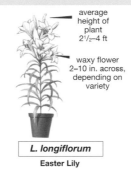

average
height of
plant
2½–4 ft

waxy flower
2–10 in. across,
depending on
variety

L. longiflorum

Easter Lily

TYPES

Lilium longiflorum (Easter Lily) is a popular choice — white 5 in. (12 cm) wide summer flowers. Bowl-, trumpet- and turk's cap-shaped varieties are available.

Lilium longiflorum

LILIUM
POT PLANT (see page 5)

The introduction of dwarf hybrids such as the Pixie series has made Lilies more popular as indoor plants. They are usually bought in flower and thrown away after flowering. You can keep the bulbs for planting next year, but the flowers will be small. Plant immediately in autumn, covering the tip with 1½–2 in. (4–5 cm) of compost. Keep cool, moist and dark until shoots appear.

SECRETS OF SUCCESS

Temperature: Cool — minimum 35°F (2°C) in winter.
Light: Bright light away from direct sunlight.
Water: Keep compost moist at all times during the growing season.
Air Humidity: Mist leaves occasionally.
Care After Flowering: Reduce watering when leaves turn yellow — keep compost just moist and repot bulbs in autumn.

Lisianthus russelianus

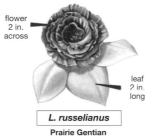

flower
2 in.
across

leaf
2 in.
long

L. russelianus

Prairie Gentian

TYPES

Just one species is sold — labelled **Lisianthus russelianus** or **Eustoma grandiflorum**. Compact varieties 1–1½ ft (30–45 cm) high rather than the tall-growing species are the types on offer.

LISIANTHUS
POT PLANT (see page 5)

These pot plants are offered for sale in flower during the summer months — double and single varieties are available in blue, purple, mauve and white. Technically the erect bushy plants are perennials, but they will have been treated with a growth-retardant by the nursery for the indoor plant market. The Poppy-like blooms appear in clusters. Not an easy plant to keep from one season to the next.

SECRETS OF SUCCESS

Temperature: Average warmth — keep cool in winter.
Light: Brightly lit spot — some sun is beneficial.
Water: Water thoroughly, then leave until compost is moderately dry.
Air Humidity: Mist leaves frequently.
Care After Flowering: Plants are usually discarded.
Propagation: Sow seeds in spring or divide plants in autumn.

Lotus berthelotii

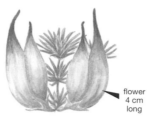

flower 4 cm long

L. maculatus

Lotus

TYPES

Lotus maculatus has orange-tipped yellow flowers — you are more likely to find **L. berthelotii** which has silvery-green leaves and red flowers.

LOTUS
HOUSE PLANT
(see page 5)

A trailing plant which is an excellent choice for a hanging basket. The leaves are divided into small narrow leaflets and the flowers are eye-catching. There are two species grown as house plants, and both bear blooms which are distinctly claw-like — the flowers appear along the 2 ft (60 cm) long stems in early summer. Lotus is not an easy plant to grow.

SECRETS OF SUCCESS

Temperature: Cool or average warmth — at least 45°F (7°C) in winter.
Light: Brightly lit spot — some direct sun.
Water: Keep moist during the growing season but water very sparingly in winter.
Air Humidity: Mist leaves occasionally.
Repotting: Repot, if necessary, in spring.
Propagation: Take stem cuttings in spring.

LYCASTE — 81 • MAMMILLARIA — 74

Mandevilla sanderi rosea

leaf 2 in. long

trumpet-shaped flower 3 in. across

twining woody stems

M. sanderi rosea

TYPES

Mandevilla (Dipladenia) sanderi rosea is grown for its yellow-throated pink flowers. **M. splendens** is larger-leaved with pink-throated blooms.

MANDEVILLA
HOUSE PLANT
(see page 5)

Large flowers appear in summer on the twining stems. Mandevilla can be grown as a climber, reaching 10 ft (3 m) or more, or it can be pruned back once flowering is finished in order to maintain it as a bush. The pink blossoms appear on the plant while it is still small, and the glossy leaves make it attractive all year round, but it has never become popular.

SECRETS OF SUCCESS

Temperature: Warm — minimum 55°F (13°C) in winter.
Light: Bright light or semi-shade — not direct sun.
Water: Water regularly from spring to autumn. Water sparingly in winter.
Air Humidity: Mist regularly, especially when in bud or flower.
Repotting: Repot in spring every year.
Propagation: Take stem cuttings in spring. Use a rooting hormone and provide bottom heat.

Maranta tricolor

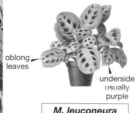

oblong leaves

underside usually purple

M. leuconeura kerchoveana

Prayer Plant
(Rabbit's Tracks)

TYPES

The ones you are likely to find will be varieties of **Maranta leuconeura**. The red-veined type is **erythrophylla**, sold as **M. tricolor**. The variety **massangeana** has white veins.

MARANTA
HOUSE PLANT
(see page 5)

The outstanding feature is the spectacular foliage, bearing coloured veins or prominent blotches on a background which may range from near white to almost black. It rarely exceeds a height of 8 in. (20 cm) and it has the habit of folding and raising its leaves at night. Maranta is not particularly difficult to grow, but it is not a plant for a beginner.

SECRETS OF SUCCESS

Temperature: Average warmth — minimum 50°F (10°C) in winter.
Light: Partial shade — do not expose to direct sunlight. Move to a well-lit spot in winter.
Water: Keep compost moist at all times with soft, tepid water. Reduce watering in winter.
Air Humidity: Mist leaves regularly.
Repotting: Repot in spring every 2 years.
Propagation: Divide plants at repotting time.

Medinilla magnifica

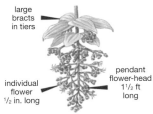

large bracts in tiers

individual flower ½ in. long

pendant flower-head 1½ ft long

M. magnifica

Rose Grape

TYPE

Medinilla magnifica is the only species grown. The oval leaves are prominently veined, the stems are winged and the flowers are as spectacular as anything to be seen indoors.

MEDINILLA

HOUSE PLANT (see page 5)

The pride of any collection, but you will need a warm greenhouse or conservatory. The leathery leaves of this 3 ft (1 m) tropical shrub are borne in pairs and in late spring the magnificent flower-heads appear. Temperature must be carefully controlled and the air must be kept constantly moist.

SECRETS OF SUCCESS

Temperature: Warm — 65°–75°F (18°–24°C) in summer and 60°–65°F (16°–18°C) in winter.
Light: Brightly lit spot screened from direct sun.
Water: Water moderately from spring to autumn. Water sparingly in winter.
Air Humidity: Mist leaves frequently — stand pot on a pebble tray (see page 115).
Repotting: Repot in spring every 1–2 years.
Propagation: Very difficult. Take stem cuttings in spring. Use a rooting hormone and provide bottom heat.

MILTONIA — 81

Monstera deliciosa variegata

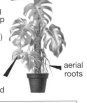

moss stick: tube of rolled plastic netting filled with damp moss or peat (see page 141)

foliage on young plant undivided — later cut and often perforated

aerial roots

M. deliciosa
(Philodendron pertusum)

Swiss Cheese Plant

TYPES

Monstera deliciosa can reach 10 ft (3 m) or more. The young leaves are heart-shaped — the mature leaves are up to 1½ ft (45 cm) wide. The variety **variegata** has cream-splashed leaves.

MONSTERA

HOUSE PLANT (see page 5)

The Swiss Cheese Plant has been a favourite for many years — with reasonable care a young plant will soon develop the characteristic lobed and perforated leaves. A sturdy support is necessary. The aerial roots must be pushed into the compost if you wish to grow a tall plant.

SECRETS OF SUCCESS

Temperature: Average warmth — minimum 50°F (10°C) in winter.
Light: Choose a moderately bright spot away from direct sunlight.
Water: Water thoroughly — keep the compost almost dry in winter.
Air Humidity: Mist and occasionally wash leaves.
Repotting: Repot in spring every 2 years.
Propagation: Remove and pot up stem tip when the plant becomes too tall.

Musa coccinea

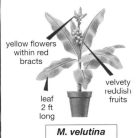

yellow flowers within red bracts

velvety reddish fruits

leaf 2 ft long

M. velutina

Banana

TYPES

Musa velutina grows about 4 ft (1.2 m) high — the yellow flowers are followed by attractive but inedible fruit. Even smaller is the 3 ft (1 m) Flowering Banana (**M. coccinea**).

MUSA

HOUSE PLANT (see page 5)

The Victorians gave pride of place to the Banana Plant in their conservatories, but only recently has there been a revival of interest. Few other leaves give such a tropical look to an indoor collection, but this plant is much more suited to the greenhouse than the living room. Even under glass you have to choose the variety with care. Bananas are best regarded as decorative rather than fruit-producing plants indoors.

SECRETS OF SUCCESS

Temperature: Warm — minimum 60°F (16°C) in winter.
Light: Bright light with some direct sun.
Water: Keep compost very moist at all times.
Air Humidity: Mist leaves frequently.
Repotting: Repot, if necessary, in spring or summer.
Propagation: Not practical in the home.

Nerium oleander La Aitana

fragrant flower 2 in. across

willow-like leaf 6–8 in. long

N. oleander

Oleander

TYPES

Nerium oleander may look compact in the garden centre, but remember that it will grow into a spreading shrub about 6 ft (2 m) tall. White, pink, red and yellow varieties are available.

NERIUM

HOUSE PLANT (see page 5)

Oleander needs a large room or conservatory. The fragrant blooms appear in summer and are borne in clusters above the Willow-like foliage. The wood and sap are poisonous. Oleander is not an easy plant to care for when it is large — the pot or tub must be moved to an unheated room in winter and it benefits from a summer vacation in the garden. In autumn cut back the stems which have flowered.

SECRETS OF SUCCESS

Temperature: Average warmth — minimum 45°F (7°C) in winter.
Light: Choose sunniest spot available.
Water: Water liberally in spring and summer. Water sparingly in winter. Use tepid water.
Air Humidity: Do not mist leaves.
Repotting: Repot, if necessary, in spring.
Propagation: Take stem cuttings in spring or summer.

Nertera depressa

creeping stems with tiny leaves. Glassy orange berries cover surface in autumn

N. depressa

Bead Plant

TYPE

The mat of creeping stems and 1/4 in. (0.5 cm) leaves of **Nertera depressa** might be mistaken for Helxine at first glance, but it is immediately recognisable once the pea-sized berries appear.

NERTERA

POT PLANT (see page 5)

Tiny white flowers in late spring are followed by berries which should last throughout the autumn and winter. Provide plenty of water, fresh air and bright light. Nearly all of them are discarded once the display of berries is finished. With care, however, this plant can be kept for several years.

SECRETS OF SUCCESS

Temperature: Cool — minimum 40°F (4°C) in winter.
Light: Bright light with some direct sun.
Water: Keep compost moist at all times — water sparingly in winter.
Air Humidity: Mist leaves occasionally.
Care After Flowering: Keep cool and rather dry during winter — increase watering when new growth appears. Place outdoors from late spring until the berries have appeared. Bring indoors for display.
Propagation: Divide plants in spring before placing outdoors.

POTTED PERFUME

CITRUS	JASMINUM POLYANTHUM
CONVALLARIA	LILIUM (some)
CYTISUS CANARIENSIS	MANDEVILLA
DATURA	NARCISSUS (some)
EUCHARIS	NERIUM
FREESIA	OLEANDER
GARDENIA	ORCHID (some)
HOYA	PLUMERIA
HYACINTH	SPATHIPHYLLUM
IRIS RETICULATA	STEPHANOTIS

Nolina tuberculata

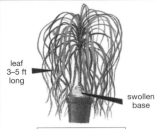

leaf 3–5 ft long

swollen base

N. tuberculata

Pony Tail
(Elephant Foot)

NOLINA
HOUSE PLANT
(see page 5)

Pony Tail is useful if you want a tall specimen plant which will not require a lot of attention. The swollen bulb-like base stores water, so occasional dryness at the roots will do no harm. The plume of long strap-like leaves gives the plant its common name. It is a rarity in Britain but is popular in the U.S. It may be labelled Beaucarnea recurvata.

TYPE

One species is sold — **Nolina tuberculata**. It grows slowly, but with time the trunk will reach 7 ft (2 m) or more and the base will be swollen like a huge bulb.

SECRETS OF SUCCESS

Temperature: Average warmth — minimum 50°F (10°C) in winter.
Light: Brightly lit spot — some sun is beneficial.
Water: Water thoroughly, then leave until compost is moderately dry. Avoid overwatering.
Air Humidity: Misting is not necessary.
Repotting: Repot, if necessary, in spring.
Propagation: Plant up offsets at repotting time. Not easy — best to buy plants.

NOTOCACTUS — 74 • ODONTOGLOSSUM — 81 • ONCIDIUM — 82 • OPUNTIA — 74 • OXALIS — 71 • PACHYPHYTUM — 89

Pachystachys lutea

golden flower-head 5 in. long

oval leaf 4 in. long

P. lutea

Lollipop Plant

PACHYSTACHYS
HOUSE PLANT
(see page 5)

The Lollipop Plant bears cone-shaped flower-heads above the oval leaves. The main appeal is the long flowering season — from late spring until autumn if the plant is liberally watered and fed regularly. Leaf fall is a sign of dryness at the roots. This shrubby plant can get out of hand if it is not pruned in the spring. The stem tips which are removed can be used as cuttings.

TYPE

Pachystachys lutea grows about 1½ ft (45 cm) high, with flower-heads made up of golden bracts and white blooms peeping through. The leaves are prominently veined.

SECRETS OF SUCCESS

Temperature: Average warmth — minimum 55°F (13°C) in winter.
Light: Brightly lit spot away from direct sun in summer.
Water: Water liberally from spring to late autumn. Water sparingly in winter.
Air Humidity: Mist leaves in summer.
Repotting: Repot in spring every year.
Propagation: Take stem cuttings in spring or summer.

Pandanus veitchii

leaf 2–3 ft long

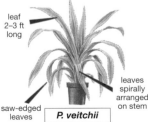

leaves spirally arranged on stem

saw-edged leaves

P. veitchii

Screw Pine

PANDANUS
HOUSE PLANT
(see page 5)

The spiny-edged narrow leaves are quite similar to those of the Pineapple plant and they are arranged spirally around the stem — hence the common name Screw Pine. It is a slow-growing plant, but it develops into a showy false palm several feet high, with a corkscrew-like trunk and long, arching leaves.

TYPES

Pandanus veitchii is wide-spreading and reaches a height of about 3 ft (1 m). The serrated leaf edges are sharp — grow the variety **compacta** to keep the foliage out of harm's way. **P. baptistii** has smooth-edged leaves.

SECRETS OF SUCCESS

Temperature: Average warmth — minimum 55°F (13°C) in winter.
Light: Brightly lit spot away from direct sun in summer.
Water: Water liberally from spring to autumn. Water very sparingly in winter. Use tepid water.
Air Humidity: Mist leaves frequently.
Repotting: Repot in spring every 2–3 years.
Propagation: Remove basal suckers when they are about 6 in. (15 cm) long and treat as stem cuttings. Use a rooting hormone and provide bottom heat.

Passiflora caerulea

ornate flower 3 in. across

hand-like leaf 4 in. across

P. caerulea

Passion Flower

TYPES

There are several Passifloras, including the Granadilla (**Passiflora quadrangularis**) which bears large yellow fruit, but only **P. caerulea** is grown as a house plant.

PASSIFLORA

HOUSE PLANT
(see page 5)

The Passiflora flower has an intricate structure — despite the delicacy of the flower there is nothing delicate about the plant. It is a rampant climber which will outgrow its welcome if it is not cut back hard each spring. The stems bear deeply-lobed leaves, tendrils and short-lived flowers all summer long.

SECRETS OF SUCCESS

Temperature: Average warmth. Keep at 40°–50°F (4°–10°C) in winter.
Light: Choose sunniest spot available.
Water: Keep compost moist at all times — may need daily watering in summer. Reduce watering in winter.
Air Humidity: Mist leaves occasionally.
Repotting: Repot in spring every year.
Propagation: Take stem cuttings in summer. Sow seeds in spring.

PELARGONIUM: see Geranium — 28 • PELLAEA — 78

Pellionia pulchra

oval, green leaf with pale central area

P. daveauana

TYPES

Trailing **Pellionia daveauana** (Watermelon Pellionia) bears a pale central band on each leaf — the outer margin may be olive or bronzy-green. **P. pulchra** (Satin Pellionia) has very dark veins on the upper surface and is purple below.

PELLIONIA

HOUSE PLANT
(see page 5)

The two types of Pellionia make useful additions to the terrarium or bottle garden, but when used in a hanging basket or as ground cover between other plants they are more demanding than easy trailers like Tradescantia. The Pellionias require moist air and winter warmth. They are unusually sensitive to draughts.

SECRETS OF SUCCESS

Temperature: Average warmth — minimum 55°F (13°C) in winter.
Light: Semi-shade or bright indirect light.
Water: Keep compost moist at all times — reduce watering in winter. Use soft water.
Air Humidity: Mist leaves frequently.
Repotting: Repot in spring every 2 years.
Propagation: Divide plants at repotting time. Stem cuttings root easily.

Pentas lanceolata K. Schum

flower-head 3–4 in. across

hairy leaf 2–3 in. long

P. lanceolata

Egyptian Star Cluster

TYPES

Pentas lanceolata (P. carnea) is the basic species. The flower-head bears numerous tubular starry blooms — there are named varieties in white, pink, red and mauve.

PENTAS

HOUSE PLANT
(see page 5)

Not a plant you are likely to find in your local garden shop, but it is well worth growing in a sunny window if you can obtain one. The growth becomes straggly if you fail to pinch out the stem tips regularly. Keep the plant about 18 in. (45 cm) high. The flowers may appear at any time of the year — winter is the most usual. Pentas is easy to grow.

SECRETS OF SUCCESS

Temperature: Average warmth — minimum 50°F (10°C) in winter.
Light: Bright light with some direct sun.
Water: Keep compost moist at all times — reduce watering in winter.
Air Humidity: Mist leaves occasionally.
Repotting: Repot in spring every year.
Propagation: Take stem cuttings in spring — use a rooting hormone.

Peperomia magnoliaefolia variegata

mound of heart-shaped leaves

P. caperata

TYPES

The three favourites are **Peperomia caperata** (1 in./ 2.5 cm wide corrugated leaves), **P. hederaefolia** (2 in./ 5 cm wide quilted leaves) and **P. magnoliaefolia variegata** (2 in./5 cm waxy leaves).

PEPEROMIA — HOUSE PLANT (see page 5)

Peperomias are slow growing, compact and provide colourful or novel foliage where space is limited — the flower-head is an upright 'rat-tail' covered with tiny greenish flowers. There are a few trailing species but the popular ones are bushy types with a wide range of leaf shapes and colours. The Peperomias are not difficult and will flourish in a centrally-heated room, but it is necessary to take care when watering.

SECRETS OF SUCCESS

Temperature: Average warmth — minimum 50°F (10°C) in winter.
Light: Bright or semi-shade, away from direct sunlight.
Water: Allow compost to dry out to some extent between waterings — apply very little in winter.
Air Humidity: Mist occasionally in summer — never in winter.
Repotting: In spring only if necessary.
Propagation: Take leaf cuttings in spring.

PHILODENDRON — HOUSE PLANT (see page 5)

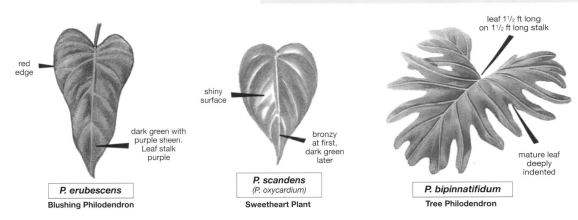

red edge

dark green with purple sheen. Leaf stalk purple

P. erubescens
Blushing Philodendron

shiny surface

bronzy at first, dark green later

P. scandens (P. oxycardium)
Sweetheart Plant

leaf 1½ ft long on 1½ ft long stalk

mature leaf deeply indented

P. bipinnatifidum
Tree Philodendron

TYPES

The leathery foliage of the climbing types varies widely in shape (entire to deeply cut), colour (pale green to rich red) and texture (glossy to velvety). **Philodendron scandens** is one of the easiest to grow — thin stems bear 3–5 in. (8– 12 cm) leaves. The general foliage pattern for the large-leaved Philodendrons is a 6–16 in. (15–40 cm) arrow-shaped leaf with a glossy surface. The favourite species for interior decorators include **P. hastatum**, **P. erubescens** and its hybrids, the velvety **P. melanochrysum** and the variegated **P. ilsemannii**. The non-climbing types, such as **P. bipinnatifidum**, spread to 8 ft (2.5 m) or more.

There are two basic types of Philodendron. Climbers are the more popular group — some of the tallest and most spectacular of all indoor plants are found here. The favourite one, however, is the Sweetheart Plant which is compact enough for even a tiny room. Aerial roots are a feature of these plants — push them into the compost to provide moisture for the upper leaves. See page 141 for instructions on how to make a moss stick. Most of the non-climbing types are capable of growing into immense plants and are therefore not suitable for the average home.

SECRETS OF SUCCESS

Temperature: Average warmth — minimum 55°F (13°C) in winter.
Light: Usual requirement is moderate brightness or light shade — P. scandens will grow in shady conditions. Keep out of direct sunlight.
Water: Water thoroughly and regularly — keep compost just moist in winter.
Air Humidity: Mist leaves regularly.
Repotting: Repot in spring every 2–3 years.
Propagation: Take stem cuttings in summer.

Philodendron scandens

Pilea Norfolk

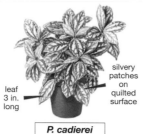

leaf
3 in.
long

silvery
patches
on
quilted
surface

P. cadierei
Aluminium Plant

TYPES

Pilea cadierei (1 ft/30 cm) is the most popular species — the varieties **Norfolk** and **Bronze** have coloured leaves. **P. Moon Valley** has quilted green leaves with prominent brown veins.

PILEA

HOUSE PLANT
(see page 5)

Nearly all Pileas are either bushy or trailing plants. The bushy ones are compact and not difficult, but they soon become leggy with age. As cuttings root easily it is a good idea to start new plants each spring. There are a few trailing species, including P. nummularifolia, P. depressa (Creeping Jenny) and the ferny Artillery Plant (P. microphylla).

SECRETS OF SUCCESS

Temperature: Average warmth — minimum 50°F (10°C) in winter.
Light: Bright light or semi-shade — protect from direct summer sun.
Water: Water liberally from spring to autumn — water sparingly in winter. Use tepid water.
Air Humidity: Mist leaves regularly.
Repotting: Repot retained plants in spring.
Propagation: Take stem cuttings in spring or summer.

PLATYCERIUM — 78

Plectranthus coleoides
marginatus

underside
and leaf
edge
rosy-purple

prominent
white
veins

P. oertendahlii
Swedish Ivy

TYPES

The most popular type (**Plectranthus oertendahlii**) bears colourful 1 in. (2.5 cm) wide leaves. The 1 in. (2.5 cm) long flowers are mauve. The largest leaves occur on **P. coleoides marginatus**.

PLECTRANTHUS

HOUSE PLANT
(see page 5)

Popularly known as Swedish Ivy, but it looks more like a small and plain Coleus rather than an Ivy. The trailing stems are covered by the foliage and they are fast growing. It is a pity that this plant is not more popular as it has many good points. It will survive in dry air, it will withstand occasional dryness at the roots and it will sometimes flower. Pinch out tips occasionally to keep the plant bushy.

SECRETS OF SUCCESS

Temperature: Average warmth — minimum 50°F (10°C) in winter.
Light: Bright light or semi-shade — avoid direct sunlight.
Water: Keep compost moist at all times — reduce watering in winter.
Air Humidity: Mist leaves occasionally.
Repotting: Repot in spring every 2 years.
Propagation: Take stem cuttings in spring or summer.

Plumbago auriculata

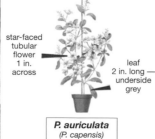

star-faced
tubular
flower
1 in.
across

leaf
2 in. long —
underside
grey

P. auriculata
(P. capensis)

Cape Leadwort

TYPES

Grow **Plumbago auriculata** as a trailer or tie it to supports as a climber — the stems will reach 3 ft (1 m). Cut back old shoots in early spring. A white variety (**alba**) can be bought.

PLUMBAGO

HOUSE PLANT
(see page 5)

Clusters of sky blue flowers appearing throughout summer and autumn make the Cape Leadwort an outstanding house plant when trained around a window. This vigorous climber can be kept as a specimen plant on a sunny windowsill. The secret of success is to keep it cool throughout the winter and early spring.

SECRETS OF SUCCESS

Temperature: Cool or average warmth — minimum 45°F (7°C) in winter.
Light: Bright light with some direct sun.
Water: Keep compost moist at all times. Water sparingly in winter.
Air Humidity: Mist leaves occasionally.
Repotting: Repot, if necessary, in spring.
Propagation: Take stem cuttings in autumn. Sow seeds in spring.

Plumeria rubra

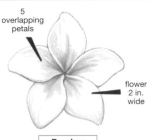

5 overlapping petals

flower 2 in. wide

P. rubra

Frangipani

TYPE

A single species (**Plumeria rubra**) is grown as a house plant. The pointed leaves are long and oval and the heavily scented flowers are white or pink.

PLUMERIA
HOUSE PLANT (see page 5)

Frangipani is a popular shrub in sub-tropical regions but it is a rarity indoors in temperate countries. It is sometimes recommended as a house plant, but it grows 7 ft (2 m) or more in a tub and is better suited to the conservatory. The glory of the plant is the large clusters of flowers borne at the ends of the branches.

SECRETS OF SUCCESS

Temperature: Average warmth — minimum 50°F (10°C) in winter.
Light: Bright light with some direct sun.
Water: Water liberally from spring to autumn. Water very sparingly in winter.
Air Humidity: Mist leaves occasionally.
Repotting: Repot in spring every 2 years.
Propagation: Take stem cuttings in spring. Use a rooting hormone and provide bottom heat.

Euphorbia pulcherrima

flower-head up to 1 ft across

lobed leaf 5 in. long

Euphorbia pulcherrima

Poinsettia

TYPES

All Poinsettias are varieties of **Euphorbia pulcherrima**. Red is the favourite colour but pink and white are available. The most unusual is deep cream with a rosy heart.

POINSETTIA
POT PLANT (see page 5)

Before the 1960s the Poinsettia was a tall-growing shrub which was difficult to keep in leaf and flower. Things have changed — today's Poinsettia is compact (1–1½ ft/30–45 cm), much more attractive and much less delicate. With care the display should last for 2–5 months if the plant was not stood outdoors and the tiny flowers were in bud at the time of purchase.

SECRETS OF SUCCESS

Temperature: Average warmth — minimum 55°F (13°C) when in flower.
Light: Maximum light during winter.
Water: Water thoroughly — wait until compost is moderately dry before watering again.
Air Humidity: Mist leaves frequently during the flowering season.
Care After Flowering: Plant should be discarded.
Propagation: Leave it to the keen hobbyist.

POLYPODIUM — 78

Polyscias balfouriana marginata

leaf 8 in. long

feathery leaves

P. fruticosa

Ming Aralia

TYPES

Polyscias balfouriana (Dinner Plate Aralia) has 3 in. (8 cm) wide grey-speckled leaves — **pennockii** is a yellow-veined variety. The leaves of the Ming Aralia are 8 in. (20 cm) long.

POLYSCIAS
HOUSE PLANT (see page 5)

The Aralias make attractive specimen plants when placed in decorative containers — the twisted stems and the attractive foliage give the plants an Oriental look. They are not popular, however, as they are expensive and readily shed their leaves if their needs are not fully met. The Dinner Plate Aralia is the one you are most likely to find.

SECRETS OF SUCCESS

Temperature: Average or warm — minimum 60°F (16°C) in winter.
Light: Bright — avoid direct sunlight.
Water: Water moderately from spring to autumn — sparingly in winter.
Air Humidity: Mist leaves frequently.
Repotting: Repot in spring every 2 years.
Propagation: Difficult. Take stem cuttings in spring — use a rooting hormone and provide bottom heat.

PRIMULA

POT PLANT
(see page 5)

• TENDER TYPES

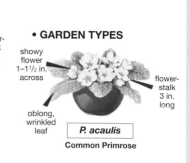

flower-
stalk
1½ ft
long

green-eyed
flower 1–1½ in.
across

flower-
stalk
1 ft
long

frilly flower
1–1½ in.
across

flower-
stalk
1 ft
long

yellow-
eyed
flower
½ in.
across

oval,
toothed
leaf

heart-shaped,
coarse leaf

lobed,
toothed
leaf

• GARDEN TYPES

showy
flower
1–1½ in.
across

flower-
stalk
3 in.
long

oblong,
wrinkled
leaf

P. malacoides	**P. obconica**	**P. sinensis**	**P. acaulis**
Fairy Primrose	Poison Primrose	Chinese Primrose	Common Primrose

Primula kewensis

TYPES

Primulas bear large numbers of flowers during the winter months. Two garden types are grown indoors to brighten up the winter windowsill. They are **Primula acaulis** (Common Primrose) with flowers on very short stalks, and **P. variabilis** (Polyanthus) with colourful flowers on 1 ft (30 cm) stalks. The most popular tender type is **P. malacoides** which bears tiers of fragrant flowers on 1½ ft (45 cm) stalks. **P. obconica** has fragrant flowers which are available in a wide range of colours, the **P. sinensis** flowers are yellow-eyed and usually red. **P. kewensis** is the only yellow tender Primula.

The garden Primulas bear clusters of winter or spring flowers in the centre of the leaf rosette or on tall flower stalks. Common Primrose and Polyanthus make colourful pot plants which can be planted in the garden after flowering, but it is usually the tender species which are grown indoors — the flowers are smaller and are borne on stalks. The Fairy Primrose is the daintiest, the Chinese Primrose is the frilly one and the Poison Primrose is the one not to touch.

SECRETS OF SUCCESS

Temperature: Cool — keep at 55°–60°F (13°–16°C) in the flowering season.
Light: Maximum light, but protect from direct sunlight.
Water: Keep compost moist at all times during the flowering season.
Air Humidity: Mist leaves occasionally.
Care After Flowering: Plant P. acaulis and P. variabilis in the garden — others are generally discarded. P. obconica and P. sinensis can be kept — repot and keep in light shade throughout summer. Water very sparingly — in autumn resume normal watering.
Propagation: Sow seeds in midsummer.

PTERIS — 44

PUNICA

POT PLANT
(see page 5)

The ordinary Pomegranate is not suitable for the living room but the Dwarf Pomegranate makes an excellent pot plant for a sunny window. The flowers may be followed by bright orange fruit, but they will not ripen. In summer the pot can be stood outdoors and in winter a cool spot is required. During the dormant period the leaves will drop.

SECRETS OF SUCCESS

Temperature: Average warmth — minimum 40°F (4°C) in winter.
Light: Bright light — some direct sun is essential.
Water: Water liberally from spring to autumn. Water very sparingly in winter.
Air Humidity: Mist leaves occasionally in summer.
Repotting: Repot, if necessary, in spring.
Propagation: Take stem cuttings in summer. Use a rooting hormone and provide bottom heat.

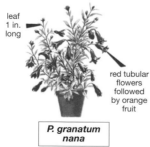

leaf
1 in.
long

red tubular
flowers
followed
by orange
fruit

**P. granatum
nana**

Dwarf Pomegranate

TYPE

Punica granatum nana grows about 3 ft (1 m) high. The leaves are glossy and bright scarlet flowers appear in summer. Ball-like fruit develop … if you are lucky.

Punica granatum nana

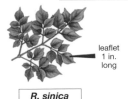

R. sinica

RADERMACHERA

HOUSE PLANT (see page 5)

leaflet 1 in. long

A house plant of the 1980s — it was introduced to Europe from Taiwan at the beginning of the decade, and its popularity as a specimen indoor tree has increased. It may be labelled simply as 'foliage plant', but you can't mistake the large compound leaves bearing shiny, deeply-veined leaflets with long tapering points. Central heating is no problem because it tolerates dry air.

TYPES

There is much confusion over the naming of the Radermachera grown as a house plant. It may be labelled as **Radermachera sinica**, **R. Danielle** or **Stereospermum suaveolens**. A variegated form is available.

SECRETS OF SUCCESS

Temperature: Average warmth — minimum 50°–55°F (10°–13°C) in winter.
Light: Bright, but protect from midday summer sun.
Water: Keep compost moist at all times — avoid waterlogging.
Air Humidity: Misting is not necessary.
Repotting: Repot, if necessary, in spring.
Propagation: Take stem cuttings in summer.

Radermachera sinica

REBUTIA — 74 • RHAPIS — 86 • RHIPSALIDOPSIS — 75

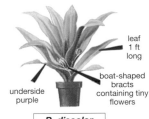

leaf 1 ft long

boat-shaped bracts containing tiny flowers

underside purple

R. discolor

Boat Lily

RHOEO

HOUSE PLANT (see page 5)

The short stem bears fleshy, lance-shaped leaves. Their colouring is unusual — glossy green or green-and-yellow above, purple below. An added feature of interest is the presence of small white flowers in purple 'boats' at the base of the lower leaves. Remove side shoots if grown as a specimen plant. It needs winter warmth and freedom from draughts.

TYPES

Rhoeo discolor is the only species — the popular variety is **vittata** which bears green leaves with bold yellow stripes. The 'boat' flowers are responsible for one of the common names — Moses in the Cradle.

SECRETS OF SUCCESS

Temperature: Average warmth — minimum 50°–55°F (10°–13°C) in winter.
Light: Bright or semi-shade — no direct sun in summer.
Water: Keep compost moist at all times — reduce watering in winter.
Air Humidity: Mist leaves frequently.
Repotting: Repot in spring every year.
Propagation: Use side shoots as cuttings in spring or summer. Bushy plants can be divided.

Rhoeo discolor vittata

flowers single, semi-double or double

plant 6–12 in. high

flower ½–1½ in. across

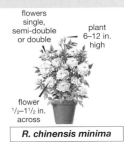

R. chinensis minima

Miniature Rose (Fairy Rose)

ROSA

POT PLANT (see page 5)

It may seem strange that very few homes have a Miniature Rose — it cannot be because of a lack of appeal. The problem is that they have special needs. Follow the rules below, and in autumn repot and stand the plant outdoors. Bring back in mid-winter — cut off top half of the stems and move to its display spot.

TYPES

Miniature Roses are hybrids of **Rosa chinensis minima**, blooming from spring to late summer. Choose a variety listed as 1 ft (30 cm) tall or less. Choose a plant grown from a cutting.

SECRETS OF SUCCESS

Temperature: Average warmth — keep at 50°–70°F (10°–21°C) during the growing season.
Light: Maximum light — a sunny window is ideal.
Water: Water liberally when indoors. Allow to dry out slightly between waterings.
Air Humidity: Mist leaves frequently.
Care After Flowering: See above.
Propagation: Take stem cuttings in early spring — use a rooting hormone.

Rosa Judy Fischer

Saintpaulia Rhapsodie No. 3

round or heart-shaped leaf usually 2–4 in. across

violet-like flower usually 1–1¹/₂ in. across

fleshy foliage with velvety surface

S. hybrida

African Violet

SAINTPAULIA
HOUSE PLANT (see page 5)

The original African Violet was notoriously difficult to grow, but modern varieties are much more robust and freer flowering. They are world-wide favourites — the main attractions are their compact size and the ability to produce several flushes of flowers each year. The basic needs are steady warmth, careful watering, good light, high air humidity and regular feeding. Remove dead flowers and leaves immediately.

TYPES

There are thousands of varieties of **Saintpaulia hybrida**. Widths range from less than 3 in. (8 cm) to more than 16 in. (40 cm) — flower forms include singles, doubles, frilled, bicolours and stars.

SECRETS OF SUCCESS

Temperature: Average warmth — minimum 60°F (16°C) in winter.
Light: Bright light: E- or S-facing window in winter — W-facing window in summer. Shade from sun.
Water: Keep compost moist — use tepid water.
Air Humidity: High air humidity is essential — see page 155.
Repotting: Repot, only if essential, in spring.
Propagation: Take leaf cuttings in spring.

Sansevieria Golden hahnii

sword-like foliage

golden-edged leaves

S. trifasciata laurentii

Mother-in-Law's Tongue

SANSEVIERIA
HOUSE PLANT (see page 5)

Mother-in-Law's Tongue is the most popular type. It is seen on windowsills and in Pot Groups everywhere. It is almost indestructible — the upright succulent leaves withstand draughts, dry air, bright sunshine, dense shade and direct sunlight. Under good conditions it bears sprays of fragrant, small white flowers.

TYPES

Sansevieria trifasciata is the all-green basic species, with 1–3 ft (30 cm–1 m) high leaves — the variegated type **laurentii** is much more popular. **S. Golden hahnii** is a 6 in. (15 cm) dwarf.

SECRETS OF SUCCESS

Temperature: Average warmth — minimum 50°F (10°C) in winter.
Light: Bright light with some sun, but will grow in shade.
Water: Water moderately from spring to autumn — every 1–2 months in winter.
Air Humidity: Misting is not necessary.
Repotting: Seldom required — repot if pot cracks.
Propagation: Remove offset by cutting off at base — allow to dry before inserting in compost.

Saxifraga sarmentosa

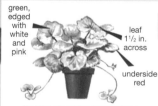

green, edged with white and pink

leaf 1¹/₂ in. across

underside red

S. sarmentosa tricolor

Mother of Thousands (Magic Carpet)

SAXIFRAGA
HOUSE PLANT (see page 5)

The outstanding feature is the production of long, slender red runners which bear miniature plants at their ends. Clusters of insignificant flowers appear in summer. You can choose from two varieties: S. sarmentosa is easy to care for — S. sarmentosa tricolor is more attractive, but it is unfortunately slow growing and more tender.

TYPES

Saxifraga sarmentosa (S. stolonifera) bears olive green leaves with silvery veins. These plants grow about 8 in. (20 cm) high, and the pendant runners can reach 2–3 ft (60 cm–1 m). The colourful variety **tricolor** is smaller.

SECRETS OF SUCCESS

Temperature: Cool or average warmth — minimum 40°–45°F (4°–7°C) in winter.
Light: Brightly lit spot, away from direct sunshine.
Water: Water liberally from spring to autumn. Water sparingly in winter.
Air Humidity: Mist leaves occasionally.
Repotting: Repot in spring every year.
Propagation: Very easy. Peg down plantlets in compost — cut stem when rooted.

Schefflera actinophylla

leathery, glossy leaflets

leaf-stalk attached to tree-like stem

S. actinophylla
(Brassaia actinophylla)

Umbrella Tree

SCHEFFLERA

HOUSE PLANT
(see page 5)

In subtropical gardens it is known as the Octopus Tree because of its spectacular tentacle-like flowers. Unfortunately it does not bloom under room conditions and the indoor plant form is known as the Umbrella Tree, which refers to the finger-like glossy leaflets radiating like umbrella spokes. Schefflera is not difficult to grow.

TYPES

Schefflera actinophylla is an attractive bush when young — a 6–8 ft (1.8–2.5 m) tree when mature. The number of leaflets per stalk increases from 4 to 12 with age. Less easy to find are the smaller **S. digitata** and the distinctly-veined **S. octophyllum**.

SECRETS OF SUCCESS

Temperature: Average warmth — minimum 55°F (13°C) in winter. If possible avoid temperatures above 70°F (21°C).
Light: Bright light, away from direct sunshine.
Water: Water liberally from spring to autumn. Water sparingly in winter.
Air Humidity: Mist leaves frequently.
Repotting: Repot in spring every 2 years.
Propagation: Difficult. Take stem cuttings in summer. Use a rooting hormone and provide bottom heat.

Schizanthus hybrida

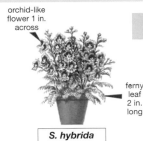

orchid-like flower 1 in. across

ferny leaf 2 in. long

S. hybrida

Poor Man's Orchid

SCHIZANTHUS

POT PLANT
(see page 5)

Poor Man's Orchid is an apt name for this plant — exotic multicoloured blooms can be obtained for the price of a packet of seed. Sowings are made in spring for late summer flowering or in autumn for blooming in spring. Pinch out the tips of young plants to induce bushiness. Move seedlings into larger pots — 5 in. (12 cm) for compact varieties, 7 in. (18 cm) for taller types. Keep the plants cool, well lit and provide fresh air on warm days.

TYPES

Schizanthus hybrida bears unevenly lobed and yellow-eyed flowers. Choose a compact variety (10–15 in./25–38 cm) such as **Hit Parade**, **Star Parade** or **Dwarf Bouquet**.

SECRETS OF SUCCESS

Temperature: Cool or average warmth — keep at 50°–65°F (10°–18°C).
Light: Bright light with some direct sun.
Water: Keep compost moist at all times.
Air Humidity: Mist leaves occasionally.
Care After Flowering: Plant should be discarded.
Propagation: Sow seeds in spring or autumn.

SCHLUMBERGERA — 75 • SCILLA — 68

TRY GARDEN PLANTS INDOORS

There are many plants in the outdoor garden section of the garden centre which are not included in this book but which can be grown as house- or pot-plants. Listed below are some which are readily available.

AGAPANTHUS

ASTILBE

BEDDING PLANTS

BUXUS

CALLISTEMON

HEBE

LAURUS

MYRTUS

NANDINA

VIBURNUM

Scindapsus aureus

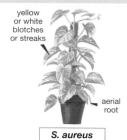

yellow or white blotches or streaks

aerial root

S. aureus

TYPES

Treat **Scindapsus (Epipremnum) aureus** as a climber or trailer — a moss stick (page 141) is an ideal support. Stems may reach 6 ft (2 m) or more. Varieties are more difficult to grow than the species.

SCINDAPSUS

HOUSE PLANT
(see page 5)

A great favourite on both sides of the Atlantic — not a difficult plant to grow, but it has difficulty with its name. It is Scindapsus aureus (Devil's Ivy) in Britain's garden centres, Golden Pothos in the U.S and Epipremnum aureus to the botanist. The leaves are blotched with yellow or white.

SECRETS OF SUCCESS

Temperature: Average warmth — minimum 50°–55°F (10°–13°C) in winter.
Light: Well-lit but sunless spot. Variegation will fade in poor light.
Water: Water liberally from spring to autumn — water sparingly in winter.
Air Humidity: Mist leaves frequently.
Repotting: Repot, if necessary, in spring.
Propagation: Take stem cuttings in spring — use a rooting hormone. Keep in dark until rooted.

SEDUM — 89

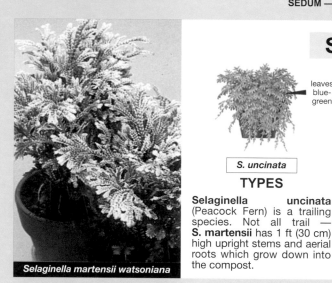

Selaginella martensii watsoniana

leaves blue-green

S. uncinata

TYPES

Selaginella uncinata (Peacock Fern) is a trailing species. Not all trail — **S. martensii** has 1 ft (30 cm) high upright stems and aerial roots which grow down into the compost.

SELAGINELLA

HOUSE PLANT
(see page 5)

Selaginella (Creeping Moss) is a plant for the glass garden — it is much less happy away from this protection, its tiny leaves shrivelling in the dry air of hot rooms. You can try it in a shallow, well-drained pot in semi-shade. Use soft water for watering and misting. The Resurrection Plant (S. lepidophylla) is a novelty — it is bought as a dry ball and restored to life by soaking in water.

SECRETS OF SUCCESS

Temperature: Average warmth — minimum 55°F (13°C) in winter.
Light: Semi-shade.
Water: Keep compost moist at all times — reduce in winter. Use soft water.
Air Humidity: Mist, but do not soak, leaves regularly.
Repotting: Repot, if necessary, in spring.
Propagation: Take stem cuttings in spring or summer.

SEMPERVIVUM — 89

Senecio macroglossus variegatus

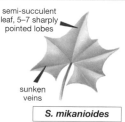

semi-succulent leaf, 5–7 sharply pointed lobes

sunken veins

S. mikanioides

German Ivy (Parlour Ivy)

TYPES

Senecio macroglossus variegatus is the Cape Ivy — 2 in. (5 cm) long yellow-edged leaves on stems up to 10 ft (3 m) long. **S. mikanioides** (German Ivy) can also reach 10 ft (3 m) — the leaves are 3 in. (8 cm) wide.

SENECIO

HOUSE PLANT
(see page 5)

Senecio is a confusing genus. There are the familiar flowering one (page 16), the Succulent species (page 89) and the Ivy-like climbers described here. Like the true Ivies the leaves are lobed and the stems trail or are trained up canes or wires, but these lobes are more pointed and fleshier. It is surprising that they are not popular — they are better able to cope with dry air than true Ivies.

SECRETS OF SUCCESS

Temperature: Average warmth — minimum 50°F (10°C) in winter.
Light: Bright light — some direct sun beneficial in winter.
Water: Keep compost moist at all times — reduce watering in winter.
Air Humidity: Mist leaves occasionally.
Repotting: Repot in spring every 2 years.
Propagation: Take stem cuttings in spring or summer.

Smithiantha hybrida Cathedral

pendant flower 2 in. long

mottled leaf 4 in. long

S. hybrida

Temple Bells

TYPES

Smithiantha zebrina is a tall-growing plant — it is better to choose one of the varieties of **S. hybrida** (12–15 in./30–38 cm). The flowers are a blend of yellow, orange and/or pink.

SMITHIANTHA

POT PLANT (see page 5)

Temple Bells describes the pendant bell-like flowers which appear on long stalks in autumn above the mottled velvety leaves. Smithiantha is not an easy plant to grow in the average room — it needs the warm humid conditions of a conservatory. It is raised from rhizomes planted on their sides in potting compost in late winter — they should be 1/2 in. (1 cm) below the surface.

SECRETS OF SUCCESS

Temperature: Warm or average warmth — minimum 60°F (16°C).
Light: Brightly lit spot away from direct sun.
Water: Keep compost moist at all times.
Air Humidity: Mist frequently but do not wet the leaves.
Care After Flowering: Stop watering and leave the rhizome to overwinter in the pot. Repot in late winter.
Propagation: Divide rhizomes at repotting time.

Solanum pseudocapsicum

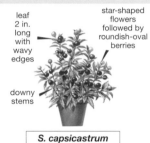

leaf 2 in. long with wavy edges

star-shaped flowers followed by roundish-oval berries

downy stems

S. capsicastrum

Winter Cherry

TYPES

Solanum capsicastrum is the Winter Cherry. The 4 in. (10 cm) wide berries are orange-red. The Jerusalem Cherry (**S. pseudocapsicum**) is taller (1½–2½ ft/45–75 cm high) and the berries are larger.

SOLANUM

POT PLANT (see page 5)

The plants bear tiny flowers in summer and are followed in autumn by green berries. As winter approaches they change colour and become a familiar sight at Christmas. If the bush is placed on a sunny windowsill in a cool room, the display should last for months. A word of warning — the fruits can be poisonous.

SECRETS OF SUCCESS

Temperature: Cool — keep at 50°–60°F (10°–16°C) in winter.
Light: Bright light with some direct sun.
Water: Keep compost moist at all times.
Air Humidity: Mist leaves frequently.
Care After Flowering: Usually discarded. Can be kept by keeping almost dry until spring, repotting, and standing outdoors in summer and then bringing indoors in autumn.
Propagation: Sow seeds.

Sollya heterophylla

flower 1 in. across

S. heterophylla

Australian Bluebell

TYPE

Sollya heterophylla is available at some garden centres and can be used to clothe a tall foliage plant.

SOLLYA

HOUSE PLANT (see page 5)

Many of the climbers described in this book are giants which are more at home in the conservatory than in the living room, but this is a modest plant which grows to about 3 ft (1 m). The groups of nodding bell-shaped flowers open in summer — their colour is sky-blue and they are followed by purple fruits. Not an easy plant to find, but one worth looking for.

SECRETS OF SUCCESS

Temperature: Cool or average warmth — at least 45°F (7°C) in winter.
Light: Brightly lit spot or light shade.
Water: Keep moist at all times during the growing season, but water more sparingly in winter.
Air Humidity: Mist leaves occasionally.
Repotting: Repot, if necessary, in spring.
Propagation: Take stem cuttings in spring.

golden-centred
flower 1½ in.
across

downy
leaf
9 in.
long

S. africana

House Lime

TYPES

Sparmannia africana is tree-like, quickly growing several feet high. The flowers appear in long-stalked clusters. Cut back after blooming has finished — repeat flowering may occur.

Sparmannia africana

SPARMANNIA

HOUSE PLANT
(see page 5)

The pale downy leaves make a pleasant contrast to the dark leathery foliage of Philodendron or Ficus. It grows quickly and may need repotting more than once a year. Keep growth in check by pinching out the stem tips of young plants. Sparmannia blooms in early spring if it has been kept in direct sunlight during winter.

SECRETS OF SUCCESS

Temperature: Average warmth — minimum 45°F (7°C) in winter.
Light: Brightly lit spot away from direct sun in summer.
Water: Keep compost moist at all times — may require daily watering in summer. Water more sparingly in winter.
Air Humidity: Mist leaves occasionally in summer.
Repotting: Repot in spring every year.
Propagation: Stem cuttings root easily in spring or summer.

arum-like
flower 3 in.
long

lance-shaped
leaf 6 in.
long

S. wallisii

Peace Lily

TYPES

Spathiphyllum wallisii grows about 1 ft (30 cm) high — a dwarf variety (**Petite**) is available. **S. Mauna Loa** is larger (2 ft/60 cm) and less hardy. White flowers turn pale green with age.

Spathiphyllum wallisii

SPATHIPHYLLUM

HOUSE PLANT
(see page 5)

The Peace Lily is a good choice if it can be kept out of direct sunlight in a room which is reasonaly warm in winter. There must be no cold draughts and the pot should be surrounded by moist peat or stood on a pebble tray (page 115). The glossy leaves grow directly out of the compost; in spring and sometimes again in autumn the flowers appear.

SECRETS OF SUCCESS

Temperature: Warm or average warmth — minimum 55°F (13°C) in winter.
Light: Semi-shade in summer — bright light in winter. Strong sunlight will damage the leaves.
Water: Keep compost moist at all times — reduce watering in winter.
Air Humidity: Mist leaves very frequently.
Repotting: Repot in spring every year.
Propagation: Divide plants at repotting time.

glossy
leaf
4 in.
long

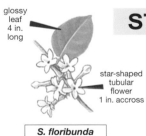

star-shaped
tubular
flower
1 in. accross

S. floribunda

Wax Flower
(Madagascar Jasmine)

TYPES

The stems of **Stephanotis floribunda** can reach 10 ft (3 m) or more, but is usually sold twined around a wire hoop. The heavily scented waxy flowers appear in summer.

Stephanotis floribunda

STEPHANOTIS

HOUSE PLANT
(see page 5)

Stephanotis is usually associated with bridal bouquets, but it can also be grown as a free-flowering house plant. Its vigorous climbing stems must be trained on a support. A beautiful but difficult plant — it hates sudden changes in temperature, needs constant cool conditions in winter and is attractive to scale and mealy bug.

SECRETS OF SUCCESS

Temperature: Average warmth — keep at 55°–60°F (13°–16°C) in winter.
Light: Brightly lit spot away from direct sun in summer.
Water: Keep compost moist at all times. Water sparingly in winter.
Air Humidity: Mist leaves occasionally.
Repotting: Repot in spring every 2 years.
Propagation: Take stem cuttings in summer. Use a rooting hormone and provide bottom heat.

Strelitzia reginae

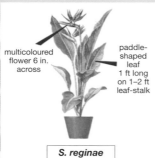

S. reginae

Bird of Paradise

TYPE

Strelitzia reginae is the species grown indoors. The flowers usually appear in spring, but sometimes occur earlier or later.

multicoloured flower 6 in. across

paddle-shaped leaf 1 ft long on 1–2 ft leaf-stalk

STRELITZIA

HOUSE PLANT
(see page 5)

Surely the most spectacular of all the flowers which can be grown in the home. The vivid flowers last for several weeks on top of tall stalks, surrounded by large leaves. It needs patience (new plants take 4–6 years before flowering starts) and space (mature plants in a 10 in./25 cm pot grow 3 ft/1m high), but is surprisingly easy to grow.

SECRETS OF SUCCESS

Temperature: Average warmth — keep at 55°–60°F (13°–16°C) in winter.
Light: As much light as possible, but shade from hot summer sun.
Water: Water thoroughly, then leave until the compost surface is dry. Water sparingly in winter.
Air Humidity: Mist leaves occasionally.
Repotting: Repot young plants in spring.
Propagation: Divide plants at repotting time.

Streptocarpus Constant Nymph

S. hybrida

Cape Primrose

TYPES

Flowers are white, blue, purple, pink or red with prominently-veined throats. The blooms of **Streptocarpus Constant Nymph** are lilac with violet veins.

trumpet-shaped flower 2 in. across

strap-shaped leaf 8–12 in. long

STREPTOCARPUS

HOUSE PLANT
(see page 5)

Many hybrids have appeared but the old favourite Constant Nymph still remains the most popular Streptocarpus. When growing conditions are satisfactory a succession of blooms appear above the rosette of coarse leaves throughout the summer. It needs a shallow pot, moist air, bright light and freedom from draughts and cold air in winter.

SECRETS OF SUCCESS

Temperature: Average warmth — minimum 55°F (13°C) in winter.
Light: Brightly lit spot away from direct sun in summer.
Water: Water freely, then leave until the compost surface is dry. Reduce watering in winter.
Air Humidity: Mist occasionally. Do not wet the leaves.
Repotting: Repot in spring every year.
Propagation: Divide plants at repotting time. Seeds may be sown in spring.

Streptosolen jamesonii

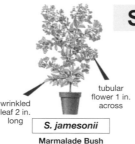

S. jamesonii

Marmalade Bush

TYPE

Streptosolen jamesonii will grow 3–7 ft (1–2 m) high if left unpruned. The branches are weak — the best way to grow this rambling shrub in a conservatory is to train it against a wall.

wrinkled leaf 2 in. long

tubular flower 1 in. across

STREPTOSOLEN

HOUSE PLANT
(see page 5)

The main feature of Streptosolen is the large clusters of marmalade-coloured flowers borne at the tip of each branch in spring or summer. The stems require some form of support — you can stake the main stem and train it as a standard (page 142). Streptosolen becomes leggy with age — this is most marked when the compost is not kept constantly moist. A well-lit spot is essential, especially in winter.

SECRETS OF SUCCESS

Temperature: Average warmth — minimum 50°F (10°C) in winter.
Light: Bright light, away from direct sun in summer.
Water: Keep compost moist at all times.
Air Humidity: Mist leaves occasionally.
Repotting: Repot, if necessary, after flowering.
Propagation: Take stem cuttings in spring or summer.

semi-adult
form —
adult form
has 4 lobes

**S. podophyllum
Green Gold**

*Syngonium podophyllum
Emerald Gem*

SYNGONIUM

HOUSE PLANT
(see page 5)

The unusual feature of this plant is the change in leaf shape as it gets older. The young leaves are arrow-shaped — at this stage the variegation is at its brightest. As the plant gets older it acquires a climbing habit and the leaves become lobed. Aerial roots are produced and a moss stick (page 141) makes an excellent support.

TYPES

The basic species is the all-green **Syngonium (Nephthytis) podophyllum**. The variegated types are the popular ones, ranging from near all-green to the near all-white (**S. p. Imperial White**).

SECRETS OF SUCCESS

Temperature: Average warmth — minimum 60°F (16°C) in winter.
Light: Well-lit spot away from direct sunlight.
Water: Keep compost moist at all times — reduce watering in winter. Avoid overwatering.
Air Humidity: Mist leaves regularly.
Repotting: Repot in spring every 2 years.
Propagation: Take stem cuttings bearing aerial roots in spring. Use a rooting hormone.

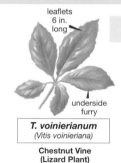

leaflets
6 in.
long

underside
furry

T. voinierianum
(Vitis voinieriana)

**Chestnut Vine
(Lizard Plant)**

Tetrastigma voinierianum

TETRASTIGMA

HOUSE PLANT
(see page 5)

This giant member of the Grape family comes with a warning — it is too large and too vigorous to grow as a house plant, and unlike the Kangaroo Vine it suffers in direct sunlight and in an unventilated room. It belongs in the conservatory or greenhouse where it can be used to cover large areas with its glossy saw-edged leaves. You will have to provide stout supports for the fast-growing stems.

TYPE

Tetrastigma voinierianum is the only species you will find at the garden centre. Each leaflet measures about 1 ft (30 cm) across and it can grow 5–7 ft (1.5–2 m) a year.

SECRETS OF SUCCESS

Temperature: Cool or average warmth — minimum 45°–55°F (7°–13°C) in winter.
Light: Bright light away from direct sunlight.
Water: Water liberally from spring to autumn — sparingly in winter.
Air Humidity: Mist leaves occasionally.
Repotting: Repot, if necessary, in spring.
Propagation: Take stem cuttings in spring or summer.

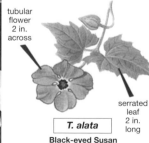

tubular
flower
2 in.
across

serrated
leaf
2 in.
long

T. alata

Black-eyed Susan

Thunbergia alata

THUNBERGIA

POT PLANT
(see page 5)

One of the best pot plants for covering a large area quickly and for providing summer colour. A few seeds sown in early spring will produce enough plants to clothe a screen or trellis with twining stems several feet long. When grown as a climber some form of support is essential — it can also be grown as a trailing plant in a hanging basket. Pinch out tips of young plants. Remove faded flowers before they produce seed.

TYPE

Sow seeds or buy a plant of **Thunbergia alata** in spring. Throughout the summer the brown-throated flowers appear, with petals of white, yellow or orange.

SECRETS OF SUCCESS

Temperature: Average warmth — minimum 50°F (10°C) in winter.
Light: Bright light with some direct sun.
Water: Keep compost moist at all times.
Air Humidity: Mist leaves occasionally, especially in hot weather.
Care After Flowering: Plant should be discarded.
Propagation: Sow seeds in early spring.

Tolmiea menziesii

leaf
2 in. across

leaf
stalk
4 in.
long

T. menziesii

Piggyback Plant

TYPE

Tolmiea menziesii is the most popular of the types which bear plantlets on their leaves — it is easy to grow in poor conditions. The long leaf stalks give the plant a trailing appearance.

TOLMIEA

HOUSE PLANT
(see page 5)

Tolmiea is a compact mound of downy, bright green leaves about 9 in. (22 cm) high. This plant gets its common name from the plantlets which form at the base of mature leaves. It is one of the hardiest of all house plants and actually relishes a cold, well-ventilated and sunless environment. Its enemy is hot, dry air.

SECRETS OF SUCCESS

Temperature: Cool to average warmth — minimum 40°F (4°C) in winter.
Light: Bright light preferred, but will grow in shade.
Water: Keep compost moist at all times — reduce watering in winter.
Air Humidity: Mist leaves occasionally.
Repotting: Repot in spring every year.
Propagation: Peg down plantlets in compost — cut stems when rooted.

*Tradescantia fluminensis
Quicksilver*

leaf
2–3 in.
long

base of
leaf
clasps
pendant
stem

T. fluminensis

**Wandering Jew
(Inch Plant)**

TYPES

Variegated forms of **Tradescantia fluminensis** include **variegata** (cream-striped) and **Quicksilver** (white-striped). **T. albiflora tricolor** leaves have white and mauve stripes.

TRADESCANTIA

HOUSE PLANT
(see page 5)

Tradescantia is the most popular member of the Wandering Jews or Inch Plants — Tradescantia, Zebrina and Callisia. The oval leaves are plentiful, provided you have the plant in a well-lit position. The creeping stems may occasionally bloom indoors, but the short-lived flowers add little to the display. Pinch out the growing tips regularly to encourage bushiness.

SECRETS OF SUCCESS

Temperature: Average warmth — minimum 45°F (7°C) in winter.
Light: Bright light is essential.
Water: Water thoroughly from spring to autumn. Water sparingly in winter.
Air Humidity: Mist leaves occasionally.
Repotting: Repot, if necessary, in spring.
Propagation: Take stem cuttings between spring and autumn.

TULIPA — 68

Vallota speciosa

sword-
like
leaf
1 ft
long

bell-like
flower 3 in.
across

V. speciosa

Scarborough Lily

TYPES

Vallota speciosa is excellent for a sunny windowsill. The leaves are evergreen and the red flowers are borne on 1–2 ft (30–60 cm) flower-stalks. White and salmon varieties are available.

VALLOTA

HOUSE PLANT
(see page 5)

In spring plant the bulb firmly in a 5 in. (12 cm) pot — leave the top half uncovered. Vallota is an easy plant — keep it cool during winter, remove dead flowers and leaves, and let the compost dry out slightly between waterings. In late summer clusters of flowers appear. Don't repot until the clump of bulbs becomes overcrowded.

SECRETS OF SUCCESS

Temperature: Average warmth — keep at 50°–55°F (10°–13°C) in winter.
Light: Bright light with some direct sun.
Water: Water thoroughly when the compost begins to dry out. Water sparingly in winter.
Air Humidity: Sponge leaves occasionally.
Repotting: Repot in spring every 3–4 years.
Propagation: Divide plants at repotting time, or detach offsets from mature plants and pot up in summer.

Yucca elephantipes

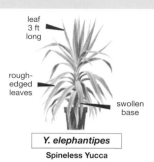

leaf 3 ft long

rough-edged leaves

swollen base

Y. elephantipes

Spineless Yucca

TYPES

The 3–5 ft (1–1.5m) woody trunk bears a crown of long, leathery leaves. Choose **Yucca elephantipes** — safer that **Y. aloifolia** (Spanish Bayonet) with sword-like leaves.

YUCCA
HOUSE PLANT
(see page 5)

A mature Yucca is a fine False Palm for a hallway or large room. A large Yucca is expensive and should be treated properly. It will need a deep, well-drained container which can be moved outdoors in summer. In winter it will require an unheated and well-lit spot. White bell-shaped flowers may appear after a number of years.

SECRETS OF SUCCESS

Temperature: Average warmth — keep cool in winter (minimum 45°F/7°C).
Light: Provide as much light as possible.
Water: Water liberally from spring to autumn. Water sparingly in winter.
Air Humidity: Misting is not necessary.
Repotting: Repot in spring every 2 years.
Propagation: Remove and pot up offsets, or root cane cuttings.

Zamioculcus zamifolia

leaflet 4 in. long

Z. zamifolia

Zamioculcas

TYPE

Zamioculcas zamifolia is the only species. The stout leaves grow about 2 ft (60 cm) high. Be careful not to overwater.

ZAMIOCULCAS
HOUSE PLANT
(see page 5)

You will not find this member of the arum family in the standard house plant textbook, but it is sold by some garden centres. It has become popular with interior decorators as a focal point in a large room — the upright leaves arise directly out of the compost and each one of these leaves bears shiny leaflets arranged in a herringbone fashion.

SECRETS OF SUCCESS

Temperature: Warm or average warmth — at least 60°F (16°C) in winter.
Light: Light shade.
Water: Allow upper part of compost to dry out between waterings — water sparingly in winter.
Air Humidity: Mist leaves occasionally.
Repotting: Repot, if necessary, in spring.
Propagation: Divide plants at repotting time.

ZANTEDESCHIA — 71

Zebrina pendula quadricolor

leaf 2–2½ in. long

base of leaf clasps pendant stem

underside purple

Z. pendula

Wandering Jew (Inch Plant)

TYPES

The leaves of the basic species **Zebrina pendula** are green and silver edged with pink. The variety **purpussii** is green and purple, and **quadricolor** is green, silver, pink and red.

ZEBRINA
HOUSE PLANT
(see page 5)

Zebrina is a close relative of Tradescantia and requires the same sort of room conditions. Zebrina, however, does require some direct sunlight to bring out the full beauty of its foliage. These oval leaves have a glistening surface which is multicoloured above and purple below. As with all the Tradescantia relatives small flowers may appear — Zebrina bears pale purple ones. Pinch out stem tips to encourage bushiness.

SECRETS OF SUCCESS

Temperature: Average warmth — minimum 45°–50°F (7°–10°C) in winter.
Light: Bright light — some direct sunlight is beneficial.
Water: Water liberally from spring to autumn. Water sparingly in winter.
Air Humidity: Mist leaves occasionally.
Repotting: Repot, if necessary, in spring.
Propagation: Take stem cuttings between spring and autumn.

Chapter 3

INDOOR PLANTS : SPECIAL GROUPS

Within the vast array of indoor plants there are some which have important features in common and so can be grouped together. The common feature may be the way they are grown (Bonsai), the way they survive their dormancy (Bulbs), the fleshiness of their bodies (Succulents) or in most cases their family relationship (Bromeliads, Cacti, Ferns, Orchids and Palms). The types available and the secrets of success are set out in this chapter.

BONSAI

It is hard to resist a mature and well-trained bonsai at the garden centre. A miniature tree with its roots clinging to a rock, or a conifer with gnarled branches on a stout twisted trunk, may seem to be an ideal house plant. The price may put you off, but the thought of root pruning, stem pruning, pinching and wiring should not be a deterrent — these are simple and enjoyable occasional tasks. Nor should you be concerned at the thought of having to keep the pot outdoors for most of the time during the summer and winter months — many varieties can be kept indoors all year round.

A couple of points you should consider carefully before buying. There is no such thing as a 'bargain' Bonsai. It will either be an attractive but untrained seedling or a naturally dwarf variety. Secondly, regular watering is essential and that can mean every day during summer. Still, you may think that this chore is a small price to pay in order to have such an attractive feature in your home. A well-grown Bonsai in the right situation is sure to be a focal point.

Acer palmatum

OUTDOOR BONSAI

HOUSE PLANT
(see page 5)

The word bonsai simply means 'a plant in a tray'. The miniaturisation, however, is not achieved by keeping the plant in a pot and leaving it there to cramp the roots. According to the official definition a bonsai is "a tree encouraged to conform in all aspects with ordinary trees, except for its miniature size. The technique consists of keeping the tree confined to its pot by pinching out the top growth and pruning the roots to strike a balance between the foliage above and the roots below, and at the same time to develop a satisfactory shape."

The Outdoor Bonsai on offer at the nursery will usually be about 4 years old. During the basic training period the plant will have been kept in a pot and each year both root and stem pruning will have taken place. In addition the branches will have been trained into attractive shapes by using stiff wire known as 'bonsai wire'. When the bonsai was about 3-4 years old it will have been moved to a shallow frost-proof tray or pot which has drainage holes.

Growing Outdoor Bonsai is a fascinating hobby, but you must know what you are doing. First of all, it is essential to know that they are *not* true house plants. They are brought inside for two or three days at a time — they suffer if kept indoors for more than a few days. The air in the average room is too hot and too dry. Outdoors some form of protection is needed against wind and rain. Next, you must realise that growing bonsai requires time and money. Even a modest collection can cost £100 or more.

Chamaecyparis pisifera

Juniperus chinensis

TYPES

The favourite subjects for classical bonsai are conifers — the leaves are generally small and evergreen and the plants are remarkably long-lived. Popular types include **Juniperus chinensis**, **Chamaecyparis pisifera**, **Larix kaempferi**, **Cryptomeria japonica** and **Pinus sylvestris**. Not all the favourite ones are evergreens — **Acer palmatum** (Japanese Maple) and **Zelkova serrata** (Grey-bark Elm) are widely grown. Flowering and fruiting trees are especially interesting, and there is a long list of subjects which are known to produce attractive bonsai — Cherry, Apricot, Peach, Japanese Azalea, Quince, Magnolia, compact Roses, Wisteria, Apple (especially the Crab varieties), Laburnum and Pyracantha are examples. In fact nearly any hardy tree can be treated in this way, so you can use an Oak, Beech, Birch or Sycamore seedling from the garden.

Pyracantha angustifolia

INDOOR BONSAI

HOUSE PLANT
(see page 5)

Ficus benjamina

Indoor Bonsai is a relatively new idea which has not come from Japan. The centre of interest appears to have been Germany and it has spread around the world. You can buy Indoor Bonsai trees from garden centres and nurseries throughout Britain.

The basic difference from the traditional Outdoor Bonsai is that non-hardy trees and shrubs are used here. Indoor Bonsai are generally much better suited than hardy types to the conditions found in the average home, and of course they *must* be kept indoors during the winter. Thus they can be regarded as true house plants, although during the summer months they should be given the standard bonsai treatment. This calls for keeping them outdoors and then bringing them inside for a few days at a time.

Obviously the easiest plan is to buy a mature and trained specimen but they are expensive. If you have the time and patience you can begin from scratch. Pot up the chosen seedling or rooted cutting in the ordinary way and care for it as advised in the appropriate section of this A-Z guide. When the main stem has reached the desired height the growing point should be pinched out. Remove some of the lower branches and pinch out the tips of upper side branches to encourage bushiness at the head of the tree. After 2 years repotting is necessary and so is root pruning — see page 60.

Like their hardy outdoor counterparts, Indoor Bonsai are fascinating to grow but their needs on page 60 have to be met for them to thrive.

Sageretia theezans

Punica granatum

TYPES

Several of the house plants described in this A-Z section can be cultivated and trained as Indoor Bonsai. **Ficus benjamina** (Weeping Fig) is the favourite one — others include **Heptapleurum** (Parasol Plant), **Bougainvillea**, **Acacia**, **Hibiscus**, **Allamanda**, **Gardenia**, **Ixora**, **Jasminum primulinum** (Primrose Jasmine), **Schefflera** (Umbrella Tree), **Punica granatum** (Pomegranate) and **Crassula argentea** (Jade Plant). Some of the Indoor Bonsai are sub-tropical or tropical trees which are grown only in this dwarfened form — examples here are **Sageretia theezans**, **Carmona microphylla** (Fukien Tea), **Pistacia** (Pistachio), **Sterculia**, **Tamarix**, **Swietenia** (Mahogany) and **Olea** (Olive). Seedlings of these trees can be bought for training from specialist nurseries. Cheapest of all are Oranges, Lemons and Coffee raised from pips or unroasted beans at home.

Carmona microphylla

BUYING YOUR BONSAI

Bonsai varieties are not natural dwarfs. They are ordinary trees which will grow to their natural size if they are not properly pruned.

The plant will be expensive. You can raise one from scratch but it will take a number of years. A cheap bonsai will either be young in need of further training or it will be poor quality. It may be ordinary nursery stock which has been cut back, potted and partly trained.

You can go to a traditional plant supplier such as a large garden centre, but seek out a specialist nursery if you plan to become a dedicated bonsai grower.

Make sure you get its name — a label stating 'bonsai' will not do. Find out if it is an indoor or outdoor variety — ask for an information sheet.

Look at the plant — it should be trained in one of the basic styles and the leaves should be green and healthy. Check that the branches are not suffering from die-back. Check that wire is not embedded in the trunk and make sure that the plant is not loose in its pot.

Look at the soil — the surface should be fairly loose, not compacted and waterlogged. The surface should be free of weeds and liverworts.

Look at the pot — the inside should not be glazed and there should be adequate drainage holes in the base.

BONSAI STYLES A–Z

BROOM (Illustrated) Garden tree-like form — regularly branching stems radiate from trunk top

CASCADE (Not illustrated) Drooping trunk — reaches below bottom of pot

EXPOSED ROOT (Illustrated) Mature roots visible well above the compost surface in the pot

FORMAL UPRIGHT (Not illustrated) Vertical trunk — branches horizontal or drooping

GROUP (Illustrated) A collection of individual trees, each with its own root system

INFORMAL UPRIGHT (Not illustrated) Curved vertical trunk — branches on outside of curves

LITERATI (Illustrated) Branches restricted to upper part of attractively shaped trunk

RAFT (Illustrated) A collection of branches rising from a horizontal trunk

ROOT-OVER-ROCK (Not illustrated) Rock replaces pot — roots grow into hollows or crevices

SEMI-CASCADE (Not illustrated) Drooping trunk — not reaching bottom of pot

SLANTING (Not illustrated) Straight or slightly curved trunk sloping to one side

TWIN TRUNK (Not illustrated) Two trunks, one smaller than the other, joined at base

TWISTED TRUNK (Illustrated) Trunk distinctly twisted — branches horizontal or drooping

WEEPING (Not illustrated) Straight or curved vertical trunk — branches all distinctly drooping

WINDSWEPT (Not illustrated) Sloping trunk with all branches on one side

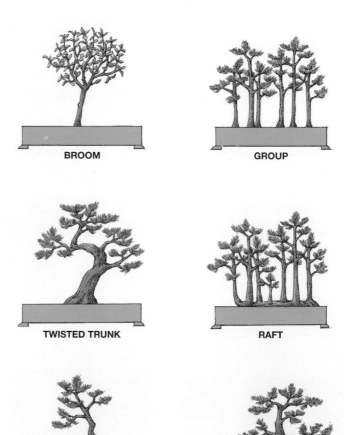

BROOM

GROUP

TWISTED TRUNK

RAFT

LITERATI

EXPOSED ROOT

BONSAI AT ITS BEST

Display

With Indoor Bonsai the general rules of house plant display apply. Place them where their basic light, temperature and humidity needs can be met — see page 60. They are ideally set at close to eye level so that the spaces between the tiers of branches can be clearly seen. Rotate plants occasionally to ensure even growth.

With Outdoor Bonsai there are several ways to display your trees. The simplest technique is to stand the bonsai pot on the patio or on a coarse sand-covered area in the border. The serious collector, however, requires something more — the usual choice is to stand the pots on slatted staging which is set close to a wall or fence for wind protection. Some form of shading may be erected above, but this must not cut out sunlight for at least part of the day.

Platform-topped posts ('monkey poles') are sometimes used to support individual trees. Eye-catching — but strong winds can topple the pots if they are not secured in some way.

Pots

A bonsai pot has a number of special features. First of all, it is shallow. The exception is the deep cascade pot. Both earthenware and stoneware pots are available — make sure that it is frost-proof if it is to be used for an outdoor variety. Look at the drainage holes — there should be at least twice as much drainage area as you would find at the bottom of an ordinary plant pot. The outside may be glazed or unglazed, but the inside must be unglazed — subdued browns, greens, greys or blues are the experts' choice. Make sure that there are feet at the base of the pot to allow free drainage.

Remember that the appearance of both the tree and the pot are important — read the note on pots above.

Compost

Ordinary garden soil is definitely unsuitable — the easiest plan is to buy a ready-mixed bonsai compost. Ordinary potting compost will not do — the medium for bonsai must be rather coarse and highly absorbent. Enthusiasts generally make their own mixture, often adapting the formula to suit the individual plant's needs. The standard recipe is 50% organic matter and 50% grit. The organic material is sifted to provide particles 2–4 mm wide. It may be peat, leaf mould or bark. The grit may be washed coarse sand, or flint grit. Some growers add calcined or Akadama clay to the mixture to help water retention.

The tree should look as if it has been taken from a site where it has grown naturally. It may look windswept, the trunk may be contorted, but it should never look obviously pruned and trained.

•

The experts recommend that in a rectangular pot the plant should be closer to one end than the other, but it is a matter of taste. Pot size is important — it must be large enough to look balanced but not so large as to overwhelm the bonsai. Bear in mind that ease of cultivation increases with size of container. Objects (Chinese figures, etc) are a matter of personal taste.

•

Anything which makes the tree look old is desirable. Exposed roots have this effect and sharis and jins (page 61) can add to the feeling of maturity.

•

In an upright style the groups of branches are generally horizontal or drooping to give a cloud effect. There should be air spaces between the 'clouds'.

CARING FOR YOUR BONSAI

Temperature

The average plant requires the warmth of a standard living room in summer and the cooler conditions you would find in an unheated room in winter. The grown-up sisters of some of the Indoor Bonsai on page 57 are listed in the A-Z guide where specific temperature requirements are given. Nearly all bonsai can be stood outdoors in summer. Outdoor Bonsai are hardy, but some require protection in a period of heavy frost.

Light

Most Indoor Bonsai require a brightly lit spot but only some flourish in direct sunlight. All should be protected from hot summer sun. As a general rule a spell outdoors is beneficial in summer, but there should be a transition period — move the pots out for just a short time at first and extend this outdoor period until the plants can be left out for their summer break. For both Outdoor and Indoor Bonsai there should be some shade from the hot midday sun.

Food

The general rules for feeding pot plants set out on page 156 apply to bonsai, although the need for regular feeding is generally greater — the pot is unusually small and the compost contains virtually no nutrients. As a general rule use a well-balanced fertilizer in the active growing season but change to a low-nitrogen one in autumn. Feed sparingly in winter. A modern development is the slow-release pellet which removes the need for frequent feeding.

Water

Water when the surface dries out — scratch the compost if you are not sure. Expect to water frequently, perhaps every day, if the container is small, the leaf area is large, the air is warm or the plant has not been repotted for some time. Use rainwater if you can on lime-hating plants. A watering can fitted with a fine rose is the recommended method, although some growers occasionally immerse the pot in a bowl of water for a brief time. Whichever method you use, take care not to keep the compost constantly saturated. With Outdoor Bonsai you may still have to water after rain if there is a dense canopy of leaves. Watering regularly does not remove the need to maintain a moist atmosphere around the leaves. Frequent misting of the leaves of Indoor Bonsai is helpful — the most effective method is to stand the pots on a pebble tray (see page 115).

Root pruning & Repotting

The purpose of root pruning is to ensure that the growth above ground and the root system below ground remain in balance. The purpose of repotting is to provide a fresh supply of compost. As a general rule new plants are root pruned yearly and mature plants are treated every 2 – 5 years. The best time is in spring when the buds are beginning to swell — deal with evergreens in March. The exceptions are spring-flowering trees — root prune when flowering has finished.

Remove the tree and gently remove some of the old compost and comb out the outer roots — the traditional tool is a chopstick. About half the compost should be removed. Cut back the roots — about 1/3 of the root system should be removed.

Thoroughly wash and dry the pot or use a slightly larger one. Cover the drainage holes with fine mesh from your bonsai supplier. Push two wires or pieces of string through the holes and secure on the mesh pieces.

Cover the base of the pot with a thin layer of grit or calcined clay — your pot should now look like the illustration. Put the plant in position and secure it by twisting the wires over the trunk base. Now add fairly dry compost and work it in between and above the roots with your fingers — do not leave any air pockets. Water in gently but thoroughly — keep out of sunlight and do not feed for a month or two.

Wiring

The basics of wiring are simple. Wire is wrapped around a branch which is then bent to the desired position. After a period of time the wire is removed and the branch retains its new shape. In practice it is not so simple — it takes a lot of experience to become an expert. Before tackling your bonsai try your hand on a twig in the garden. Use anodised aluminium wire — start with the thickest branches first. Choose wire which is about one quarter the width of the branch and cut a piece about 1½ times its length. Turn the wire anti-clockwise to grip but not bite into the wood. Bend the wired wood slowly and gently. The right time to remove the wire depends on several factors. As a rough guide wait 1 year for a conifer and about 3 months for a deciduous tree — always remove the wire before it cuts deeply into the wood. Use pincers and remove it piece by piece — do not try to unwind.

Pruning

Maintenance pruning is carried out on an established bonsai in late winter or early spring. Its purpose is to maintain the basic shape and avoid congestion. The first task is to remove some of the outer twigs to leave room for next year's growth, and to remove or shorten branches which are crossing over others and spoiling the shape. Branches which have started to grow upwards can soon spoil the cloud effect of a conifer bonsai and so need to be removed. Be careful with conifers. A cut shoot which is leafless will not produce new growth. Every few years it will be necessary to remove a few of the larger branches to allow twigs to develop. Make sure your tools are sharp. Use scissors or shears for twigs — larger branches will require secateurs or pincer-like branch cutters. Large cuts should be covered with a cut paste sealant.

Branch pruning is usually carried out in autumn and involves the removal of an unwanted branch. Use secateurs, a small saw or a branch cutter to cut off most of the branch to leave a small stub. Remove the stub with a branch cutter to leave a shallow hole — fill this depression with a cut paste sealant.

Generative pruning is carried out on deciduous trees (not conifers) in midsummer. Its purpose is to stimulate the production of new branches. Cut off the trunk or a thick branch at the desired length — in a short time a number of shoots will develop around the cut area. These should be thinned to the desired number in autumn.

Pinching

This technique is carried out during the summer months to maintain the shape of an established tree and to reduce the size of the leaves. Shoot tips are nipped out with your fingernails although you might need a small pair of scissors. The standard routine with deciduous trees is to remove the leaf bud on the shoot tips at regular intervals — with flowering trees it is important not to remove the flower buds.

Sharis & Jins

As illustrated a shari is a dead area of the trunk which has lost its bark. This decorative effect makes the bonsai look older than it really is, and is created by peeling away a strip of bark near the base of the tree — make sure that it is above ground level and does not circle the tree. Seal the edges of the cut area with a cut paste sealant. A jin is a dead branch from which the bark has been stripped.

BROMELIADS

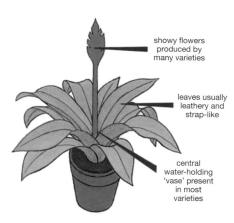

showy flowers produced by many varieties

leaves usually leathery and strap-like

central water-holding 'vase' present in most varieties

SECRETS OF SUCCESS

Temperature: High temperatures (above 75°F/24°C) may be required to bring plants into flower, but average warmth (minimum 50°F/10°C) is satisfactory for foliage types or plants in flower.

Light: Most Bromeliads require a brightly lit spot away from direct sunlight. Pineapple and the Earth Stars will thrive in full sun.

Water: Never overwater, and ensure that there is good drainage. Keep the central 'vase' filled with water — use rainwater in hard water areas. Empty and refill the 'vase' every 1-2 months. Water the compost only when it dries out. With non-vase varieties keep the compost moist, but never wet.

Air Humidity: Mist leaves in summer. Feeding through the leaves is the natural method of nutrition, so occasionally use dilute liquid fertilizer instead of water in the sprayer.

Repotting: Rarely, if ever, necessary.

Propagation: Offsets appear at the base of the plant. When the offset is several months old remove it with some roots attached and plant shallowly in Seed & Cutting Compost. Keep warm until established.

Two groups of this fascinating family are suitable for room decoration. The third one, the Earth Stars, require to be grown in a glass container. Bromeliads come in all shapes and sizes, but they have one key feature in common. In their natural habitat most of them grow attached to trees rather than in the soil, and they have a tiny root system. This means that overwatering and overpotting can be fatal.

The Flowering Rosette group is by far the most popular. The usual form is illustrated above — large and dramatic flower-heads borne on stalks. This floral display lasts for months and when it is gone there are attractive and sometimes coloured leaves. These varieties are generally undemanding plants which require neither regular misting nor repotting. They will tolerate some neglect and thrive within a wide temperature range. Not surprisingly the Flowering Rosettes are looked upon by interior decorators as an important part of their modern decor schemes.

The second group suitable for room cultivation are the Air Plants, which literally live on air! You will find them at the garden centre attached to coral, driftwood etc. The long and narrow leaves absorb moisture from the air, and nutrients from the dust which settles on the foliage.

deep orange bract 2 in. long — droops to reveal yellow-tipped flowers

arching, saw-edged leaf 1½ ft long

A. chantinii

Amazonian Zebra Plant

AECHMEA

TYPES

The Aechmeas are typical Bromeliads with leathery, arching leaves and a distinct central 'vase' from which a stout stalk bearing a bold flower-head emerges. **Aechmea fasciata (A. rhodocyanea)** is by far the most popular one. It is good enough to be the showpiece of any living room or florist window — the arching 2 ft (60 cm) grey-green leaves are banded with silvery powder and the floral spike which appears when the plant is a few years old is striking. The pink floral ball appears in midsummer and lasts until early winter. This showy Urn Plant is one of the easiest Bromeliads to grow, but there are other Aechmeas worth considering. **A. chantinii** is rather larger and the flower-head is brighter and more open.

Aechmea fasciata

ANANAS

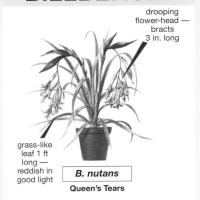

sharply saw-edged leaves

A. comosus

Pineapple

TYPES

Pineapples are grown as house plants for their foliage and not their fruit. Choose **Ananus comosus variegatus** or **A. bracteatus striatus** with brightly striped 1-2 ft (30-60 cm) arching leaves.

AIR PLANTS

TYPES

The Air Plants are the Grey Tillandsias, which differ from their green relatives (see page 64) by bearing absorbent furry scales on their foliage. As noted on page 62, these plants require neither watering nor feeding — they are regarded as focal points because of their novelty and not their beauty, although some do produce flower-heads. The most widespread species is Spanish Moss **(Tillandsia usneoides)** which is a familiar sight hanging from trees in the warmer regions of America — for use indoors see page 142. **T. caput-medusae** is the most popular house plant type — the flower-heads are made up of red bracts and small blue blooms. **T. ionanthe** forms a compact rosette of arching silvery leaves. It grows about 2 in. (5 cm) high — the inner foliage turns red when the stalkless flowers appear. **T. argentea** is another silvery-leaved Air Plant — the short leaves spread untidily outwards as the plant develops.

BILLBERGIA

drooping flower-head — bracts 3 in. long

grass-like leaf 1 ft long — reddish in good light

B. nutans

Queen's Tears

TYPES

Billbergia nutans is the best-known Billbergia and is by far the easiest Bromeliad to grow — young plants flower quite readily. **B. windii** is larger — the flower-stalks are 18 in. (45 cm) long and the foliage is grey-green. Billbergia can withstand winter temperatures as low as 35°-40°F (2°-4°C).

Ananas bracteatus striatus

Tillandsia argentea

Billbergia windii

GUZMANIA

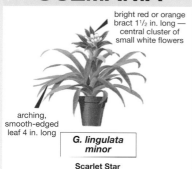

bright red or orange
bract 1½ in. long —
central cluster of
small white flowers

arching,
smooth-edged
leaf 4 in. long

G. lingulata minor

Scarlet Star

TYPES

The Guzmanias are generally grown for their showy flower-heads. **Guzmania lingulata** (leaves 1½ ft/ 45 cm long) bears orange and red bracts — so does its variety **minor** which is much more compact. **G. zahnii** is the giant with 2 ft (60 cm) long leaves — some types (e.g **G. Omer Morobe** and **G. musaica**) are grown for their striped or banded foliage.

Guzmania lingulata Broadway

NEOREGELIA

saw-edged
leaves

N. carolinae tricolor

Blushing Bromeliad

TYPES

The favourite variety, **Neoregelia carolinae tricolor**, blushes at the centre when about to flower, whereas **N. spectabilis** (Fingernail Plant) reddens at the leaf tips. The glossy leaves are 1 ft (30 cm) long, and with age the foliage of the **tricolor** variety becomes suffused with pink.

Neoregelia spectabilis

TILLANDSIA

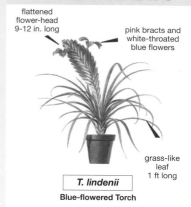

flattened
flower-head
9-12 in. long

pink bracts and
white-throated
blue flowers

grass-like
leaf
1 ft long

T. lindenii

Blue-flowered Torch

TYPES

The two most popular Tillandsias have grassy leaves, but their flowers are different. **Tillandsia lindenii** is shown above — **T. cyanea** has a more compact flower-head. A group of Tillandsia species (the Air Plants) have a completely different growth habit — see page 63.

Tillandsia cyanea

flower-head
up to 2 ft
long —
bracts
bright red

arching,
smooth-edged
leaf 1–1½ ft
long

**V. splendens
(V. speciosa)**

Flaming Sword

TYPES

The usual one is **Vriesea splendens** with its all-red, sword-like flower-head. Other types generally have more spreading flower-heads.

VRIESEA

V. splendens

V. hieroglyphica

V. fenestralis

Vriesea carinata

BULBS — Garden Types

Many of the popular bulbs which flower in the garden during the spring months can be grown indoors. For many people, helping to plant up a bowl of Tulips or Hyacinths was their first introduction to the world of indoor gardening, and for them the bulb bowl remains an essential part of early spring room decoration. There are two basic growing techniques. Large bulbs are nearly always 'forced' so that they will bloom well ahead of their garden counterparts — this **forcing technique** involves keeping them cold and dark to make the roots grow and then providing more light and warmth for leaf and flower development. Hyacinths are the most reliable — Tulips the least satisfactory.

The second growing method (the **non-forcing technique**) is used for both large and small bulbs and is simpler than forcing. The pots are placed outdoors after planting and then simply brought indoors when the flower buds have formed and are ready to open. In this case flowering will only be a few days ahead of similar bulbs grown in the garden. With both techniques the bulbs stored after flowering is over can be planted in the garden in autumn.

Following the instructions on this page should ensure success, but there is a vital first stage. Buy as early in the season as you can to ensure a wide selection, and choose bulbs which are good-sized, sprout-free, firm and disease-free.

FORCING TECHNIQUE

Place a layer of moist Seed & Cutting Compost in a bowl and set the bulbs on it — they should not touch the sides of the bowl. Fill up with more compost, pressing it firmly around the bulbs — the tips should be above the surface and the top of the compost should be about 1/2 in. (1 cm) below the rim.

The bulbs now need a period of complete darkness in an unheated place. Put the container in a black polythene bag and stand in a cellar or shed. This stage lasts for about 6-10 weeks. Check occasionally to see if the compost is still moist.

Move the bowl into a cool room indoors when the shoots are 1–2 in. (3–5 cm) high. Place in a shady spot — after a few days move to a place near to a window. In a few weeks the flower buds will appear — move to a bright but not sunny spot, free from draughts and not too warm — 60°–70°F (16°–21°C) is ideal. Turn the bowl occasionally.

After flowering cut off flowers, not flower-stalks. Continue watering until leaves have withered. Remove bulbs and allow to dry, then remove dead foliage and store in a cool, dry place.

NON-FORCING TECHNIQUE

Choose a container with adequate drainage holes. Place crocks at the bottom and add a layer of Seed & Cutting Compost. Plant the bulbs closely together and add more compost — the tips should be completely covered.

Place the pot in the garden. Bring it indoors when flower buds are present. For care during growth and after flowering see the Forcing Technique instructions.

BULBS AT CHRISTMAS

It is quite simple to raise Hyacinths, Narcissi and Tulips which will be in bloom on Christmas Day. The essential step is to buy bulbs which have been specially prepared for early flowering. These bulbs must be planted as soon as possible after purchase. September is the usual time for planting, and the forcing technique should be followed. Bring the pots indoors when the shoots are 1 in. (3 cm) high — this should not be later than December 1.

CHIONODOXA

flower-stalk 6 in. long

C. luciliae

Glory of the Snow

TYPES

The popular Chionodoxa is **Chionodoxa luciliae** — 10 white-centred, blue starry flowers appear on each slender stalk in late winter. **C. sardensis** has all-blue flowers, and the largest blooms (1½ in./4 cm across) are borne by **C. gigantea**. Plant the bulbs in September.

Chionodoxa sardensis

CONVALLARIA

bell-like flower ¼ in. long

oval leaf 8 in. long

C. majalis

Lily of the Valley

TYPES

The dainty white bells and heavy fragrance are well known. For Christmas flowers you will have to buy specially-prepared crowns ('pips') and plant in mid November.

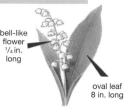

Convallaria majalis

CROCUS

Crocus chrysanthus Cream Beauty

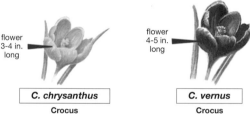

flower 3-4 in. long

C. chrysanthus

Crocus

flower 4-5 in. long

C. vernus

Crocus

TYPES

Crocus corms are planted in the autumn for flowering in early spring. The varieties of **Crocus chrysanthus** are often yellow (**Cream Beauty**, **E. A. Bowles**, **Goldilocks**, etc), but pale blues and mauves also occur, often with a golden base — **Blue Pearl**, **Princess Beatrix**, and so on. Flowering time is January-February. The varieties of **C. vernus** bloom a few weeks later, the flowers are larger, and blues and whites predominate. Popular types include **Vanguard** (silvery-pink) and **Pickwick** (mauve, striped purple).

Crocus vernus Vanguard

ERANTHIS

star-shaped flower 1 in. across

flower-stalk 3 in. long

E. hyemalis

Winter Aconite

TYPES

Many of the bulbs in this section are instantly recognisable by the average gardener, but not **Eranthis hyemalis**. The bright yellow flowers have a frilly, leafy collar — plant in September for flowering in January alongside the Snowdrops. For 2 in. (5 cm) flowers grow **E. tubergenii**.

Eranthis tubergenii

GALANTHUS

Galanthus Neil Frazer

pendant flower 1 in. long

green-tipped inner petals

flower-stalk 6 in. long

G. nivalis

Snowdrop

TYPES

Planting time is September — flowering time is January. The one you are most likely to see is the Common Snowdrop (**Galanthus nivalis**). The best variety is **S. Arnott** (9 in./23 cm).

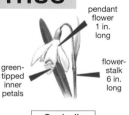

GALTONIA

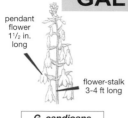

pendant flower 1½ in. long

flower-stalk 3-4 ft long

G. candicans
Summer Hyacinth

TYPE

This imposing plant is in marked contrast to the dainty dwarfs in this section. Bulbs are planted in large pots in September and each flower-stalk bears 20 or more white bells in May-June.

Galtonia candicans

GLADIOLUS

trumpet-shaped flower 3 in. across

flower-stalk 2 ft long

G. Columbine

TYPES

Gladioli are not usually thought of as indoor bulbs, and the large-flowering types are not suitable. Choose one of the Primulinus or the Miniature Hybrids such as **Columbine**, **Robin** or **Bo Peep**, or pick a low-growing species such as **G. colvillii** (1-2 ft/ 30-60 cm).

Gladiolus primulinus Robin

HYACINTHUS

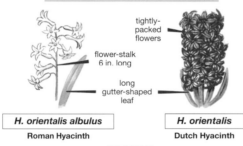

tightly-packed flowers

flower-stalk 6 in. long

long gutter-shaped leaf

H. orientalis albulus
Roman Hyacinth

H. orientalis
Dutch Hyacinth

TYPES

The flower-stalks of the Dutch Hyacinth bear 30 or more bell-like flowers on a single stalk. The 1-2 in. (3-5 cm) long blooms last for 2-3 weeks. Bulbs for January-March flowering are planted in October. Roman Hyacinths produce 2 or 3 stalks and the flowers are smaller and less tightly packed. Plant in August-September for December-January flowering.

Hyacinthus orientalis albulus

Hyacinthus Jan Bos

IRIS

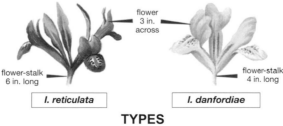

flower 3 in. across

flower-stalk 6 in. long

I. reticulata

flower-stalk 4 in. long

I. danfordiae

TYPES

Dwarf Irises are excellent for growing indoors, producing large blooms in January and February. They have never gained the popularity of Crocuses, Hyacinths, etc, but there are at least 3 species which are well worth cultivating in the house. Plant the bulbs in September and provide plenty of light once the leaves have appeared above the compost. Choose from **Iris histrioides major** (deep blue, white centres), **I. reticulata** (purple, yellow centres — fragrant) and **I. danfordiae** (yellow — fragrant).

Iris reticulata

Iris danfordiae

NARCISSUS

Narcissus Dutch Master

N. hybrida

Daffodil

N. tazetta

Tazetta Narcissus

TYPES

Nearly all types of Narcissi can be grown indoors. Plant in August-October for January-April flowers. Daffodils such as **Narcissus Dutch Master** (1-1½ ft/30-45 cm) are the ones with trumpets at least as long as the petals. Most of them are suitable, but perhaps the best group of all are the Tazettas (e.g **N. Geranium**). They produce bunches of flowers on each stem at Christmas or the New Year.

Narcissus Geranium

MUSCARI

urn-shaped flower ¼ in. long

strap-like leaf

M. armeniacum

Grape Hyacinth

TYPES

Plant in September for January-March flowers. The usual species is **Muscari armeniacum** (8 in./20 cm, blue flowers with white rims) — for sky blue flowers pick **M. botryoides** (6 in./ 15 cm).

Muscari armeniacum

SCILLA

Scilla tubergeniana

strap-like leaf

pendant flower ½ in. long

S. siberica

Bluebell

TYPES

Some garden species can be grown indoors — plant in September-October for blooming in January-March. **Scilla tubergeniana** (3 in./8 cm) is the earliest species — **S. siberica** (6 in./15 cm) is the popular one.

TULIPA

Tulipa hybrida Keizerskroon

T. hybrida

Single Early Tulip

T. hybrida

Double Early Tulip

TYPES

The most satisfactory Tulips to grow indoors are the Single Earlies and Double Earlies — both grow to 8-16 in. (20-40 cm). Some Species Tulips such as **Tulipa kaufmanniana** (6-10 in./15-25 cm) and **T. greigii** (6 in.-1 ft/15-30 cm) are also suitable. Plant in September for January-April flowers. Tall-growing Tulip varieties are much less satisfactory — the best ones are the strong-stemmed Darwin Tulips.

Tulipa kaufmanniana Stresa

BULBS — Indoor Types

A large number of indoor plants produce swollen underground organs which are used for propagation. There are the true bulbs, such as Tulips and Daffodils, which bear scale leaves, but there are also corms, tubers and rhizomes.

Some retain their foliage (see the list on this page), but most of the flowering bulbs have a dormant period when they lose their leaves. These are the ones we commonly refer to as Bulbs.

These temporary-display bulbs are divided into two groups. There are the Garden Bulbs which must be subjected to cold conditions during the rooting stage and are brought into the room only when flower buds have formed. Here we are dealing with the second group — the Indoor Bulbs which cannot tolerate frost. They are left in the pot when the foliage dies down — the compost is kept almost dry until growth starts again. A few, such as Canna, are treated differently.

The list of Indoor Bulbs is an impressive one, as stated earlier for countless children the task of planting Daffodils or Crocuses in a bowl was their first venture in horticulture, and the appeal remains. A bowl of early-flowering bulbs is an ever-popular and unfailing focal point — it tells us that spring is on its way.

OTHER INDOOR BULBS

Some bulb-forming plants keep their foliage all year round and are generally regarded as 'Pot Plants' rather than as 'Bulbs'. A number of these (see below) are dealt with in Chapter 2.

Canna hybrida J.B. van der Schoot

Freesia hybrida Marie Louise

Hippeastrum hybrida Kolibri series

gladiolus-like flower 4-5 in. across

lance-shaped leaf 1½ ft long

flower-head 1 ft long

oval leaf 6-9 in. long

Canna hybrida

Indian Shot

Eucomis comosa

Pineapple Lily

fragrant flower 1-2 in. across

strap-like leaf 9 in. long

Freesia hybrida

1½ ft strap-like leaf, at or shortly after flowering

funnel-shaped flower 5-6 in. across

Hippeastrum hybrida

Amaryllis

fragrant flower 4 in. across

strap-like leaf 1 ft long

Hymenocallis festalis

Spider Lily

Canna hybrida plants are big, bold and colourful. The large flowers are borne on a 2-3 ft (60 cm-1 m) stalk, and specialist growers can offer a bewildering array of varieties — plain, striped or spotted. There is also a choice of leaf colour.

Eucomis comosa needs lots of space. The long leaves form a large rosette and the cylindrical spike of small flowers bears a leafy crown.

Freesia hybrida has funnel-shaped flowers on one side of the 1-1½ ft (30-45 cm) wiry stems. All varieties are sweet-smelling.

Hippeastrum hybrida bulbs produce hollow stalks which bear terminal clusters of 3-6 flowers. This is the popular 'Amaryllis' offered for sale in autumn. Its hybrids are available in a wide variety of flower shades — the petals may be edged or striped in other colours.

Hymenocallis festalis bears fragrant blooms in late spring or summer. These flowers look like Daffodils with long and narrow petals, borne on 2 ft (60 cm) stalks.

Ipheion uniflorum is a low-growing plant, its starry blooms appearing on top of the 6 in. (15 cm) stems in spring. The blue or white flowers have a pleasant aroma.

star-like flower 1 in. across

Ipheion uniflorum

Spring Starflower

Hymenocallis festalis

Ipheion uniflorum Wisley Blue

Nerine sarniensis

star-shaped
flower 2 in.
across

sword-
like
leaf
1 ft
long

Ixia hybrida

African Corn Lily

lily-like
flower 3 in.
across

sword-like
leaf 1 ft
long —
develops
as flowers
open

clover-like
leaf 3 in.
across

Nerine flexuosa

star-shaped
flower ½ in.
across

Oxalis deppei

Rosette Clover

flower-head
4 in. tall

wavy-edged
leaf 1 ft
long

Veltheimia capensis

Forest Lily

trumpet-shaped
flower 6-9 in.
long

arrow-shaped
leaf 1½ ft
long

**Zantedeschia
aethiopica**

Calla Lily

crocus-like
flower 3 in.
across

strap-like
leaf 5 in.
long

**Zephyranthes
grandiflora**

Zephyr Lily

Ixia hybrida is noted for its gaily-coloured flowers, but it is much less popular than Freesia. You can recognise Ixia by its distinctive 6-petalled, dark-centred blooms on upright wiry stalks. Flowers appear in early summer.

Nerine sarniensis is the Guernsey Lily, its narrow-petalled white, orange or red flowers are tightly clustered at the top of the stalks. The leaves appear after flowering. N. flexuosa is much less common — a cluster of wavy-petalled pink or white bells on 2 ft (60 cm) flower-stalks in autumn.

Oxalis deppei bears red flowers in spring — O. cernua (Bermuda Buttercup) has yellow blooms, and O. bowiei is pale purple. Oxalis has never become popular despite its 'shamrock' leaves. The foliage closes at night.

Veltheimia capensis is a good choice for indoors. Plant the large bulb in early autumn, and after 3 or 4 months the 1 ft (30 cm) flower-stalk arises from the centre of the leaf rosette. This stalk bears about 60 small bell-shaped flowers.

Zantedeschia aethiopica is one of the most eye-catching indoor blooms and is widely used by professional interior decorators. The upturned trumpets of Calla Lily are borne on 3 ft (1 m) stalks in early spring. Hybrids are available in many colours. Z. rehmannii (pink) is a related species.

Zephyranthes grandiflora produces 6 in. (15 cm) flower-stalks in early summer, each bearing a crocus-like bloom which opens into a star. There are several large-flowering hybrids.

Veltheimia capensis

Zantedeschia aethiopica

Zephyranthes grandiflora

CACTI — Desert Types

Cacti have been part of the Indoor Plant scene for generations, but most interior decorators do not regard them as an important element of their designs.

There are advantages for the collector-minded householder — a long-lasting and varied group can be easily assembled. For the not-so-keen indoor gardener they are plants which do not need regular watering, pruning, transplanting, misting etc in order to survive on a windowsill.

For the interior decorator there is the problem of spines and the danger to viewer and indoor gardener. Wear thorn-proof gloves or use a band of folded newspaper when handling. Another problem is cost — a fully mature Cleistocactus straussii or Cereus peruvianus monstrosa can certainly provide a focal point as a Stand-alone Plant (page 103) but it can be prohibitively expensive.

An alternative approach to having a Stand-alone Cactus is to make a special type of Indoor Garden (page 122). This desert garden can be any type of receptacle ranging from a large floor-standing Designer Planter to a Dish Garden on the windowsill. Begin with a layer of compost topped with sand and perhaps some stones and pebbles if space

permits. In this is planted a varied selection of the most long-suffering of the Special Groups — the Cacti.

As noted above they will survive with little attention, but that approach has no place in interior design. In order to have specimen plants worthy of attention and perhaps in bloom you should read the information in the adjoining column.

SECRETS OF SUCCESS

Temperature: Average warmth from spring to autumn. Keep cool in winter — 50°-55°F (10°-13°C) is ideal but no harm will occur at 40°F (4°C). Windowsill plants should be brought into the room at night if the weather is very cold and there is no artificial heat.

Light: Choose the sunniest spot available, especially in winter. In the greenhouse some shading may be necessary in the hottest months.

Water: Increase watering in spring, and in the late spring-late summer period treat as an ordinary house plant by watering thoroughly when the compost begins to dry out. Use tepid water. In late summer give less water and after mid autumn keep almost dry — just enough water to prevent shrivelling.

Air Humidity: Do not mist in summer (exception: Cleistocactus). The main requirement is for fresh air — open windows on hot summer days.

Repotting: Repot annually when young; after that only repot when essential. Transfer in spring into a pot which is only slightly larger than the previous one.

Propagation: Cuttings of most varieties root easily. Take stem cuttings or offsets in spring or summer. It is vital to let the cuttings dry for a few days (large cuttings for 1-2 weeks) before inserting in peat-based compost. Another propagation method is seed sowing — germination temperature 70°-80°F (21°-27°C).

HOW TO MAKE A CACTUS BLOOM

Chamaecereus

Gymnocalycium

Mammillaria

Rebutia

Although some cacti, especially the ones illustrated, will bloom when the plant is still quite young, there are others, such as Opuntia and Cereus, which are more difficult to bring into bloom.

About half the cactus varieties can be expected to flower indoors by the time they are three or four years old. They will continue to bloom each year, and although spring is the usual flowering season even a modest collection can be selected to provide a few blooms all year round.

The secret lies in the fact that most cacti will only flower on new growth. This calls for summer care and winter 'neglect' as described in Secrets of Success. Another point to remember is that flowering is stimulated when the plant is slightly pot-bound.

slender green stems and brown spines. Pink tubular flowers

globular white-flaked stem with prominent ribs and curved spines

columnar stem with prominent ribs and brown spines

finger-like stems and white spines

Aporocactus flagelliformis

Rat's Tail Cactus

Astrophytum capricorne

Goat's Horn Cactus

Cereus peruvianus

Column Cactus

Chamaecereus silvestrii

Peanut Cactus

slender many-ribbed columnar stem covered with fine white bristles

columnar stem with numerous ribs and small comb-like spines

Aporocactus flagelliformis is a popular and easy Cactus — the ½ in. (1 cm) wide stems grow several inches a year and the 3 in. (8 cm) flowers appear in spring. Good for hanging baskets.

Astrophytum capricorne begins life as a ribbed ball but becomes cylindrical with age. Yellow daisy-like flowers are produced in summer on mature specimens, which reach 6 in.-1 ft (15-30 cm) depending on the species. A. capricorne has curved spines — A. ornatum has long straight ones.

Cereus peruvianus is one of the most important of all Stand-alone Cacti for the interior decorator. The stem reaching 2-4 ft (60 cm-1 m) in time and bearing 6 in. (15 cm) long flowers in summer. C. peruvianus monstrosus is a slow-growing grotesque mutation — the real eye-catcher of the family.

Chamaecereus sylvestrii is an old favourite — it spreads rapidly, the 3 in. (8 cm) long stems readily producing red flowers in early summer. If you think Cacti never bloom, try this one.

Cleistocactus straussii is another Cactus which features on the designers' list. When fully grown it reaches 3-4 ft (1 m) or more. The wool and spines covering the surface are white, giving the plant a silvery appearance and its common name.

Echinocereus pectinatus produces a 10 in. (25 cm) high column clothed with spines. E. salm-dyckianus bears fragrant bright flowers — see below.

Cleistocactus straussii

Silver Torch Cactus

Echinocereus pectinatus

Hedgehog Cactus

Aporocactus flagelliformis

Cereus jamacaru

Echinocereus salm-dyckianus

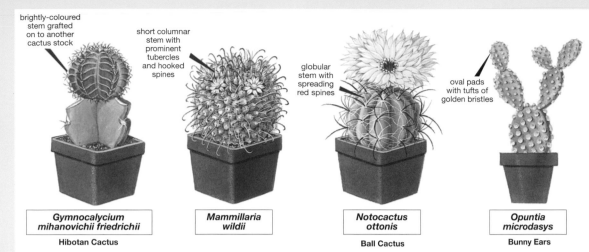

brightly-coloured stem grafted on to another cactus stock

short columnar stem with prominent tubercles and hooked spines

globular stem with spreading red spines

oval pads with tufts of golden bristles

Gymnocalycium mihanovichii friedrichii

Hibotan Cactus

Mammillaria wildii

Notocactus ottonis

Ball Cactus

Opuntia microdasys

Bunny Ears

globular stems and short white spines

Rebutia miniscula

Mexican Sunball

Gymnocalycium mihanovichii friedrichii is the Hibotan or Red Cap Cactus. Its coloured stem is grafted on to a green Cactus. It is an eye-catching novelty.

Mammillaria bocasana is the favourite species of the genus — it is a cluster-forming silvery plant which bears a ring of small white blooms around the stem in spring. M. wildii is similar, but it is oval rather than round.

Notocactus ottonis is a typical Notocactus — spherical, fiercely spined and bearing 3 in. (8 cm) wide blooms when a few years old. N. leninghausii is different — it is grown for its columnar stem rather than flowers.

Opuntia microdasys is the favourite member of the genus — it grows about 1 ft (30 cm) high and bears tiny hooked spines. These may be red or white, depending on the species. Opuntias come in various shapes and sizes.

Rebutia miniscula forms 2 in. (5 cm) wide balls. Not much to look at, but popular in small collections because it can be relied upon to produce its deep orange, tubular flowers every summer. R. senilis is a 3-4 in. (8-10 cm) ball.

Trichocereus candicans is an imposing plant when mature — a 3 ft (1 m) tall column which branches freely as it gets older. T. spachianus forms a bristly column reaching 5 ft (1.5 m) or more.

columnar stem with long yellow spines

Trichocereus candicans

Torch Cactus

Gymnocalycium mihanovichii friedrichii

Notocactus leninghausii

Rebutia senilis

CACTI — Forest Types

In their natural home the Forest Cacti are attached to trees in woodlands and jungles, and so it is not surprising that they are so different in form and requirements from the spine-covered Desert Cacti.

The typical Forest Cactus has leaf-like stems and a trailing growth habit, making it suitable for hanging baskets. A few, such as Rhipsalis, are grown for their stem form but their main attraction is their flowers. The most spectacular group are the Epiphyllums, with their fragrant saucer-size blooms.

Unfortunately the Forest Cacti can be shy bloomers, and there are rules to follow if you want a good display every year. Provide a cool and dry resting period, never move a plant once buds appear and allow stems to harden outdoors during summer. There are specific needs for each type — see below.

SECRETS OF SUCCESS

Temperature: Ideal temperature range is 55°-70°F (13°-21°C). During resting period keep at 50°-55°F (10°-13°C).

Light: Choose a well-lit spot, shaded from direct sunlight for most varieties. Epiphyllum thrives on an east-facing windowsill.

Water: Increase watering when resting period is over and buds begin to form. Treat as an ordinary house plant when flowers appear and during active growth — water liberally when compost begins to dry out. Use rainwater if tap water is very hard.

Air Humidity: Mist leaves frequently.

Repotting: Repot annually shortly after flowering has finished. Epiphyllum is an exception — flowering is encouraged by pot-bound conditions so do not repot annually.

Propagation: Cuttings of most varieties root easily. Take stem cuttings in summer, using a terminal 'leaf' pad or stem tip. Allow cutting to dry for a few days before inserting in peat-based compost.

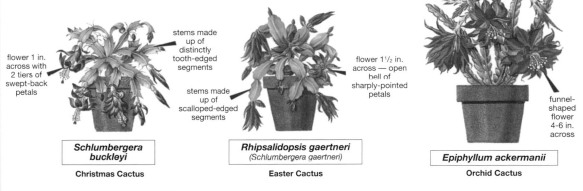

flower 1 in. across with 2 tiers of swept-back petals

stems made up of distinctly tooth-edged segments

stems made up of scalloped-edged segments

flower 1½ in. across — open bell of sharply-pointed petals

notched stem 2 ft long

funnel-shaped flower 4-6 in. across

Schlumbergera buckleyi

Christmas Cactus

Rhipsalidopsis gaertneri
(Schlumbergera gaertneri)

Easter Cactus

Epiphyllum ackermanii

Orchid Cactus

Rhipsalidopsis gaertneri

Schlumbergera buckleyi is the familiar Christmas Cactus. Its branching and arching stems are composed of 1-2 in. (3-5 cm) long flattened segments — along the edges are pointed projections. Between November and late January the flowers appear — white, pink, red and purple varieties are available.

Rhipsalidopsis gaertneri is its sister plant—the Easter Cactus which blooms in April or May. Its growth habit and general appearance are similar to Christmas Cactus, but the flowers which range from pink to dark red do not have swept-back petals and the segment edges are shallowly scalloped.

Shop-bought specimens of Christmas and Easter Cactus generally produce abundant blooms during the flowering season and are then kept for next year. Unfortunately in unskilled hands they never flower again. The reason is that they need to be stood outdoors between June or July and mid-September. They should then be brought indoors and given a resting period by being kept cool and dryish. About a month or two before the expected flowering time restore normal treatment described in Secrets of Success.

Epiphyllum ackermanii is an untidy plant like all Epiphyllums. The strap-like stems sprawl outwards, but its unattractive appearance is more than made up by the flowers which appear in May or June — flaring, multi-petalled trumpets which can be as wide as a saucer. Many colours are available.

FERNS

In Victorian times they were extremely popular and large collections were grown in conservatories and in specially constructed glass cases. But very few varieties were grown as ordinary living room plants, because gas fumes and coal fire smoke are extremely toxic to nearly all Ferns. It was the advent of central heating with its freedom from fumes which led to the revival of interest, but radiators in turn have their problems. Few Ferns can tolerate hot dry air. However, most Ferns are not really difficult to grow in the modern home, but they will not tolerate neglect. The compost must never be allowed to dry out, and the surrounding air needs to be kept moist.

There is a bewildering choice of varieties. Nearly two thousand are suitable for growing indoors, but comparatively few are available commercially. The classical picture of a Fern is a rosette of much divided, arching leaves (correctly referred to as 'fronds') but there are also Ferns with spear-shaped leaves, holly-like leaflets and button-like leaflets. There is also a wide choice of ways to display your collection. Many of them are ideal for a hanging basket and some, such as Boston Fern and Bird's Nest Fern, are large enough and bold enough to be displayed as specimen plants on their own. Delicate Ferns, such as Delta Maidenhair, are best planted in a Glass Garden. When grouping Ferns with other plants make sure that they are not crushed — the fronds are fragile and need room to develop. In addition ensure that all dead and damaged fronds are removed so that new ones can grow.

HOW TO CHOOSE A FERN

Easiest to grow	**Davallia** **Pteris cretica** **Nephrolepis** **Asplenium nidus** **Pellaea rotundifolia**
For hanging baskets	**Nephrolepis** **Adiantum**
For bold display as a specimen plant	**Nephrolepis** **Asplenium nidus** **Blechnum gibbum**

SECRETS OF SUCCESS

Temperature: Average warmth — cool but not cold nights are desirable. The best temperature range is 60°-70°F (16°-21°C) — the minimum for most types is about 50°F (10°C) and ferns may suffer at more than 75°F (24°C).

Light: Despite popular opinion, ferns are not shade lovers indoors as most varieties originated in the dappled brightness of tropical woodland. Good indirect light is the proper location — an east- or north-facing windowsill is ideal.

Water: Compost must be kept moist at all times and never allowed to dry out. This does not mean constantly soggy compost — waterlogging will lead to rotting. Reduce watering in winter.

Air Humidity: Moist air is necessary for nearly all ferns. Mist fronds regularly and use one or other of the techniques described on page 155.

Repotting: Repot in spring when the roots fill the pot — most young specimens will probably require annual repotting. Do not bury the crown of the plant.

Propagation: The simplest way is to divide the plant into 2 or 3 pieces in early spring if it produces rhizomes. Some ferns produce young plants at the ends of runners (example — Boston Fern) or on fronds (example — Mother Fern). It is possible, but not always easy, to raise plants from spores obtained from the underside of mature fronds.

FERN LEAF LANGUAGE

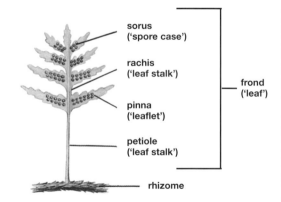

sorus ('spore case')

rachis ('leaf stalk')

pinna ('leaflet')

petiole ('leaf stalk')

frond ('leaf')

rhizome

ADIANTUM

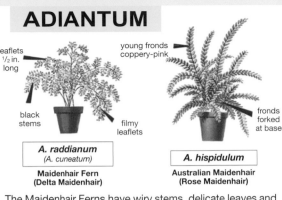

Adiantum raddianum

Adiantum capillus-veneris

leaflets ½ in. long

young fronds coppery-pink

black stems

filmy leaflets

fronds forked at base

A. raddianum
(A. cuneatum)

Maidenhair Fern
(Delta Maidenhair)

A. hispidulum

Australian Maidenhair
(Rose Maidenhair)

The Maidenhair Ferns have wiry stems, delicate leaves and a delicate constitution. They need moist air, warmth and shade — plants for the terrarium or shaded conservatory rather than the living room. **Adiantum raddianum** is perhaps the easiest to grow — the arching **A. tenerum farleyense** is the most attractive. **A. hispidulum** is quite distinctive and **A. capillus-veneris** grows wild in Britain.

ASPLENIUM

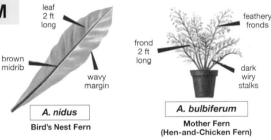

Asplenium nidus

Asplenium bulbiferum

leaf 2 ft long

feathery fronds

brown midrib

wavy margin

frond 2 ft long

dark wiry stalks

A. nidus

Bird's Nest Fern

A. bulbiferum

Mother Fern
(Hen-and-Chicken Fern)

The Aspleniums or Spleenworts need shade and a moist atmosphere. There are 2 basic types which are cultivated as house plants, and they look nothing like each other. Firstly there is the Bird's Nest Fern — **Asplenium nidus**. Its spear-like leaves surround the fibrous 'nest' at the centre. Not difficult, but you must not handle the young fronds. The other type of Asplenium is the Mother Fern. The fronds are finely divided and when mature bear numerous tiny plantlets. **A. bulbiferum** is the usual one — **A. viviparum** is smaller and the fronds are more arching.

BLECHNUM

large palm-like crown of stiff fronds; trunk develops with age

B. gibbum

A distinct trunk develops with age — the crown has a 3 ft (1 m) spread. The most popular species is **Blechnum gibbum** — in a large collection you might find the Brazilian Tree Fern (**B. braziliense**).

DAVALLIA

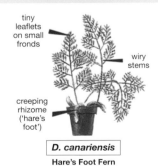

tiny leaflets on small fronds

wiry stems

creeping rhizome ('hare's foot')

D. canariensis

Hare's Foot Fern

Davallia is grown for its thick rhizomes which grow over the edge of the pot. Common names include Hare's Foot, Squirrel's Foot and Rabbit's Foot. **Davallia canariensis** has Carrot-like foliage.

DICKSONIA

dull green leathery leaflets

black trunk

D. squarrosa

New Zealand Tree Fern

Dicksonia squarrosa is a pretty pot plant when small, but forms a tall tree when mature. It produces a 10-20 ft (3-6 m) high trunk when mature. Dicksonia belongs in a large conservatory.

NEPHROLEPIS

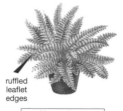

lacy leaflet edges

ruffled leaflet edges

N. exaltata Fluffy Ruffles
Feather Fern

N. exaltata whitmanii
Lace Fern

If you can have only one Fern, choose a variety of Nephrolepis. In Victorian times the stiff species **Nephrolepis cordifolia** and **N. exaltata** were popular, but not any more. Now it is the Boston Fern **N. exaltata bostoniensis** and its many varieties which are the favourites. The leaflets are sometimes divided even further to give a feathery or lacy effect.

Nephrolepis cordifolia

Nephrolepis exaltata bostoniensis

PELLAEA

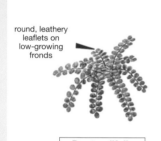

round, leathery leaflets on low-growing fronds

P. rotundifolia
Button Fern

Pellaea has an unusual feature for a Fern — it prefers dry surroundings. **Pellaea rotundifolia** is easy to grow — long arching fronds arise from a creeping rootstock. **P. viridis** is much more fern-like.

PLATYCERIUM

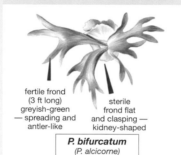

fertile frond (3 ft long) greyish-green — spreading and antler-like

sterile frond flat and clasping — kidney-shaped

P. bifurcatum
(P. alcicorne)
Staghorn Fern

These Ferns bear large and spectacular fronds, usually divided at their ends into antler-like lobes. The fronds are of two distinct types. **Platycerium bifurcatum** is the popular and easy-to-grow species.

POLYPODIUM

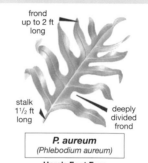

frond up to 2 ft long

stalk 1½ ft long

deeply divided frond

P. aureum
(Phlebodium aureum)
Hare's Foot Fern

Polypodium aureum has deeply cut leaves on thin stalks. There are unusual features — the rhizome creeps along the surface and it will grow in dry air. The most attractive variety is **mandaianum**.

PTERIS

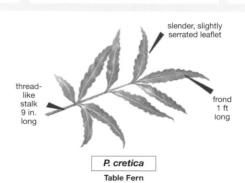

slender, slightly serrated leaflet

thread-like stalk 9 in. long

frond 1 ft long

P. cretica
Table Fern

The most popular types are varieties of **Pteris cretica** in a range of colours and forms. **Albolineata** has cream-centred leaves and **alexandrae** has cockscomb-tipped leaflets. **P. ensiformis victoriae** with its silver-centred leaflets is the prettiest. **P. tremula** is quite different with its 3 ft (1 m) long stalks and feathery leaflets. **P. vittata** has long leaflets borne like the rungs of a ladder.

Pteris ensiformis victoriae

Pteris vittata

ORCHIDS

Orchids were once just for the rich and knowledgeable, but not any more. Once they were found only in greenhouses and conservatories, but not any more — Orchids are now one of the top three in the list of our favourite house plants. There are several reasons for this dramatic increase in the popularity of these exotic plants. First of all, there is now a large selection of varieties for growing in the home and some of the newer hybrids are much more tolerant of ordinary room conditions than the traditional ones. Next, these Orchids are now widely available — you will find them in garden centres, supermarkets, florists, DIY superstores and on market stalls everywhere. Finally there has been the realisation that the blooms can last for months and even a modest collection can provide flowers all year round. You can grow Cymbidium for autumn to spring flowers, Paphiopedilum for spring to autumn flowers and Phalaenopsis for flowers at various times during the year.

Always check the requirements of a genus you have not grown before. Bright light Orchids generally need a windowsill and all will require the extra moisture provided by a humidity tray. There are other Orchid sites apart from the windowsill. A tea trolley with a pebble tray (page 115) makes an excellent home.

There are two approaches to Orchid growing. You can treat them as long-lasting pot plants to be disposed of after flowering, and that makes care a simple matter. Or you can aim to keep them as permanent house plants which will bloom year after year — this calls for more attention to air humidity, feeding, repotting etc. Work to do, then, but the results are so rewarding. As a Stand-alone Plant or part of an Indoor Garden, Orchids always attract attention.

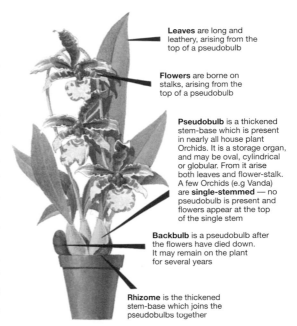

Leaves are long and leathery, arising from the top of a pseudobulb

Flowers are borne on stalks, arising from the top of a pseudobulb

Pseudobulb is a thickened stem-base which is present in nearly all house plant Orchids. It is a storage organ, and may be oval, cylindrical or globular. From it arise both leaves and flower-stalk. A few Orchids (e.g Vanda) are **single-stemmed** — no pseudobulb is present and flowers appear at the top of the single stem

Backbulb is a pseudobulb after the flowers have died down. It may remain on the plant for several years

Rhizome is the thickened stem-base which joins the pseudobulbs together

BRASSIA

It is not difficult to see why B. verrucosa is called the Spider Orchid. The thread-like petals and sepals give it a most unusual appearance for an Orchid, and yet it is one of the easiest to grow. The 4 in. (10 cm) wide pale green flowers are borne on graceful sprays — the aroma is either sweet or unpleasant, depending on personal taste. Flowering begins in late spring, and there should be a period of rest when the blooming period is over — give less water until growth restarts. It will thrive at ordinary room temperatures and it can be kept cool in winter — minimum 50°F (10°C). Place the pot in a bright spot away from direct sunlight. A number of hybrids of Brassia are available.

CAMBRIA

You will find the name Cambria on the label of long-stemmed plants which are available wherever Orchids are sold, but you will not find it in most books. It is a plant which does not occur in nature — it is a hybrid of other Orchid genera and is more correctly known as Vuylstekeara. The long-lasting flowers are available in various shapes and sizes — the flower stalks require support. A windowsill is a favourite site for this plant — provide shade against direct sunlight in summer. Cambria should be kept in a room which is lit after dark in winter. The minimum winter temperature is 55°F (13°C). The compost must never be allowed to dry out — reduce but do not stop watering in winter.

CATTLEYA

The white Cattleya bloom is the Corsage Orchid — the largest of all Orchid flowers in cultivation. Waxy and with a frilled and colourful lip it is the showpiece of the Orchid world, but not all Cattleyas are giants. There are miniature ones and there is a wide range of colours — always choose a hybrid as they are much easier to grow than the species. Flowering times range from spring to autumn, depending on the variety — the flowers last for about 3 weeks. Let it rest after flowering for about 6 weeks by giving less water. The minimum winter temperature should be 55°F (13°C) — place the pot in a bright spot with morning or evening sun. Wipe the leaves occasionally with tepid water.

CYMBIDIUM

The original hybrids were large ungainly plants — these have now been replaced by the mini varieties as house plants which are available in a wide range of colours. Mini-Cymbidiums are recommended for beginners as they will withstand more neglect than other types. There are 20 or more blooms on each upright stem and the flowers last for 8–12 weeks. The flowering period is autumn and winter — let it rest after flowering by giving less water. Put the plant outside in a semi-shady spot in summer, and in winter keep it in a cool room with a minimum temperature of 50°F (10°C). Cymbidium needs a bright spot with some morning or evening sun.

DENDROBIUM

The genus Dendrobium is an author's nightmare. There is a multitude of species with a variety of heights, flower shapes and colours, and flowering times which range from early spring to late winter. Some can thrive in a winter temperature as low as 50°F (10°C) whereas others need 60°F (16°C) or more. Finally, your plant is probably evergreen but it may lose its leaves after flowering. As a general rule keep the plant in a bright spot away from direct sunlight and let it rest after flowering, but the best advice is to make sure you buy a named variety with instructions. The most popular ones are the D. nobile varieties with white or pink flowers in spring. Keep cool and dry in winter.

LYCASTE

L. aromatica can be used to add variety to your Orchid collection. The all-yellow flowers are borne singly on 8 in. (20 cm) high stems, and they are noted for their strong scent. The plant grows actively in summer and needs both warmth and ample water. It must be kept cool and very little water is needed in winter when the flowers appear and the leaves fall. Mist the leaves regularly when the plant is growing and keep it in an area where there is light shade. The largest flowers (6 in./15 cm across) are borne by L. virginalis which is the easiest species to grow — this plant should be kept completely dry in winter. In addition to the species there are many large-flowered hybrids in a range of colours.

MILTONIA

Miltonia species are difficult to care for and are best left to the commercial grower or Orchid enthusiast with a greenhouse. They do not like temperature fluctuations and demand constantly moist air. Fortunately there are Miltonia hybrids nowadays and these are much less demanding — stand the pot in a bright spot away from direct sunlight and ensure a minimum temperature of 55°F (13°C) in winter. The fragrant blooms measure 2–3 in. (5–8 cm) across and have a pansy-like appearance — hence the common name Pansy Orchid. The usual colours are white, pink and red and the usual flowering time is May-July. The arching stems may need some support.

ODONTOGLOSSUM

Many of the species, such as O. crispum and O. cervantesii, have beautiful flowers but are not easy to grow. The problem is that their native home is in the mountains and not in the jungle, and so they need cool conditions in order to thrive — they suffer when the temperature exceeds 65°–70°F (18°–21°C). The hybrids are less demanding and can be grown in the living room. Put the pot in a bright spot away from direct sunlight and increase the interval between watering when they are not in flower. Aim for a winter temperature of at least 55°F (13°C). Odontoglossum varieties are not as popular as many of the plants described here — some (the Tiger Orchids) have striped petals.

ONCIDIUM

Some of the Oncidium species are quite spectacular with their butterfly-like flowers — O. papilio and O. tigrinum are examples. The problem is that they are difficult to grow and are best avoided for growing in the home. The hybrids, however, will succeed in a bright but sunless location if you provide good ventilation and some means of increasing the humidity around the plants during the growing season. Allow the plant to rest after flowering by reducing watering and keeping the pot in a cool room. Aim for a minimum winter temperature of 50°F (10°C). The tall spikes of the hybrid varieties bear numerous flowers which are usually quite small.

PAPHIOPEDILUM

The well-known Slipper Orchid with its pouched flowers differs from other popular house plant types in two ways. There are no pseudobulbs, so it must be kept reasonably moist throughout the year. It is also the only common Orchid which grows on the ground and not attached to trees. Each flower stalk bears a single 2–4 in. (5–10 cm) wide bloom which lasts for 8–12 weeks — there are many hybrids from which to make your choice. If you have a warm, centrally-heated room pick one with mottled leaves — all-green varieties are for cool locations. A minimum winter temperature of 55°F (13°C) is required. A brightly lit spot away from direct sun is necessary.

PHALAENOPSIS

You will find Phalaenopsis everywhere that Orchids are sold. The flat-faced flowers are borne on arching stems, each bloom lasting for about a month. The hybrids on offer are easy to grow, and with proper care will flower intermittently all year round. Popularly known as the Moth Orchid, it needs a bright but sunless spot with a minimum winter temperature of 65°F (18°C) — Phalaenopsis does not enjoy the cool nights favoured by some other types. It will grow quite happily with day temperatures as high as 82°F (28°C), but give it a rest period by putting it in a room with a lower temperature than its usual home for a few weeks in autumn. Do not cut off the roots growing outside the pot.

ZYGOPETALUM

Zygopetalum is not one of the popular group of Orchids so don't expect to find it at your local garden centre or DIY superstore. It is, however, worth looking for if you are building up a varied collection as it has a heavy fragrance and the flower lip has unusual violet-coloured stripes. The petals and sepals are green with large brown blotches. They are generally large plants with flower spikes reaching a height of 1½–2 ft (45–60 cm). The flowers usually appear in winter and last for about a month. Do not mist the leaves — use some other method for creating high humidity around the plant. For guidance on temperature, water and light requirements see the rules for Cymbidium on page 80.

CARING FOR YOUR ORCHIDS

Each Orchid has its own cultural requirements — Paphiopedilum is easy to care for but the beautiful Cattleya is a challenge. There are some general requirements, and these are shown below. Resting is an additional need if you want your plants to bloom again. There are four general hates — draughts, strong summer sun, poor drainage and direct radiator heat.

Temperature

There are cool-growing types which require a minimum temperature of 50°F (10°C) and at the other end of the scale the tropical-growing ones need a minimum of 65°F (18°C). As a general rule your Orchids will thrive at a temperature where you are comfortable — ideally there should be at least a 10°F (5°C) difference between the day and night temperature. Most types benefit from a spell outdoors between June and September in a sheltered spot out of the sun.

Light

From spring to autumn the general requirement is a brightly lit spot away from direct sunlight. There are exceptions — plants from the forest floor such as the Jewel Orchid will thrive in quite shady conditions whereas Cymbidium needs summer sun when not in flower. In winter it will be necessary to move the plant closer to the window as some direct sun is no longer a problem. Always grow Orchids in a room which is lit at night during winter.

Water

You can water either by the immersion method (see page 153) or in the traditional way with a watering can. It is essential to allow the plant to drain fully before putting it back on its saucer or in its holder — root rot resulting from standing water is one of the main causes of Orchid death. Aim to keep the compost moist at all times, although the surface may be dry. Water about once a week — more in summer, less in winter. Use tepid soft water.

Air Humidity

Orchids need a moist atmosphere and that can be a problem in a centrally-heated room. With an 'easy' type such as Paphiopedilum you can get away with misting the leaves frequently in summer and occasionally in winter, or by surrounding the pot with other house plants. For more demanding Orchids, however, a Pebble Tray is necessary, as described and illustrated on page 115. Sponging the leaves occasionally with tepid water will provide additional help, but for some tropical varieties the only satisfactory answer is to grow them in a glass-sided container. The Orchidarium is shown on page 120.

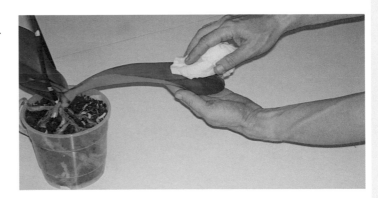

Food

Orchid compost does not contain fertilizer. Avoid the temptation to overfeed — as a general rule feed with an orchid fertilizer or half-strength pot plant fertilizer with every third watering — decrease in spring and autumn and stop in winter. Do not feed a newly-potted plant for at least a month.

Dead-heading

With most Orchids you should cut off flowering stems near the base once the blooms have faded. With Phalaenopsis the stem should be cut a little below the bottom flower so that it will be able to flower again on the same stalk.

Repotting

Don't be in a rush to repot — this should take place about every 2 years when the pseudobulbs have reached the rim of the container. Spring is the recommended time. The new pot should not be much larger than the old one and you will need to buy a special orchid compost. This will be a bark mix, a rockwool mix or sphagnum peat plus perlite. Gently pull the plant out of its pot (as illustrated) and cut away any damaged roots. Pot up in the usual way as described on page 159, taking care not to press the compost down too tightly. Lightly water from the top to settle the Orchid into the new pot before returning it to its home. Use soft tepid water.

PALMS

Palms have a vital role to play in Roomscaping. They come in a wide range of leaf shapes, sizes and prices. To buy a small Parlour Palm for a Pot Group on the sideboard will certainly not be expensive, but a stately Kentia Palm to serve as the head-high centrepiece of a large display would be costly. Such impressive features are widely used by interior decorators on both sides of the Atlantic, but the plan for the rest of us who want a large Palm is to buy a small one and grow it on, repotting as necessary.

These two Palms are ideal if you want an elegant specimen plant with a cast-iron constitution. Both are remarkably easy to look after in an average room, provided you don't regard them as lovers of tropical sunshine and desert-dry air. In fact they require cool winters, moist summers and protection from direct sunlight. All Palms are generally regarded as purely foliage plants, although the Parlour Palm produces tiny ball-like flowers.

Long and narrow leaflets are the key family feature, but width varies greatly, from the very narrow Dwarf Coconut Palm to the spear-like leaflets of the true Coconut Palm. The plants in this group do vary widely, but they all have one feature in common. If you try to cut a stem back you will kill it.

CANE PALMS

deep green narrow leaflets

yellowish-green leaflets

deep green broad leaflets

cane-like stems

Chamaedorea seifrizii	*Chrysalidocarpus lutescens* (Areca lutescens)	*Chamaedorea erumpens*
Reed Palm	Areca Palm (Butterfly Palm)	Bamboo Palm

A small group of Palms produce tall reed-like stems which look rather like Bamboo canes when mature.

Chamaedorea seifrizii and C. erumpens can grow 7–10 ft (2–3 m) tall under good conditions.

Chrysalidocarpus lutescens is the Areca Palm which like Chamaedorea is an impressive plant — its arching fronds may measure 3 ft (1 m) or more.

Rhapis excelsa (page 86) and R. humilis are Fan Palms, but are sometimes called Bamboo Palms as their slender stems can grow 7 ft (2 m) high.

SECRETS OF SUCCESS

Temperature: Average warmth — minimum 50°F (10°C) in winter. Winter night temperature should not exceed 60°F (16°C) for Parlour and Kentia Palms.

Light: A few delicate Palms revel in sunshine, but the popular varieties should be kept in partial shade. Both Parlour and Kentia Palms can thrive in low light conditions.

Water: The first need is for good drainage — all Palms detest stagnant water at the roots. During winter keep the soil slightly moist. Water more liberally in spring and summer.

Air Humidity: Mist leaves if room is heated. Occasionally sponge mature leaves. Avoid draughts.

Repotting: Only repot when the plant is thoroughly pot-bound, as Palms dislike disturbance. Compact the compost around the soil ball.

Propagation: From seed. A temperature of 80°F (27°C) is required, so propagation is difficult.

Chrysalidocarpus lutescens

FEATHER PALMS

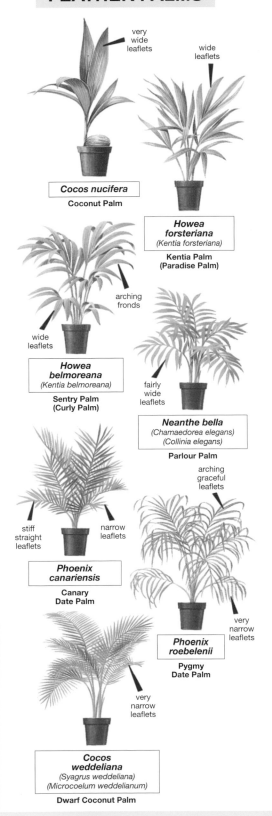

very wide leaflets

Cocos nucifera
Coconut Palm

wide leaflets

Howea forsteriana
(Kentia forsteriana)

Kentia Palm
(Paradise Palm)

arching fronds

wide leaflets

Howea belmoreana
(Kentia belmoreana)

Sentry Palm
(Curly Palm)

fairly wide leaflets

Neanthe bella
(Chamaedorea elegans)
(Collinia elegans)

Parlour Palm

arching graceful leaflets

stiff straight leaflets

narrow leaflets

Phoenix canariensis
Canary Date Palm

very narrow leaflets

Phoenix roebelenii
Pygmy Date Palm

very narrow leaflets

Cocos weddeliana
(Syagrus weddeliana)
(Microcoelum weddelianum)

Dwarf Coconut Palm

The fronds are divided on either side of the midrib into leaflets — these leaflets may be soft and drooping or stiff and erect. **Neanthe bella**, the most widely grown of all indoor Palms, belongs to this group. It may be listed as **Collinia elegans** or **Chamaedorea elegans** in the textbooks, but all these names refer to the old favourite Parlour Palm which is usually bought as a 6-12 in. (15-30 cm) specimen. After a few years it will reach its adult height of about 2 ft (60 cm) and tiny yellow flowers and small fruit appear if grown in good light. The dwarf nature of Neanthe makes it ideal for small rooms and bottle gardens — for a much bolder display the usual choice is one of the Howea (Kentia) Palms. These are the traditional Palm Court plants which grow up to 9 ft (3 m) tall. It is not too easy to distinguish between the 2 species — **Howea forsteriana** is the British favourite and is quicker growing but less arching than **H. belmoreana**. The true Date Palm (**Phoenix dactylifera**) is less attractive though quicker growing than the species of Phoenix sold as house plants — **P. canariensis** (6 ft/2 m) and **P. roebelenii** (3 ft/1 m). The true Coconut Palm (**Cocos nucifera**) unfortunately dies after a couple of years indoors. Its near relative **Cocos weddeliana** (more correctly **Syagrus weddeliana**) is sold as a house plant and is thought by some experts to be the most attractive of all the indoor Palms. But it has none of the hardiness of the popular types and needs the warmth and humidity of a conservatory.

Howea belmoreana

Phoenix canariensis

FAN PALMS

segments divided to base of large fan

segments not divided to base of large fan

drooping tips

coarsely-toothed leaf stalk

finely-toothed leaf stalk

toothed leaf stalk

Chamaerops humilis	*Trachycarpus fortunei* (Chamaerops excelsa)	*Livistona chinensis* (Latania borbonica)
European Fan Palm	Windmill Palm	Chinese Fan Palm

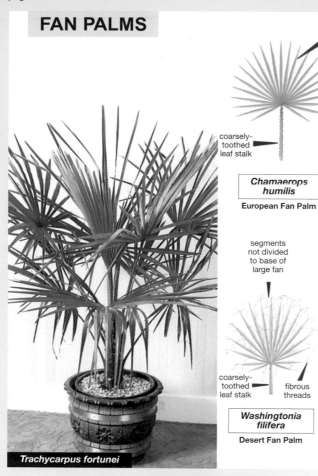

Trachycarpus fortunei

segments not divided to base of large fan

coarsely-toothed leaf stalk

fibrous threads

Washingtonia filifera

Desert Fan Palm

segments divided to base of small fan — leaflets 8 in. long

Rhapis excelsa

Little Lady Palm

The fronds are split into numerous segments radiating from a point at the base — these segments may be entirely or only partly divided. The leaf stalks are long, up to 2 ft (60 cm) or more, and are generally toothed. The Fan Palms are not widely grown as house plants — the large leaves can be dramatic in the right situation but have none of the graceful effect associated with Palms. Some are easy — **Chamaerops humilis** (the only native European Palm) is quite hardy indoors, but others are difficult to grow — **Washingtonia filifera** is short lived. The large-leaved ones are too wide spreading for the average room — it is the smaller-leaved **Rhapis excelsa** with its upright stems which is widely sold.

SAGO PALMS

ball-like base

Cycas revoluta

Sago Palm

The Sago Palms (Cycads) are distinctly Palm-like in appearance but they are not closely related to the true Palms. You will find only one species at the garden centre — **Cycas revoluta**. It is an extremely slow-growing plant, putting out just one leaf per year. In time it forms an attractive, dark green rosette.

FISHTAIL PALMS

wedge-shaped leaflets

Caryota mitis

Burmese Fishtail Palm

The Fishtail Palms get their name from the shape of the leaflets, which are about 6 in. (15 cm) long and 4 in. (10 cm) wide. **Caryota mitis** is the favourite one — lots of ragged-edged leaflets on arching fronds. **C. urens** (Wine Fishtail Palm) is less popular — its leaflets are more triangular but there are fewer of them.

Cycas revoluta

Caryota urens

SUCCULENTS

It is the leaf or stem form which is the common feature for this Special Group, rather than any family connections. Nearly forty plant families have at least one Succulent member.

Defining the word 'Succulent' is straightforward — it is a plant with thick, fleshy leaves or with thickened or fleshy stems which take the place of leaves. Much less straightforward is setting the dividing line between plants generally regarded as Succulents and other plants or groups which fit the definition but are classed elsewhere. The Cacti fit the definition perfectly, but are treated as a separate Special Group. Sansevieria and other fleshy-leaved house plants which have different requirements to the Succulent group are treated as ordinary house plants in this book. Those fleshy-leaved plants which are grown mainly for their blooms (Hoya, Kalanchoe blossfeldiana etc) are treated as Flowering house plants or Foliage house plants.

Three or four tiny pots of Succulents and a small Cactus or two are the usual starting point for a life-long interest in house plants.

The Succulents are indeed a good starting point for children as these plants are easy to care for, can withstand a great deal of neglect and mismanagement, and are amongst the easiest of all plant groups to propagate.

Hundreds of Succulents with widely differing shapes and sizes are commercially available. Most of them have a rosette shape, as the tightly-packed leaf arrangement helps to conserve water in their desert habitat. Despite the wide variety of shapes, the Succulents are remarkably consistent in their needs. They evolved in the dry areas of the world and their general requirements are related to this habitat — free-draining compost, sunshine, fresh air, water in the growing season, a period outdoors in summer and a cold and dry resting period in winter.

SECRETS OF SUCCESS

Temperature: Average warmth from spring to autumn — succulents (unlike most house plants) relish a marked difference between night and day temperatures. Keep cool in winter; 50°–55°F (10°–13°C) is ideal but no harm will occur at 40°F (4°C).

Light: A windowsill is the right spot, as some sunshine is vital. Choose a south-facing windowsill if you can, but some shade in summer may be necessary. Haworthia needs a bright but sunless site.

Water: Treat as an ordinary house plant from spring to autumn, watering thoroughly when the compost begins to dry out. In winter water very infrequently, once every 1–2 months.

Air Humidity: No need to mist the leaves. The main requirement is for fresh air — open windows in summer.

Repotting: Only repot when essential — then transfer to a slightly larger container in spring. Use a shallow pot rather than a deep one.

Propagation: Cuttings root easily. Take stem cuttings, offsets or leaf cuttings in spring or summer. It is vital to let the cuttings dry for a few days (large cuttings for 1–2 weeks) before inserting in compost. Water very sparingly and do not cover with polythene or glass. Another propagation method is seed sowing — germination temperature 70°–80°F (21°–27°C).

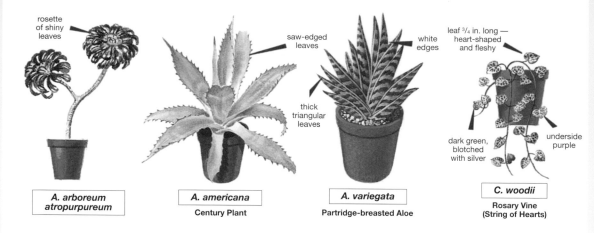

A. arboreum atropurpureum

rosette of shiny leaves

A. americana
Century Plant

saw-edged leaves

thick triangular leaves

A. variegata
Partridge-breasted Aloe

white edges

C. woodii
Rosary Vine (String of Hearts)

leaf ¾ in. long — heart-shaped and fleshy

dark green, blotched with silver

underside purple

wavy-edged leaves

silvery surface

C. undulata
Silver Crown

Aeonium arboreum atropurpureum bears rosettes of purple-brown leaves on its branched stems — flat rosette varieties such as A. tabulaeforme are available.

Agave americana is the most popular species. There are two colourful varieties — marginata has green leaves edged with yellow, and mediopicta (cream leaves edged with green). A. victoriae-reginae is a popular Agave — its 6 in. (15 cm) triangular leaves are dark green edged with white.

Aloe variegata is easy to recognise — the upright 6 in. (15 cm) leaves bear prominent bands. A. humilis is a blue-green dwarf bearing white teeth. Stemmed species such as the Tree Aloe A. ferox are available.

Ceropegia woodii is an unusual Succulent for a hanging basket — the sparsely-leaved wiry stems grow about 3 ft (1 m) long.

Cotyledon undulata has 1-2 ft (30-60 cm) stems with wavy-edged and bloom-covered leaves. C. orbiculata is a larger shrub with spoon-shaped leaves.

Crassula argentea is a favourite Succulent — the tree-like trunk can reach 3 ft (1 m). Some Crassulas (e.g C. perforata and C. repestris) have stems appearing to grow through the leaves. C. lycopodioides has stems clothed with minute fleshy scales, C. falcata has propeller-shaped leaves.

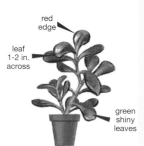

red edge

leaf 1-2 in. across

green shiny leaves

C. argentea
(C. portulacea)
Jade Plant
(Money Tree)

Aeonium arboreum atropurpureum Schwarzkopf

Agave americana marginata

Cotyledon orbiculata

pinky-
bronze
leaves

**E. gibbiflora
metallica**

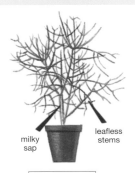

milky
sap

leafless
stems

E. tirucalli

Milk Bush

toothed
jaw-like leaves

F. tigrina

Tiger Jaws

finely-
pointed
leaves

H. fasciata

Zebra Haworthia

leaf
1 in.
long

silvery-
white
bloom

P. oviferum

Sugar Almond Plant
(Moonstones)

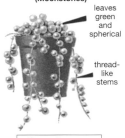

leaves
green
and
spherical

thread-
like
stems

S. rowleyanus

String of Beads

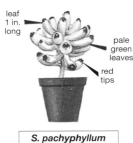

leaf
1 in.
long

pale
green
leaves

red
tips

S. pachyphyllum

Jelly Beans

dense cover
of threads

S. arachnoideum

Cobweb Houseleek

Echeveria harmsii and E. gibbiflora are rosette-topped trees. Other species grow as flattened rosettes such as the silvery ball-like E. elegans, the furry E. setosa and the pinkish-tinged E. carnicolor.

Euphorbia tirucalli is pencil-stemmed. Euphorbias come in many shapes — Cactus-like (E. grandicornis), globular (E. obesa) etc.

Faucaria tigrina has leaves which are 2 in. (5 cm) 'jaws' complete with soft teeth. The summer flowers are yellow.

Haworthia margaritifera forms a ball-like 6 in. (15 cm) rosette with white tubercles on the back of the leaves. All the Haworthias have thick and warty leaves.

Pachyphytum oviferum bears rosettes of egg-like leaves. Less popular is P. amethystinum with mauve-tinged leaves.

Sedum pachyphyllum is the most popular species. Most are low growing with branching leafy stems, but there are also shrubby types such as S. prealtum, and pendant species such as the 3 ft (1 m) long S. morganianum. Popular trailers include S. sieboldii.

Sempervivum arachnoideum is hardy — the Houseleeks are old favourites indoors and out. Many varieties are available — all seem to thrive on neglect.

Senecio rowleyanus with its pea-like foliage is one for a hanging basket or the front of a display. S. herreianus has oval foliage.

Echeveria elegans

Faucaria tigrina

Sedum sieboldii mediovariegatum

Chapter 4

ROOMSCAPING

Roomscaping — you will not have heard the word, although its brother is well known to nearly everyone.

Its brother is garden landscaping — the set of rules and techniques which are used to create attractive features outdoors. It is not about finding a home for individual plants — it is about growing some eye-catching specimens on their own and grouping others to form attractive features, such as a rockery or herbaceous border.

The gardener has no problems in finding out how to create a landscaped garden — there are magazine articles, TV programmes, show gardens to visit, and books on garden design.

With indoor plants, however, there are few books and no TV programmes to show you how to create features with House Plants and Pot Plants — for home owners it is just a matter of buying a plant which has caught their fancy and then finding a spot for the pot in the living room, kitchen or hall.

This is not because of a lack of interest in indoor plants — more than 90% of homes have at least one and there are scores of books to tell you which plants to put on the windowsill. But you would have to search to find the way to create a designer-type windowsill feature.

Roomscaping uses the accepted principles of good design to create indoor plant arrangements in the same way that the landscaper and the skilled flower arranger create their displays. There are various styles — informal, formal, cottage etc for the landscaper. For the flower arranger there are also a variety of styles (line, mass etc) and design rules such as texture, unity, balance etc. The purpose of this chapter is to describe the various styles of indoor plant features, and to outline the way to use the design principles of contrast, scale, balance etc. An indoor plant can do so much more than just stand on its own in a plastic pot on the windowsill or sideboard.

THE FIVE STEP GUIDE TO SUCCESSFUL ROOMSCAPING

STEP 1 : Read the BASICS
OF GOOD DESIGN (page 92-95)

STEP 2 : Decide on the LOCATION (page 96-101)

STEP 3 : Choose a STYLE (page 102-142)

STEP 4 : Select a suitable
RECEPTACLE (page 143-144)

STEP 5 : Buy the right PLANTS (page 145-149)

STEP 1 : Read the BASICS OF GOOD DESIGN

You will be doing nothing 'wrong' if you choose to ignore the advice in this section. The principles set out here are what the professionals regard as good design — they are ways to ensure that the knowledgeable will recognise the presence of the accepted good design concepts.

Shape, Texture & Pattern

These terms are used to describe the appearance of the foliage of a House Plant. Shape covers the size and outline of the leaf, Texture is the physical nature of its surface and Pattern is the distribution of colour. Wander around the display at a large garden centre to see the range of Shapes — tiny-leaved Mind-your-own-business to 2 ft (60 cm) wide Monstera leaves, straight-edged Crotons to feathery Asparagus Fern. The range of Textures is equally wide — smooth, spiny, dull, shiny, velvety, ruffled etc. Finally, the Patterns — all-green, variegated (green plus one other colour), multi-coloured, veined and so on. A mixture of Shapes, Textures and Patterns in your display will add interest, but too many different types in a feature can lead to confusion.

Unity

Unity refers to the way designers ensure that various items blend into a harmonious whole. This does not mean that the result should be dull or unexciting. House a blood-red Anthurium in a cylindrical stainless steel container against a stark white wall of a contemporary room and there is all the contrast you could desire — but there is also the unity of modern shapes and surfaces. Again, the shapes, colours and sizes are all different with a small Palm in a coloured ceramic pot holder on the piano in a chintzy room — but once again there is unity. There are all sorts of rules which try to help, but the simplest plan is to ask yourself two questions — does the plant seem to belong with the receptacle, and does the plant fit in with the room?

Balance

There are two aspects to the concept of balance. The first one concerns the plant or plants in the receptacle. Here there must be physical balance, which means that the receptacle and its compost must be heavy enough to prevent a one-sided arrangement from toppling over. In addition there must also be visual balance, which means that a physically-stable feature must not look as if it could topple over. You can increase the 'weight' of the lighter side of a visually-unbalanced feature by introducing plants with large dark leaves. The second aspect of balance concerns the visual impact of two nearby features, which may be quite different in style, against a wall. To see if they are balanced, imagine them on the pans of a giant pair of scales — if one side would clearly outweigh the other then the effect is not balanced.

Hue, Tint & Shade

THE WARM COLOURS
The warm colours brighten up the display. The hues are often dramatic and direct the eye away from the cool colours — the tints and shades are more subdued.

WHITE
White on its own has a calming effect — when placed next to warm colours the result is to make them look brighter.

THE COOL COLOURS
The cool colours quieten down the display. The hues are restful and provide an air of tranquility, but they are overshadowed by bright warm colours.

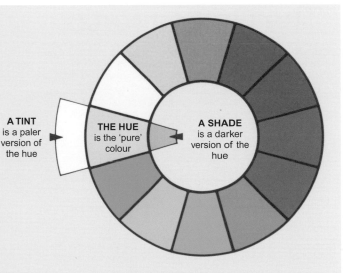

A TINT
is a paler version of the hue

THE HUE
is the 'pure' colour

A SHADE
is a darker version of the hue

MONOCHROMATIC DISPLAY
In a monochromatic scheme the various tints and shades of a single hue are the colours of the flowers and/or the non-green parts of the leaves.

ANALOGOUS DISPLAY
In an analogous scheme the two, three or four hues of the flowers and/or the non-green parts of the leaves are all neighbours on the colour wheel.

CONTRASTING DISPLAY
In a contrasting scheme the two hues of the flowers and/or the non-green parts of the leaves are directly opposite on the colour wheel.

POLYCHROMATIC DISPLAY
In a polychromatic (or rainbow) scheme the hues of the flowers and/or the non-green parts of the leaves are from all parts of the wheel.

Scale

Scale is the relationship of the plant and its container to the size and shape of the room and its furniture — the aim is to ensure that they are in proportion. A tall and spreading Palm in a small hall can look hopelessly out of place, whereas a scatter of isolated pots of small plants would spoil the appearance of a large room decorated in a contemporary style.

There are no rules to show how to ensure that the scale is right, but there are guidelines. A floor-standing tree-like plant is the best choice if you are dealing with a large, bare area. Do think big — an average-sized plant may well look lost. A specimen with wide-spreading or drooping leaves will appear to lower the ceiling — a tall, column-like plant will seem to add height to the ceiling.

Don't buy a Specimen tree on impulse. Measure the height and width you want to cover before you leave the room, and then take your tape measure to the garden centre to find a plant which will fit the bill.

The Golden Ratio

This term is used by designers to describe the ratio 1 to 1.618 — it has been used since the time of Ancient Greece to create visually pleasing effects in buildings, paintings, landscaping, room design etc. About 2500 years ago it was found that this ratio was the basis of many of the proportions found in the human body, and later it was found that it applied to flowers, trees, shells and so on. And so it was applied to art — the relationship of the width to the length of the Parthenon in Athens follows the Golden Ratio, and so do many of the features in paintings from the 14th to the 21st century.

In Roomscaping we can use a simplified version of this formula, which has been given many names including the Golden Mean, Golden Rectangle, Divine Proportion and the Golden Section. In simple terms it means that if a plant is 1½ times taller than its neighbour, then the effect will be pleasing to our inner designer eye. If you are covering an area of wall with plants, try to aim for a rectangle with one side 1½ times longer than the other. This is sometimes called the Goldilocks effect because of its not-too-little, not-too-much feel, but it is not a Golden Rule.

Movement

Movement is a simple concept which is easy to understand — it is any technique or material which moves the eye from one part of the display to another. The first thing to do is to make sure that two or more of the plants you buy for a group display are eye-catching enough to serve as focal points — these are areas to which the eye is drawn and rests there for a little time. Focal points should be separated in the arrangement. Next, aim for what flower arrangers call 'ins and outs' — the flowers/leaves should not create a level surface over a large area. Curves are very important — note how the trailing plant in the arrangement on the right moves the eye from one feature to the other. There is a final rule. One plant should not be so dominant as to distract the eye for a long time from the other plants in the group — use such a specimen as a Stand-alone Plant.

Contrast

Unity (page 92) and Contrast would seem to be opposing design ideas, but they are not. Unity means that the plant feature should fit in with the overall appearance of the room — there should never be a feeling that it doesn't belong. Within the plant/container/background combination, however, there should be some degree of contrast. This means that there should be a marked difference between one or more of these items. The degree of contrast between the plant(s) and the receptacle(s) is a matter of personal taste, but there are some points to remember. A green plant in a green pot can look boringly dull, but the use of a brightly-coloured or highly-patterned container will take attention away from the plant. Although there need not be a high degree of contrast between plant and pot there should be clear-cut contrast between the plant feature and its background — white is ideal, but other pastel shades will do. Putting a multi-coloured arrangement of indoor plants in front of a highly-patterned background is a design fault. Against such paper or curtains you should choose a display in which large green leaves dominate.

STEP 2 : Decide on the LOCATION

The standard advice for getting the best visual effect from your indoor plants is to look at their future home before you make your purchase. First of all, which room do you have in mind? There are often both advantages and pitfalls in choosing any of the six basic areas — see page 98 for a room-by-room guide.

The next task is to decide on the position for the plant or plants in the room. On page 99 you will find information on the six locations which can be used to display House Plants. There are questions you will have to ask. How much natural light would the plants receive? Is the room heated? Is the room kept warm on winter nights? Your choice of room and location within the room will affect both the display styles which would be suitable and the range of plants which would flourish there.

Of course, there may be no choice of location to be made if the plants are required to do a specific job such as covering an empty fireplace or serving as a divider between parts of a room. So location is fixed, but it is still necessary to consider the factors described above to ensure that the display will be both effective and attractive.

All this underlines the first sentence at the top of the page. As when we are dealing with the garden it is necessary to consider the location before making a purchase. However, this is often a counsel of perfection — more than half the House Plants we buy are impulse purchases. It caught our eye, and so we bought and read the label later. We all do this occasionally, and the best course of action is to look it up in Chapter 2 or 3 and find a location where it would be most likely to succeed. We should also consider whether it would be a good idea to put it with other plants to make a Pot Group or an Indoor Garden. Step 3 on page 102-130 sets out the advantages of grouping plants together.

Hardly any type of plant can be expected to flourish in every area of your house, but there are plants which can be relied upon to grow under the whole range of conditions. There is even a small group which can be grown in dark corners — see page 149.

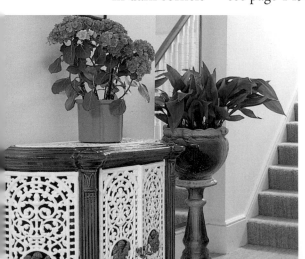

There are other factors apart from the obvious environmental ones which will affect the health and longevity of the plants. In addition the lighting and background (page 100) will affect the appearance of the display.

It is now time to think about choosing a suitable style, a receptacle and finally the plants to choose. However, it should now be obvious that looking at the location has been an important first step.

ONE PLANT — NINE APPEARANCES

Dusty leaves

Washed leaves

Polished leaves

Plain background

Mirrored background

Patterned background

Uplighting

Spotlighting

Backlighting

ROOM-BY-ROOM GUIDE

BEDROOM

The bedroom is the least popular place for indoor plants — only one in ten has them. Some designers say we spend too little time there, it is too far from the watering can, taps etc, and visitors are few. Most interior decorators take the opposite view — here you don't have to worry what the whole family and friends think, and it is an excellent place for plants which hate too much heat in the winter. Examples are Cyclamen, Beloperone, Hydrangea, Campanula, Bougainvillea and Abutilon. Fragrant plants are popular.

HALL

Beautiful leaves and flowers near the front door are an immediate indication of a well-tended home — it is therefore not surprising that only the living room and kitchen are more popular sites. A large and well-lit hall is a great opportunity for the roomscaper — here is the place for showy flowering plants. Unfortunately most halls are poorly lit, draughty, cold at night and narrow. Here you should choose from the range of flowering Pot Plants to provide a colourful and inexpensive temporary display.

BATHROOM

A feature in magazines but not in the home — only one in ten bathrooms houses an indoor plant. This is strange — it is the best room for plants requiring moist air, and no room is more in need of the softness and greenery that they bring. A pot on the windowsill or a wall-mounted holder is the usual choice for a small bathroom, but a spacious one can be used to show off exotic Specimen Plants such as Anthurium, Cymbidium and Caladium. However, make sure your scheme meets with approval from the rest of the family!

LIVING ROOM

Nearly four in every five living rooms have indoor plants. The favourite place, but in most cases the visual impact can still be improved by rearranging them and perhaps buying a few additional ones — see Step 3 for details of how this can be done. Make use of indoor plants to enliven dull areas, such as an empty hearth or a bare shelf. A moderately good place for plants, but there can be problems — low humidity in a centrally-heated room and too much heat in winter for plants which require a period of dormancy.

DINING ROOM

The place where we entertain (or impress) our friends, a location next to the kitchen for easy watering and with decor which is usually sparse, but only one dining room in four houses an indoor plant. The usual problem is a lack of space, but a plant display can be used in place of cut flowers on the table in even the most compact room. Four rules — the display must be low-growing, in good condition, odour-free and pest-free. Other places in a small dining room are the windowsill or on the wall in a suitable container.

KITCHEN

The kitchen is second only to the living room as the most popular place for plants, and this is not surprising — some members of the family may spend much of the day there, the air is moist, and the appearance of cupboards, steel sinks etc can be softened and enlivened by colourful plants. The windowsill in front of the sink is the favourite spot — lighting is good and water is close to hand. But some roomscaping is needed here — grouping can well be an advantage but an untidy jungle could spoil the view and darken the room.

PLANT SITE GUIDE

HANGING FROM THE CEILING There is no better way of displaying a trailing plant than suspending it in a container attached to the ceiling. We notice plants in a hanging basket which wouldn't receive a second glance if they were on the sideboard. Dull corners and alcove windows are the favourite sites. There is, unfortunately, a rather long list of warnings. Don't have a hanging basket in the line of traffic if the ceiling is low, and do make sure that the attachment is strong enough to hold the weight of fully grown plants and compost just after watering. Next, the plants must be in good condition — a bedraggled Ivy or a scorched Philodendron will diminish rather than enhance the beauty of the environment. Finally, do remember that upkeep is not easy — it is obviously more difficult to water a hanging basket than its floor-standing counterpart.

STANDING ON A WINDOWSILL This site is a favourite place for housing indoor plants. Interior decorators do include this site in their scheme of things, but not with a line of uncoordinated pots placed neatly along the length. It is better to use an eye-catching Specimen Plant — a low and bushy one if placed in the centre or a tall and narrow plant if placed on one side. Size must be in keeping with the surroundings — a small and insignificant plant in a large window will do nothing to enhance the decor. Choose plants with care — if the window faces east, south or west you will need a plant which can withstand some direct sun. Read the lists on page 148 before making your choice. A south-facing window will need some form of screen against the hot, summer sun.

STANDING ON THE FLOOR The place for a large Architectural Plant (see page 105) is on the floor — to place a heavy pot on a table or sideboard can make it look unsafe. There are other types which are also recommended as Stand-alone Plants — flowering standards are best displayed in this way and so are tall climbers such as Philodendron and Monstera. Such displays are a great favourite with interior designers. A matched pair on either side of a door adds symmetry to a large room — a pot stood near a patio door brings the garden indoors.

STANDING ON A PEDESTAL A number of indoor plants produce long hanging stems or arching leaves, and the display is often spoilt when the pot is stood on a sideboard or windowsill. The place for such plants is in a hanging container or on a pedestal. To house several pots in a pedestal-like arrangement you can buy a metal or cane pot stand.

STANDING ON FURNITURE Small Specimen Plants need to be raised off the ground so that they can be enjoyed at close range. The usual way to do this is to place the pot on a windowsill, shelf or sideboard.

GROWING ON A WALL The plants most usually chosen are either flowering types to provide a splash of colour against a pastel wall surface, or trailers to frame pictures, windows etc. There are several difficulties. It is not easy to keep the surrounding air moist, and frequent watering will be required. Choose a receptacle with a large and deep saucer.

THE BACKGROUND CAN BE IMPORTANT

For most plants the best background is a non-patterned, pale pastel colour. This is especially true for all-green foliage plants and for brightly coloured flowers.

Heavily variegated leaves and plants bearing masses of pale blooms may look insipid when set against a pale background. A dark surface is visually more effective.

Small leaves are often lost against an intricately-patterned background. Move such plants in front of a plain wall — use large-leaved types against patterned surfaces.

For a bold effect aim for contrasts in colour and shapes. A background with a strongly perpendicular look can be improved by placing a spreading plant in front of it.

THE LIGHTING CAN BE IMPORTANT

For life-giving illumination the plants must rely on daylight or fluorescent lighting. For display purposes the light of an ordinary bulb directed on to the foliage or flowers will greatly enhance the appearance of a Specimen Plant in the evening. The best type of bulb to use is a spotlight or floodlight, but overheating with a Filament-type bulb can be a problem. There are alternatives nowadays. Halogen bulbs are effective but emit a lot of heat — compact Fluorescent and LED bulbs give out relatively little heat.

SPOTLIGHTING A light or lights (usually spotlights recessed in the ceiling or set on a track) which are above the plant or plants. There are two benefits — plants in groups are brought into a unified whole and the details of individual plants are heightened.

UPLIGHTING A light or lights which are set at ground level in front of the plant or plants. Leaves are illuminated, but the main purpose is to cast interesting shadows against the wall. Move the light to seek the most dramatic effect.

BACKLIGHTING A light or lights which are set at ground level behind the plant or plants. The basic purpose is to turn the plant into a silhouette as clearly shown on page 97. This is not a technique for ordinary displays — you need space and large plants.

LOCATION PICTURE GALLERY

Nothing could be simpler. Just a few pots of low-growing African Violets in a casserole dish which matches the dinner service. Simple, but effective. ▷

◁ *Asplenium, Nephrolepis, Cissus ... a group of shade-loving foliage plants add interest to a fireplace in summer time.*

△ *Many shapes and sizes of plants are present in this living room and the effect can be quite stunning. But do be careful — this number and variety of plants in a colourful over-furnished room would be overpowering.*

STEP 3 : Choose a STYLE

THE STAND-ALONE PLANT
page 103–110

THE POT GROUP
page 111–120

THE INDOOR GARDEN
page 121–130

THE GLASS GARDEN
page 131–134

THE WATER GARDEN
page 135–140

THE STAND-ALONE PLANT

The Stand-alone Plant is a foliage or flowering plant which is grown as a solitary feature because of its use or attractive appearance

As described later, the standard range of indoor plants are usually more attractive, healthier and easier to care for when grouped together. However, the Stand-alone Plant is the feature favoured by interior decorators when the plant has something to say, which means that the plant is good enough to be a focal point. This is referred to as a **Specimen Plant**, and the various types are illustrated on page 105-107.

When a Specimen Plant is grown on its own there are no competing leaves or flowers to distract the viewer, but this also means that there is nothing to hide discoloured leaves, misshapen branches etc. Good quality is thus a basic need when choosing a Specimen Plant for displaying on its own. There are additional factors to consider with the Stand-alone Plant. An attractive and balanced container can enhance the effect, as shown by the illustration, and both the background and lighting (page 100) have a part to play.

Roomscapers choose Specimen Plants for stand-alone displays where they serve as focal points, but in the home we may also use an ordinary plant in a stand-alone pot. It may be used to add some flower colour or attractive foliage to a dull spot rather than serving as a focal point, or it may be grown for the owner's satisfaction rather than to add to the decor of the room. This is something we all do and is perfectly acceptable, but as a general rule ordinary plants and especially imperfect ones are more attractive when grouped together.

FOCAL POINT

A focal point is an item in a room which is attractive or unusual enough to divert attention away from nearby objects. Design experts advise that focal points should be placed at the middle point of walls and not in corners, but the corner is often the only area available for a large Architectural Plant.

ARCHITECTURAL STAND-ALONE PLANTS

These plants are sometimes referred to as Decorator Plants in the U.S — a reminder of the part they play in fashionable room decoration. They are permanent features of the room with year-round interest, so foliage ones are chosen.

In simple terms the Architectural Plant is one which is sufficiently eye-catching because of its shape to serve as a focal point in the room, although they can also be used to fill a large, empty space or to serve as a room divider. Many of them are trees with interesting shapes or spreading leaves.

Boldness is the key, and there are a few rules to follow. The choice of texture, colour and size of the container or pot holder can improve or mar the display — read page 144. As a general rule, choose a container which is about a quarter the height of the Architectural Plant. As shown on page 100 the background can affect the impact of an Architectural Plant. As the plant is a focal point it is important to keep it in peak condition. Leaves should be dust-free and any dead foliage should be removed.

In a modern minimalist room the use of a large and striking Architectural Plant is almost an obligatory feature. The problem is that the price of a large plant may be prohibitive, but that need not deter you as there are several alternative approaches. If you have the time to wait then you can buy a young plant, repot it regularly and then place it in its permanent position once it has reached the desired size. An alternative approach is to make one of the do-it-yourself displays described on page 141-142. Buying a pedestal is the only answer if you want an instant display without having to buy a large specimen. A large, spreading Fern or a fully grown Chlorophytum with cascading plantlets placed on a pedestal can provide an Architectural-type display.

This last point illustrates that the dividing line between Architectural and Non-architectural Stand-alone Plants (see overleaf) is not clear-cut.

Popular Architectural Plants

Araucaria heterophylla
Chamaedorea seifrizii
Cyperus alternifolia
Dicksonia squarrosa
Dieffenbachia
Dracaena fragrans
Dracaena marginata
Ficus benjamina
Ficus elastica decora
Ficus lyrata
Grevillea robusta
Heptapleurum arboricola
Howea belmoreana
Howea forsteriana
Philodendron bipinnatifidum
Phoenix canariensis
Schefflera actinophylla
Sparmannia africana
Yucca elephantipes

Orchids — the Stand-alone Plants *par excellence* for the living room. The Moth Orchid was once a rarity, now it is seen everywhere. After flowering cut back to 1 in. (3 cm) above a node (small bump) on the spike (stem). This usually produces a new flowering spike.

NON-ARCHITECTURAL STAND-ALONE PLANTS

It is a mistake to regard Architectural Plants as the clear-cut elite of the Stand-alone group. The foliage display provided by a mature Monstera deliciosa can be matched by few Architectural Plants, but it is excluded because it is a climber. An Anthurium or a Bird of Paradise will turn more heads than the average Rubber Plant, but these floral beauties are not classed as Architectural Plants because their display is not permanent.

Moderate-sized Palms, such as Neanthe bella, and attractive Ferns are worthy of display on their own, but it is the plants with coloured leaves that come into their own as Stand-alone Plants. Climbers deserve a special mention as they are the cheapest way to obtain a tall and wide-spreading display.

House Plants with large flowers are best displayed on their own and showy Pot Plants such as Gloxinia, Poinsettia and Azalea are usually treated this way.

Multi-coloured Foliage Plants

Begonia rex
Caladium
Codiaeum
Cordyline terminalis
Nidularium
Rhoeo

Flowering Plants

Begonia tuberhybrida
Bromeliads
Bulbs
Cyclamen
Gloxinia
Hydrangea
Orchids
Pelargonium
Poinsettia
Rhododendron simsii

Climbing Plants

Cissus
Hoya
Monstera
Passiflora
Philodendron hastatum
Rhoicissus
Scindapsus
Stephanotis
Thunbergia

Trailing Plants

Chlorophytum
Columnea
Nephrolepis
Zygocactus

STAND-ALONE PLANT PICTURE GALLERY

A traditional Stand-alone Plant display in a traditional setting — a showy Pot Plant in front of a not-in-use fireplace to provide a splash of colour for a limited period. ▷

Collections of the same type of plant can be a talking point — the popular examples are Bromeliads, ◁ Orchids and Cacti. Here is something more unusual — a Stand-alone Lemon tree with nearby Orange ones

△ Unlike the Azalea above, this Bromeliad display has a distinctly unusual appearance — glass, coloured gravel and sand provide eye-catching alternatives to compost and terracotta.

A pair of identical Stand-alone Plants can provide interest and a feeling of balance which would be missing from a single pot ▷ *display. This point is illustrated by this stair display of paired Pitcher Plants.*

Metal containers are being used on an increasing scale to replace traditional pots ◁ in contemporary settings. This stainless steel pot looks at home in this room, but would be quite wrong in a period room.

△ Pot or plant? As a general rule you should aim to have either the pot or the plant as the eye-catching feature. The two photographs above illustrate the point, but this is not an absolute rule and it is sometimes successfully ignored.

◁ One of the most popular Stand-alone trees is the variegated Weeping Fig (Ficus benjamina variegata). The leafy crowns are large but the trunks are thin — several stems are often plaited together to ensure adequate support.

Large floor-standing plants with narrow or ▷ sword-shaped leaves are popular with interior designers. Palms are the usual choice where narrow spreading leaves are required, but for broader leaves the False Palms such as this Dracaena marginata bicolor are the more usual selection.

The blooms on a flowering Pot ◁ Plant should be bold or unusual if it is to be displayed as a Stand-alone Plant rather than being part of a Pot Group or Indoor Garden. Anthurium is a good example of a plant which benefits from not being surrounded by others.

THE POT GROUP

The Pot Group is a collection of Stand-alone Plants in which the display is seen as a single unit

It cannot be denied that an outstanding plant deserves a place on its own in a receptacle which does it justice. But the average House Plant is not outstanding, and for them the Pot Group offers a number of advantages which are described and illustrated on the following pages.

There are all sorts of ways of bringing a number of pots together. The arrangement can be horizontal or vertical, and the pots may or may not be collected together in some form of open unit such as a wire jardinière or on a large drip tray. The Victorians were conscious of the value of grouping pots together and there were all sorts of multi-tiered metal units, including the popular corner stand. These pot group stands have lost their charm except as antique pieces, but all the reasons for grouping plants together remain and are listed on page 112-113. There is an additional advantage which is not listed — the creation of an attractive Pot Group gives the same sort of satisfaction which flower arrangers derive from their work.

The plants can be a restrained collection or a riot of colour — there are no rules but there is guidance on page 116. The grouping and types of pots can range from the very simple to the truly lavish. Obviously, the purpose of creating the Pot Group is to add interest and living colour to part of the room, and advice on the placing of the arrangement is given on page 114-115.

Pot Group or Stand-alone Plants?

The key feature of the Pot Group is the fact that the plants plus the pots form a single **unit** in which each plant generally has an effect on its neighbours. This can be by reducing light, increasing humidity or by preventing unrestricted growth.

Stand-alone Plants

These three plants are clearly an arrangement of separate pots — each one is seen as an individual.

Pot Group

At first glance these three plants are seen as a unit — only later do we see them as individual plants.

THE ADVANTAGES OF GROUPING

The virtue of having an eye-catching plant on its own rather than being surrounded by others was pointed out on page 103, but it is also true that most plants benefit from being grouped together. There are four basic reasons.

① Imperfections can be hidden in a group

The plants we have scattered about the room do tend to suffer as time passes. The lower leaves of some types such as Croton may have fallen because the air is too dry, and the scorched leaf tips of Palms and Dumb Canes caused by too much sun have to be removed. In addition there is the unattractive appearance of a small flower-head on a long stalk and the unbalanced effect of a plant which is lop-sided. These defects, and others, are unavoidable — the answer is to collect the plants together into a Pot Group in which the base stems, trimmed leaves and long flower stalks are hidden.

A bare-stemmed Croton and a lop-sided Syngonium plus a Begonia, Rose and Palm. Each imperfect plant is seen as a separate unit.

An attractive single unit, the Pot Group has been created by packing them together. Campanula has been added to improve the shape.

② Plants are easier to care for in a group

The ritual of looking after a number of plants scattered around the room involves moving from plant to plant — it is of course an easier task to use a watering can or mister when the plants are collected together into a Pot Group. The saving in time and effort may be small here, but there are other time-savers. Weak stems, lop-sided growth and floppy flower-heads require staking for plants in Stand-alone Pots, but when pots are grouped together these wayward stems can often be supported by their taller neighbours. In addition the task of trimming off brown tips and other imperfections is less necessary in a group as there is a variety of leaves to mask these defects.

③ **Plants usually thrive better in a group**

It has been found that many plants benefit from being placed next to others in a group rather than being grown in isolation. The usual explanation is that they benefit from the increase in humidity which is found in this microclimate — this extra humidity arises from the evaporation of the moisture from the newly misted leaves and the damp compost in the surrounding pots. This increase in humidity results in a reduction in the shrivelling of the leaves of moisture-lovers such as the delicate Ferns. In addition the general vigour of the plant is sometimes increased, and the reasons are not fully known.

The edges of the leaflets on a Fern grown as a Stand-alone Plant tend to shrivel in the dry air in winter.

The leaflets on the Maidenhair Ferns in the centre of the Pot Group have remained fresh and green.

④ **Plants usually look better in a group**

A pot containing an attractive Specimen Plant can be stood on its own or can be grouped with others — here it can serve as a focal point, providing a centre of interest. But most small-leaved and low-growing plants do not have this degree of visual appeal, and when grown as a Stand-alone Plant may appear insignificant. In a Pot Group, however, they can take on three functions which add considerably to the appearance of the group. They can add greenery between and in front of the Specimen Plants, and in addition the blooms of a modest plant may add dramatically to the display — see the yellow Chrysanthemum in the photograph. Finally, trailers can soften the front edge of the containers in a Pot Group.

POT GROUP TYPES

Standard Group

A Standard Pot Group is a collection of plants in individual pots which are placed closely together, in which the plants and not the containers are the main point of interest. To make a Pot Group which has that 'interior decorator' look calls for the use of established design principles. The Basics of Good Design section (page 92-95) will have given you some idea of what the professionals have in mind when creating a display, and the Location section (page 96-101) will have given you some idea of the best place for the display. And now it is time to think about the choice of pots for the display — the Receptacle section (page 143-144) will provide information on the types available. Be careful. Too much variety of colour, size and shape will spoil a Standard Pot Group.

It is time to buy the plants. Choose three or a larger odd number — they should all have rather similar light and temperature needs. There should be a range of heights and textures, and the usual choice is a selection of foliage plants to provide the permanent skeleton, and some flowering plants are added to provide colour to the display.

And now for the arrangement. If the Pot Group is to be viewed only from the front and sides, then as a general (but not strict) rule the taller plants should be at the back and the smaller ones at the front. Straight lines should be avoided — reduce the back row height at the sides and do have ups and downs to give a feeling of movement. Overall outline shape is a matter of personal taste — the lop-sided pyramid is popular. If the display is to be seen from all sides, the taller plants belong in the middle with the smaller ones surrounding them. Once again you must break up this overall pattern to ensure movement.

Finally, a word of warning. Do not think a riot of different colours, shapes and textures will ensure that your Pot Group will have a professional look. The displays created by interior decorators are often quite restrained and may consist solely of foliage plants.

Designer Group

Designers do sometimes produce Pot Groups which are large and exotic, filled with stunning plants and unusual containers. But size, plant type and colour are not key features of the Designer Pot Group. There are just two basic requirements.

First of all, pots of at least two different heights are used — there is a definite 3-D feel. Secondly, the appearance of the pots is just as important as the plants — it is a display where both plants and containers are decorative.

Pot holders are a basic feature — in the arrangement shown above the back pot holder contains a Kentia Palm which is much taller than the other plants. A smaller plant could be used by raising it with a block of wood under the pot. It is essential that this pinnacle plant receives maximum display. The smallest pot contains a flowering Pot Plant which is replaced when the blooms fade, and a trailing plant is grown in one of the middle receptacles, with its stems allowed to drape over the base unit.

Just 5 plants and a simple DIY base unit, but very effective. The example on page 119 is even simpler, but once again it exhibits the two key features of the Designer Pot Group.

Pebble Tray

Grouping plants within a shallow tray is an excellent technique for growing plants which need high humidity in a centrally-heated room. If you find it difficult to grow African Violets or Orchids then try them in a Pebble Tray. The tray should be about 2 in. (5 cm) high. Avoid a dangerously wide overhang if the tray is to be stood on a windowsill.

Place 1 in. (3 cm) of gravel on the bottom of the tray. Group the plants on the surface.

A favourite place for a Pebble Tray is on a radiator shelf below a window-sill. In this situation the humidity around the plants in winter will be trebled. Watering is a simple matter — allow water to run out of the pots and into the gravel. The water level must not be allowed to cover the top of the gravel.

Vertical Display

The Pot Group is nearly always horizontal, although the pots are sometimes set at different heights. The Vertical Display, however, is both easily arranged and can be extremely effective. The traditional version is a corner shelf unit with a pot on each shelf — use the same variety of colourful trailing plant to produce a column of foliage or flowers. A series of hanging baskets attached to each other can be used to give the same effect — the metal or cane plant stand which carries pots at different heights has the advantage of portability.

POT GROUP COLOUR SCHEMES

Rainbow Group

This is the Pot Group equivalent of the most popular type of flower arrangement — a multi-coloured collection of flowers in front of or within a variety of foliage. Some designers feel that this is too garish a way to use indoor plants, and it is true that the Rainbow Group is usually a mistake in a room with a complex pattern of bright colours in the carpet, wallpaper, pictures etc. In a plain room, however, it can dramatically liven up the decor.

Muted Group

Foliage plants are the dominant feature. Ferny and solid-leaved types can be used to ensure that green is the dominant colour. A few pots of plants with pastel-coloured blooms can be included to brighten the display, but the effect must always be restrained. The Muted Group is a good choice where the display is to be in front of or close to brightly-patterned wallpaper or curtains — it also has a calming effect when placed near brightly-coloured or gaudy furnishing items.

One-colour Group

A blue or white border is a well-established garden feature in Britain and blanket bedding of just one annual is popular in some European countries. Despite this acceptance outdoors the One-colour Group is an uncommon sight indoors apart from, of course, a foliage-only collection. It is strange that one of the most popular of all house plant arrangements is the One-colour Indoor Garden — a bowl filled with yellow Daffodils or pink Hyacinths.

POT GROUP
PICTURE GALLERY

One of the most popular types of Pot Group — a cluster of containers on the hearth to hide a fireplace. The flowering Pot Plants add colour to a dull area. ▷

◁ A variety of plants and pots is not essential. This grouping of identical white Kalanchoes provides an eye-catching feature in this contemporary-style room.

△ An opposite approach to the white pots above — a mixture of pots and a riot of foliage colour make up this corner arrangement. Note the central focus plant.

An example of the way House Plants can transform a room. Two groups of Stand-alone Pots containing Strelitzias provide colour and a dramatic touch. ▷

A Pot Group which differs markedly from the arrangement above. The mixed collection forms a colourful mass, but in both cases the pots are hidden. ◁

△ A classical springtime Pot Group — Hyacinths, Daffodils and Cyclamen promise things to come in the garden outside the window. Here the containers are an important feature.

DESIGNER POT GROUPS

A small table-top group, but the two basic elements of the Designer Group are there — pots of different heights have been used and the colours of the pots enhance the display. ▷

◁ *This Designer-type display has a number of good features. The Chlorophytum at the base provides contrast to the Chamaedorea Palm, Maidenhair Fern and Weeping Fig — the pale pot at the front contrasts well with the brown and green surround. These provide touches of brightness to what could have been a dull display.*

A glass fish tank can be trans-
formed into an Orchidarium to
house an Orchid collection. A 2 in.
(5 cm) layer of hydroleca
(expanded clay pellets) is placed at
the base of the tank. The pots are
stood on this layer and water is
added to cover the bottom half of
the hydroleca layer. Do not cover.
The Orchidarium provides a moist
atmosphere for the plants and it
protects them from draughts. The
tank should be placed near a
window.

▷

This arrangement clearly
demonstrates the value of creating
Movement (see page 95) wherever
◁ you can. The floor-standing pot has
been brought next to the table
display so that the plants seem to
be flowing downwards.

THE INDOOR GARDEN

The Indoor Garden is a receptacle containing more than one plant. No pots are seen — they have been removed or are hidden from sight

Indoor gardening remains an uncommon concept because there is a strange reluctance to growing indoor plants in groups rather than as spaced-out pots. Colourful plants such as Begonia semperflorens or Coleus can be bedded out in the home as they are in the garden, but they are nearly always grown in isolated pots.

The Indoor Garden is a receptacle in which more than one plant is grown, and unlike the Pot Group individual pots are not visible. It may be a simple bowl with a few plants or a forest of greenery and flowers in a multi-tiered structure, but the basic principles are the same. The plants have been either taken out of their pots and planted into the receptacle or the pots have been retained and surrounded with packing material.

As with the Pot Group this feature brings plants together rather than leaving them dotted around the room. Both styles have a number of benefits. Imperfections can be hidden, air humidity around the leaves is raised, and watering becomes easier when the plants are together.

The Indoor Garden also has its own unique advantages. Here you are truly gardening — albeit in a very small way. You are putting plants together to create a feeling of 'oneness'. The insulation of the roots helps to protect the plants from the cold of an unheated room in winter and from the baking sun on a windowsill in summer. Finally, there is the water reserve in the packing material if the pots are retained.

Unfortunately, the Indoor Garden does have a few disadvantages compared to the Pot Group. It is easy to overwater as there is no drip tray to catch the drainage water when the plants are kept in their pots, and this danger is even greater when the plants are grown in compost in the bowl or planter. These plants cannot be turned to prevent lop-sided growth, and removal is not easy when a plant has to be replaced. Still, there is something special about creating an Indoor Garden and this style should certainly be more popular.

INDOOR GARDEN TYPES

Standard Planter

The Standard Planter is the basic Indoor Garden. There are six steps covering choice and assembly which you have to follow to ensure success — these steps are set out on page 124. Avoid buying too many plants — you must allow the larger ones to display their shape and leaves without being crushed or hidden by other plants. Leave the plants in their pots rather than planting in the packing layer so that they can be easily turned or replaced if necessary.

Take care when watering. The Planter does not have drainage holes and so waterlogging is a common problem. Keep the packing layer damp but not wet. You must fit a water gauge (see page 124) or buy a moisture meter — see page 152. You will find that the Planter requires less frequent watering than Stand-alone Plants.

Designer Planter

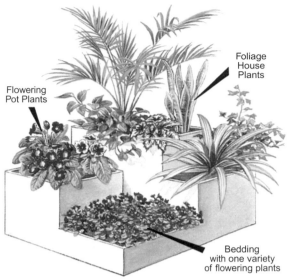

Foliage
House
Plants

Flowering
Pot Plants

Bedding
with one variety
of flowering plants

This type of Indoor Garden may be no larger than a Standard Planter and its planting may not be on a grander scale. The essential difference is that the Designer Planter is made up of two or more containers and the plants are on two or more levels.

Ready-made models are available or you could buy separate planters and stand them together. You can build your own if you are a DIY enthusiast. Each planting unit can be treated individually from both the planting and cultural standpoints — here you have the closest equivalent to outdoor gardening. The lowest unit is bedded-out with Pot Plants which are changed with the season — bulbs in spring, Poinsettias at Christmas, etc. The tall specimens at the rear form a permanent leafy backcloth.

SIX STEP GUIDE TO PLANTER SUCCESS

STEP 2 : PLANTS

Choose suitable plants The first consideration is to look for plants which have roughly the same requirements for light, heat and water — it is foolish to expect Succulents and Ferns to grow happily together. The usual plan is to have one or more pinnacle (tall) plants, a number of medium-sized ones, and then a few creeping and spreading ones to clothe part of the planter's edge. These foliage plants provide the framework — flowering types are added to provide extra colour.

STEP 4 : POTS

Stand the pots in the planter Place a thin layer of packing material (see Step 6) on top of the soakaway layer and place the pots in position. Clay pots are preferred and they must have drainage holes. The tall pots can be stood on the packing material layer but the smaller ones will need some form of support to bring them to a little below the rim of the planter. It may be necessary to stand a small pot on an upturned empty one.

STEP 5 : WATER GAUGE

Insert a water gauge Self-watering troughs with water-level indicators are available, but you can make your own water gauge. Insert a tube through the soakaway layer — the base of the tube should touch the bottom of the planter. Insert a stick in the tube and use it as a dipstick — the water level should be below the top of the soakaway.

STEP 1 : PLANTER

Choose a suitable planter Most shop-bought planters are plain oblong troughs made of white, black or green plastic. Workmanlike, but not a design feature. Wood and cane are better surfaces — a square or a wide circular shape offers more scope for an artistic arrangement. Any sufficiently tall container will do, but avoid patterned or highly coloured ones which can detract from or compete with the display.

STEP 3 : SOAKAWAY

Create a soakaway layer Place a 2-3 in. (5-8 cm) layer of gravel over the base of the planter.

STEP 6 : PACKING LAYER

Place the packing material around the pots The final step is to fill the space between the pots with damp potting compost. This packing layer must completely fill the space between the soakaway and the rim of the pots. Do not add the packing material around the stems of plants.

Planting Suggestions

Make sure that the height and shape of the plants are in keeping with the size of the planter — aim for contrast in leaf shape.

As a pinnacle plant in a small planter Sansevieria provides height without spread — Grevillea and Dizygotheca avoid the shading effect of large leaves. The choice of pinnacle plants for a large planter is easier — Palms, Dracaena, Ficus, Monstera and Philodendron are popular choices.

Coloured foliage plants are popular for the middle-size range — look for the red-leaved Cordyline, the yellow Scindapsus, Chlorophytum and Ivy. For multicoloured leaves there are Croton, Coleus and Begonia rex.

Finally, the trailers — the popular four are Ivy, Tradescantia, Ficus pumila and Zebrina.

Hanging Basket

Most cascading plants have to be seen at eye-level or above in order for their beauty to be fully appreciated. The pots can be stood on a pedestal or high shelf, but a Hanging Basket is the answer if you want to create a feature which will provide interest and colour to the upper part of a room. In front of a window where the view is not vital is a favourite site, so is a long bare wall where a bracketed support is used to hold the container. Two types are available. There is the standard water-proof container bearing holding chains or wires — a better variant is the plastic basket with a built-in drip tray.

Fixing to the ceiling or on the wall must be secure. Use plants growing in soilless compost and surround the pots with moist compost. Hanging Baskets must not be neglected — the air near the ceiling is warmer than elsewhere, and so more frequent watering may be necessary. The easiest way is to install a pulley fitting or you can use a pump-action watering can.

Don't restrict your choice to ordinary hanging plants like Ivy and Creeping Fig — do include flowering cascade types such as Fuchsia, Campanula and Lobelia.

Pot-et-Fleur

The Pot-et-Fleur is a square or round receptacle in which a small number of foliage house plants are grown in potting compost. The unique feature is that a deep glass or metal tube is pushed into the compost in front of the tallest plant and between mid-sized foliage plants. Subsequently the tube is filled with water and used for a small flower arrangement. In this way flowers from the garden, supermarket, florist etc can be used to provide an ever-changing and colourful display.

It is a mistake to regard the Pot-et-fleur as a hybrid of house plant culture and flower arranging — it is a house plant display with a few seasonal flowers to add a touch of brightness.

Built-in Garden

The Built-in Garden is the ultimate house plant feature — here we bring a garden bed indoors. It is a ground floor feature which contains soil or compost in the same way as the border in a greenhouse. In the house it belongs in a spacious hall, conservatory or garden room — in offices and public buildings it is usually constructed in the foyer. The most satisfactory type is made at the same time as the building.

The type in the photograph is, of course, out of the question once the house is built, but if the space is available and the environment is right you can construct a raised bed if the foundation below is sound. You will need a retaining wall of brick, reconstituted stone, wood or tile-covered blocks which will hold a 4 in. (10 cm) layer of gravel and a 1½ ft (45 cm) layer of compost — paint the inside with bituminous paint before filling.

Location is important. Good light is essential — glass overhead or a large window alongside is necessary. Use plants in pots to facilitate easy removal.

Bowl Garden

It may seem strange to think of a bowl of spring flowers on the windowsill as an Indoor Garden, but it does fit the definition on page 121 — 'a receptacle containing more than one plant. No pots are seen — they have been removed or are hidden from sight'.

The mixed bowl contains a variety of plants rather than a single species, and it is a longer-lasting feature than the bowl of spring bulbs. It is one of the most popular types of Indoor Garden — it is nearly always bought ready-made for standing on the sideboard or for giving as a present. The usual receptacle is a round bowl and there is a standard planting pattern. A tall plant, such as a variegated Ivy, is set at the back of the bowl. In front of it are planted a bushy or spreading plant and a flowering type. A trailer such as an Ivy or Ficus pumila may be added to soften the edge.

Watering is a major problem — the absence of drainage holes makes over-watering difficult to avoid. If you are starting from scratch it is better to use a receptacle with drainage holes and to add a layer of gravel before adding the compost. Stand the bowl on a drip tray.

The mixed bowl is often criticised because it is not a permanent display — the stage is quickly reached when it becomes over-crowded. However, it lasts longer than a flower arrangement and the plants can be removed and planted elsewhere.

Dish Garden

A small Indoor Garden can be created in a shallow dish using carefully-chosen Succulents and Cacti. The surface of the container should be plain but a varied and colourful collection of plants can make the Dish Garden a point of interest on a sideboard or shelf. A waterproof container can be used, but a dish with drainage holes will avoid the danger of overwatering. For construction details see page 142.

Living Screen

The eating area in a combined living/dining room can be separated in many ways. A wooden divider unit is sometimes used — a few pots in the open spaces will help to enliven such a unit. A living screen is preferred by many plant-lovers. A deep and reasonably wide trough is placed on the floor and a trellis or series of decorative poles secured in the compost so the support runs from floor to ceiling. Pots are then inserted in the compost — suitable plants are Cissus, Syngonium, Hedera, Ficus benjamina, Scindapsus, Philodendron scandens and Ficus pumila.

INDOOR GARDEN PICTURE GALLERY

Two black Planters make up this office feature. A range of tough foliage plants have been used — flowering Pot Plants have been excluded so as to ensure easy maintenance. ▷

A simple box Planter for the sitting room. The wide variety of shapes, colours and textures of the foliage rather than the container surface provides the interest. ◁

An arrangement incorporating a number of good design features — there are movement, balance, and marked contrasts in texture and shape.

⊲

The classic miniature Indoor Garden. A bowl with a pinnacle plant, a flowering specimen and a few delicate green fillers. A popular present, but not an ideal choice as a Roomscaping feature. One or more plants will need to be removed after a short time — so much easier if the plants are in pots or spaced out in a planter.

▷

THE GLASS GARDEN

The Glass Garden is a feature
in which the plants are partially or
fully enclosed within a glass container

Much of this Roomscaping section is devoted to the creation of areas of interest by the use of a plant or group of plants which catch the eye because of the beauty of their shape, their leaves and/or their flowers. The Glass Garden earns its place for a different reason — it has novelty value. With the Bottle Garden there is the question of how the plants got into the container, and with the Terrarium there is the chance to display delicate plants which cannot be grown under ordinary room conditions — the novelty of growing rarities.

All sorts of household items and custom-made containers can be used, as shown on the following pages. Choose glass — transparent plastic is not satisfactory. The list of suitable plants is limited — avoid quick-growing types in a small container and do not grow flowering plants in a Bottle Garden. Reject plants which need dry air conditions. In the Terrarium do take the opportunity to grow some of the tropical plants which need constantly moist air and a freedom from draughts.

In the middle of the 20th century the Bottle Garden using a second-hand carboy became a popular feature, but it is not often seen nowadays. Little watering is required, but it is a poor way of growing house plants — the Terrarium is a much better choice. Removal of dead plants is straightforward and so is replanting. Be very careful not to overwater — the period between waterings is measured in weeks and not days.

Terrarium

The key feature of this type of Glass Garden is that the plants can be reached for pruning, removal etc — this is not possible with a Bottle Garden. Many types are available, but perhaps the most satisfactory is the Fishtank Garden. Place a layer of gravel and charcoal at the bottom of the container and then add a 3 in. (8 cm) layer of compost. You can landscape it into hills and valleys.

It would be a pity to waste such a good home on commonplace plants — delicate Ferns, Croton, Fittonia, Cryptanthus, Calathea, Selaginella and Rhoeo would all flourish. You could add flowering plants between the foliage ones to provide splashes of colour — African Violets and small Orchids are ideal. Two warnings — never use Cacti or Succulents and always leave room between the plants so that they can spread.

After planting cover the top with a bevel-edged sheet of glass. Stand it in a well-lit spot away from direct sunlight. Water with care — an enclosed Glass Garden can usually be left without watering for 3-6 months. There is little else to do — remove dead or diseased leaves as they appear.

Bottle Garden

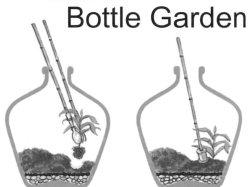

All sorts of glass bottles can be used — the carboy is the most spectacular. Insert a stiff paper cone in the mouth of the bottle and pour in a 2 in. (5 cm) layer of gravel. Add a thin layer of charcoal and finally a thick layer of seed & cutting compost. Firm with a tamper (a cotton reel at the end of a bamboo cane).

Now introduce the plants. First of all, the tall pinnacle plants — popular choices include Sansevieria, Grevillea and Dizygotheca. Fill-in plants include Cordyline terminalis, Chlorophytum, Ivy, Croton and Begonia rex. You will need about six specimens, including one pinnacle plant, and at least one trailer. The planting tools are a dessert spoon tied to the end of one cane, and a fork at the end of another. Firm the compost around each plant with the tamper.

Use a long-necked watering can to train a gentle stream of water against the glass to clean it and to moisten the surface. Insert the stopper. A further light watering will not be required for many months. Place in a spot where there is reasonably bright light but no direct sunlight.

GLASS GARDEN PICTURE GALLERY

All sorts of bottle shapes and sizes have been used to create Glass Gardens. Remember that difficulty increases as the size of opening decreases. ▷

A collection of ferns planted in a Victorian fern case. The Fern Craze was at its height in the 1860s — one catalogue listed 818 species. ◁

△ Misting can be a problem. Slide back the lid, open the door or remove the stopper until the glass clears.

△ Carnivorous plants are an excellent choice, especially if companion planting is used to create a tropical feel.

THE WATER GARDEN

The Water Garden is a feature in which the plants are grown close to or within a water container

In recent years a variety of simple table-top fountains and waterfalls have appeared — the tinkling sound of moving water is there, but plants are not.

There must be a good reason for our failure to put plants and water together indoors. It cannot be a lack of interest in water gardening — the small plant-filled pond is one of the fastest-growing features in outdoor gardening. Nor can it be the price — the cost of one of these indoor waterfalls is less than a meal for two. Finally, it cannot be a shortage of advantages — unlike its outdoor counterpart this feature helps nearby plants by increasing humidity and it provides a novelty item to impress your friends.

The basic reason would seem to be that unlike garden ponds it has been denied the magic of TV exposure and there has been virtually nothing in the magazines. Interest in indoor water gardening is increasing in the U.S — the problem in Britain is that so many of our experts believe that growing water plants indoors is not practical. Here is your chance to prove they are wrong.

The photographs on this page illustrate the range of Water Gardens. The feature can be as small as a simple bowl with a single water plant or it may be as large as the colourful conservatory jungle complete with waterfall shown on the right. Many sizes but just two groups — the In-water Display and the Around-water Display.

WATER GARDEN TYPES

Around-water Display

Ordinary house plants and not aquatic ones are used here — they are grown in pots or containers around a water feature. It is possible to incorporate a water feature within an Indoor Garden (page 121-130) — these displays are becoming increasingly popular in the U.S. However, ready-made water/indoor plant units are not available, and a simpler approach is to create a Pot Group Water Garden. The starting point is a shop-bought water feature which will have some form of moving water — a small fountain, a round bubble jet, a rock waterfall or a series of water-filled jars is the usual choice. Place it on a firm surface and have a light source which highlights the moving water.

Now place the plants in their pots around the water feature. Many of the points raised in the Pot Group section (page 111-120) apply, but there are special rules for arrangement. The tallest plants should be at the back of the display — the mid-sized ones should be at the sides to enclose the water area. A weeping plant which does not interfere with the fountain or waterfall is an effective addition. Low-growing plants and trailers may be used at the front to hide the edge of the water container.

In-water Display

In this display one or more aquatic plants are grown in the water — ordinary house plants may or may not be kept nearby. Quite simply, this is a matter of bringing the garden pond indoors. The pleasure of having Water Lilies growing indoors is of course the main attraction of having an In-water Display. Most experts feel that growing aquatics in the home is not practical. It was not always so — water gardens in the parlour were features in many Victorian houses, and for some the plants rather than the fish were the main attraction.

The critics are right to raise the drawbacks. Good light is absolutely essential. A glass-roofed conservatory is ideal but a raised area near a south-facing window should be satisfactory. Pond balance which keeps the water naturally clear outdoors does not occur indoors — the water area is too small and the temperature of the water is higher than in the garden. Finally, two outdoor features should be omitted from the In-water Display of plants if you want to grow Water Lilies — fish and water-moving features such as fountains and waterfalls have no place here.

Despite these drawbacks it is worth trying this novel approach to growing plants indoors. If Water Lilies do not succeed there are other attractive aquatics to try.

The first job is to choose the most suitable type and size. There is an enormous range from small glass bowls to large sunken pools, but the two which can be most strongly recommended are the half-barrel Minipond for the sunny living room and the Conservatory Pond for the glazed plant room.

Minipond

Any container which will hold at least 5½ gallons (25 litres) of water can be used as long as it is decorative, waterproof, non-corrosive and non-toxic. It should also be deep enough to allow the water level to be at least 6 in. (15 cm) above the top of the plant baskets. The most attractive choice is a half-barrel. You can start work between May and September. Varnish the outside and treat the inside with a sealant such as bitumen paint. Place the container in the brightest spot available.

Add tap water and then wait for at least three days before you begin planting. You will need a dwarf Water Lily plus some floaters and oxygenators to help to suppress algal growth. It is essential to have a good cover of leaves — some floaters can be removed when the Water Lily pads start to spread. There may be room for a marginal plant — see page 139 for advice on plants and planting.

Conservatory Pond

A Conservatory Pond can be a simple structure for Water Lilies as shown below or a colourful showpiece with waterfall, lighting, a range of aquatics inside and a collection of house plants outside — see page 140. The basic requirements are a sound base, a fully waterproof inner surface and a water level which is deep enough for the chosen plants. The inclusion of fish is not a good idea, nor is a fountain or waterfall if you plan to grow Water Lilies.

There are three methods of construction. The simplest plan is to buy a rigid liner and cover the sides with wooden panels or wood roll. A brick, block or reconstituted stone pond looks more substantial — brick and block walls can be tiled to improve their appearance. You may wish to install a filtration system at this stage in order to keep the water clear.

Fill with tap water and leave for three days before planting — the minimum depth required will depend on the plants which are to be grown. Your aim should be to keep about two-thirds of the surface covered with Water Lilies and/or floaters so as to suppress the development of green algae. Cleaning out the pond by siphoning out the water may be necessary every five years. Keep plants in buckets of water while this work is being undertaken.

Two words of warning. Employ an electrician if you plan to install a fountain or waterfall. Secondly, remember that an active toddler can drown in 4 in. (10 cm) of water.

Rigid liner
on sand base

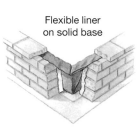

Flexible liner
on solid base

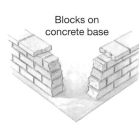

Blocks on
concrete base

RIGID LINER Use a glass fibre pond — choose a simple shape (square, rectangle, semi-circle etc) if a surrounding wall is to be built. A thinner polyethylene pre-formed pond may require a wooden frame for support. Colour is a matter of personal preference, but black is the usual choice.

FLEXIBLE LINER Use butyl sheeting — choose a simple shape. A stout wall is required — it will have to take the strain from the weight of water. Make sure that the mortar is set before filling with water. After filling, the edges and corners should be folded and then held down by some form of coping.

NO LINER It is possible to dispense with a liner if the brick or block wall is properly laid on a concrete base. The inside can be rendered with cement to improve the appearance — this is optional but painting the inside with two coats of pond paint is essential. Follow the instructions on the tin.

Planting your Pond

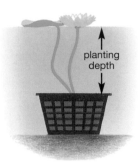

planting depth

Your pond will need several types of aquatic plants. Water Lilies are desirable but not essential in the Conservatory Pond — the requirements are strong light and still water. The main floral effect comes from the marginal plants which usually require to be set at a shallower depth than the dwarf Water Lilies. With both of these types it is necessary to house the roots and compost in open-sided baskets. Next, you will need oxygenators — these are bought in bunches from the aquatics department at your garden centre. Plant the bunch in a basket of heavy soil covered with gravel — put one basket per 10 sq. ft (1 sq. m) on the bottom of the pool. Finally there are the floaters which work with Water Lilies to cover the water surface — the roots are submerged but the stems, leaves and flowers (if any) are on or above the surface. Just drop them in the water and remove some as necessary if overcrowding takes place.

Latin Name	Common Name	Planting Depth	Description
WATER LILIES			
NYMPHAEA PYGMAEA ALBA	WHITE DWARF WATER LILY	4 – 8 in.	1 in. wide white starry flowers. Borne freely above purple-backed leaves
NYMPHAEA PYGMAEA HELVOLA	YELLOW DWARF WATER LILY	4 – 8 in.	2 in. wide pale yellow starry flowers. Leaf cover 1½ ft x 1½ ft
OXYGENATORS			
CALLITRICHE VERNA	WATER STARWORT	See above	Star-shaped leafy rosette on surface. Good in small ponds. Can be temperamental
ELODEA CANADENSIS	CANADIAN PONDWEED	See above	Narrow leaves on long stems. Very efficient but it can be invasive
FLOATERS			
AZOLLA CAROLINIANA	FAIRY MOSS	See above	Dense mats of tiny leaves spread rapidly. Whole surface may be covered
EICHHORNIA CRASSIPES	WATER HYACINTH	See above	Shiny leaves and swollen stems. Orchid-like flowers in well-lit ponds
HYDROCHARIS MORSUS-RANAE	FROG-BIT	See above	Kidney-shaped leaves and small white flowers. Growth is restrained
PISTIA STRATIOTES	WATER LETTUCE	See above	Felted leaves form floating rosettes. Flowers insignificant. Can be difficult
STRATIOTES ALOIDES	WATER SOLDIER	See above	Rosettes of small sword-like leaves come to the surface at flowering time
MARGINALS			
ACORUS GRAMINEUS	JAPANESE RUSH	4 – 6 in.	The variety Variegatus has green and yellow striped leaves. Height 8 in.
CALTHA PALUSTRIS	MARSH MARIGOLD	0 – 2 in.	Buttercup-like flowers appear above heart-shaped leaves in spring. Height 1 ft
CYPERUS VEGETUS	UMBRELLA GRASS	0 – 4 in.	Lance-shaped leaves radiate from the top of the stems. Height 1½ ft
HOUTTUYNIA CORDATA	HOUTTUYNIA	2 – 4 in.	Mats of heart-shaped leaves. Variegata has colourful foliage. Height 8 in.
IRIS LAEVIGATA	WATER IRIS	0 – 3 in.	Large flowers – various colours are available. Very popular. Height 2 ft
MENTHA AQUATICA	WATER MINT	0 – 3 in.	Creeping plant used to cover pool edge. Balls of tiny mauve flowers. Height 1 ft
MIMULUS LUTEUS	MONKEY FLOWER	0 – 2 in.	Snapdragon-like red-blotched yellow flowers in summer. Height 8 in.
PELTANDRA VIRGINICA	ARROW ARUM	2 – 6 in.	Deeply ribbed arrow-shaped leaves with arum-like flowers in summer
PONTEDERIA CORDATA	PICKEREL WEED	4 – 6 in.	Heart-shaped leaves with spikes of blue flowers in late summer. Height 2 ft
ZANTEDESCHIA AETHIOPICA	ARUM LILY	2 – 4 in.	Spectacular white trumpets in summer above arrow-shaped leaves. Height 2½ ft

WATER GARDEN PICTURE GALLERY

An excellent indoor water feature — the selection of stone and plants gives this display a natural feel. Unfortunately, it requires a lot of space (and money) to create. ▷

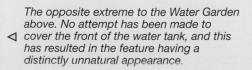

◁ The opposite extreme to the Water Garden above. No attempt has been made to cover the front of the water tank, and this has resulted in the feature having a distinctly unnatural appearance.

DO-IT-YOURSELF DISPLAYS

There are occasions when the roomscaper needs a tall plant to serve as an impressive Stand-alone Plant or as a pinnacle specimen in a Pot Group. Unfortunately tall plants are expensive, but there are ways of transforming small plants into impressive 'trees'. In addition Bromeliads and Staghorn Ferns can be used to produce novel and eye-catching displays, and lowly Succulents can be grouped together to form a Dish Garden (page 142).

HOW TO GROW A TI TREE

Ti Trees are grown by planting pieces of mature cane cut from Dracaena, Cordyline or Yucca. The crown of leaves which appears at the top of the cane gives an 'instant palm' effect. Nursery-raised Ti Trees can be obtained but you can also grow your own — Ti Canes (cut from outdoor tropical plants and dried before shipment) are becoming increasingly available.

Crown of leaves appears at the side of the cane once rooting has taken place

Dry cane planted firmly in Seed & Cutting Compost. Keep compost moist but not wet

An old Dracaena, after its top has been removed and used as a cutting, will grow as a Ti Tree.

HOW TO MAKE A MOSS STICK

A moss stick (U.S name — totem pole) is a valuable aid for growing Vines, Monstera, Philodendron and Ivies. It serves a double purpose for plants with aerial roots such as Monstera — it provides support for the weak stem and it provides moisture through the aerial roots to the upper leaves.

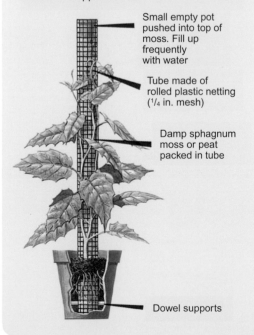

Small empty pot pushed into top of moss. Fill up frequently with water

Tube made of rolled plastic netting (¹/₄ in. mesh)

Damp sphagnum moss or peat packed in tube

Dowel supports

HOW TO MAKE AN IVY TREE

Cut the side shoots from a specimen of Fatshedera lizei and stake the stem. When it has reached 3 ft (1 m) high remove the top growth with a horizontal cut. Make crossed cuts on stem top as shown below.

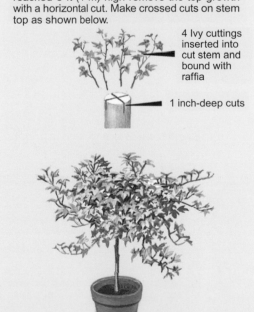

4 Ivy cuttings inserted into cut stem and bound with raffia

1 inch-deep cuts

HOW TO MAKE A BROMELIAD TREE

Leafy Bromeliad — Choose plants with a well pronounced 'cup' in the heart of the rosette. Remove from pot, wrap roots with sphagnum moss and then tightly attach with plastic-covered wire to branch

Tillandsia usneoides (Spanish Moss) — a unique Bromeliad which grows as grey-green strands in moist air. No watering required

Keep cup filled with water and spray sphagnum moss with water at weekly intervals

Branch set in Plaster of Paris and stones

Pebbles

Leafy Bromeliad

Sphagnum moss

Container

HOW TO MAKE A DISH GARDEN

Succulents are ideal plants for a dish garden. Choose carefully and aim for an attractive landscape. Once made it will require very little attention and should last for a number of years on a windowsill.

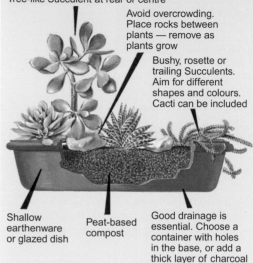

Tree-like Succulent at rear or centre

Avoid overcrowding. Place rocks between plants — remove as plants grow

Bushy, rosette or trailing Succulents. Aim for different shapes and colours. Cacti can be included

Shallow earthenware or glazed dish

Peat-based compost

Good drainage is essential. Choose a container with holes in the base, or add a thick layer of charcoal

HOW TO MAKE A FLOWERING STANDARD

Choose an upright Fuchsia variety. Use a rooted cutting and keep the plant well-lit in winter

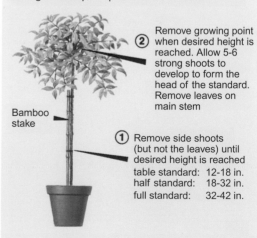

Bamboo stake

② Remove growing point when desired height is reached. Allow 5-6 strong shoots to develop to form the head of the standard. Remove leaves on main stem

① Remove side shoots (but not the leaves) until desired height is reached
table standard: 12-18 in.
half standard: 18-32 in.
full standard: 32-42 in.

HOW TO MAKE A FERN PLAQUE

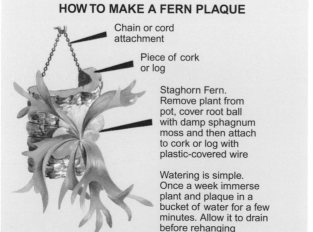

Chain or cord attachment

Piece of cork or log

Staghorn Fern. Remove plant from pot, cover root ball with damp sphagnum moss and then attach to cork or log with plastic-covered wire

Watering is simple. Once a week immerse plant and plaque in a bucket of water for a few minutes. Allow it to drain before rehanging

STEP 4 : Select a suitable RECEPTACLE

The first section of this book is devoted to hundreds of different indoor plants, and they have one feature in common. Hardly any of them can be grown if they are not planted in a suitable growing medium housed in some form of receptacle.

The words 'receptacle', 'pot' and 'container' are often used interchangeably and this can lead to confusion. The best plan is to use the word receptacle as an all-embracing term to cover the three types of housing used for one or more plants — the pot, pot holder and container. There is no 'best' type of receptacle — the one to use depends on the style you have chosen and also personal preference.

Pot

A pot is a receptacle with a hole or holes at the base. It is used for potting one or more plants. A pot holder or drip tray is necessary to catch drainage water.

The basic pot is made of clay or plastic, and each type can support perfectly good plants. The terracotta or plain plastic pot used by the supplier is usually retained, but the roomscaper who feels that the pot should add to the decor of the room must look elsewhere. Their choice is between a decorative pot into which the specimen they have bought is transplanted or a pot holder into which the pot is placed.

Clay and plastic have disadvantages and advantages as shown below, and alternative types are available. Glazed ceramic and glass pots are available, but are not popular. Semi-transparent pots are sometimes used to house Orchids, and foam plastic pots offer the virtue of insulation against summer heat and winter cold.

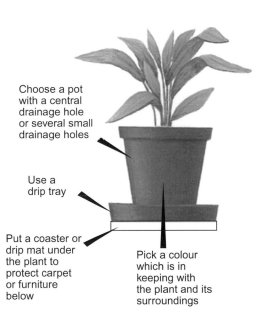

Choose a pot with a central drainage hole or several small drainage holes

Use a drip tray

Put a coaster or drip mat under the plant to protect carpet or furniture below

Pick a colour which is in keeping with the plant and its surroundings

Clay or Plastic?

Advantages:
- Heavy — much less liable to topple over.
- Waterlogging is less likely because of porous nature.
- Traditional 'natural' appearance — no chance of colour clashes.
- Damaging salts are leached away from the compost.

Advantages:
- Lightweight — much less liable to break if dropped.
- Watering is needed less often.
- Decorative and colourful forms available.
- No crocking needed — easy to clean.

Pot Holder

A pot holder or cachepot is a receptacle with a waterproof inner base and no drainage holes. It is used for holding and hiding a single pot.

The overall effect of most Stand-alone Plants is improved by being placed in a pot holder. Shop-bought ones come in a wide range of sizes, materials and prices. The ideal size is 2 in. (5 cm) wider than the diameter of the top of the pot and the height should be about 1 in. (3 cm) higher than the top of the pot when it is in place. The pot holder should be in keeping with the style of the room. Stainless steel cylinders are splendid in ultra-modern surroundings — plant-filled china pots can be charming in period rooms.

Place a layer of gravel at the base before the pot is placed inside. The space between the pot and pot holder can be filled with bark chippings etc, but that would pose a problem. The pot cannot be moved to a sink for watering, and excess water cannot be poured away.

The pot holder must be large enough to provide stability

The purpose of the pot holder is to provide a suitable base for the beauty of the plant. It should not compete with it

Container

Potting compost

Narrow layer of small lumps of charcoal

Layer of small pebbles filling the bottom ¼ of the container

A container is a waterproof receptacle with no holes at the base. It is used for potting one or more plants or for holding several pots.

The choice of a suitable pot holder is restricted because of the need to house standard-sized pots, but a container has no such limitations. The usual practice is to take the plants out of their pots and plant them directly into the compost-filled container.

Because of this all sorts of items are used as containers. At the garden centre you will find a wide range of planters, but many household receptacles can be used, such as brass coal scuttles and lined wicker baskets. The shape and colour can enhance or detract from the beauty of the plant — see the illustration above.

Container growing poses one problem. Excess water cannot escape and this means that waterlogging will occur unless you water with care. The only satisfactory solution is to use a moisture meter (page 152) or fit a dipstick (page 124).

Choose the right size

One of the few points on which professional designers agree is that the height of the pot or pot holder and the height of the plant should not be the same. It is a rule we all break sometimes, but extremes should be avoided — the pot must be large enough to make the display look stable, but small enough not to overwhelm the plant. Having a pot which is between a third and a fifth of the height of an Architectural Plant and between a half and a sixth of the width of a spreading plant are sometimes quoted as designer ideals.

STEP 5 : Buy the right PLANTS

Buying an inexpensive Pot Plant just because it looks colourful, and taking it home to brighten up the windowsill or piece of furniture is done by all of us from time to time. If on the other hand you are looking for a House Plant to be a permanent feature in a display, it is wise to find out something about it before making your purchase. Will it thrive in the location you have in mind? Will it grow to be too big? Do you have the time to meet its needs? In the A-Z guide there are plants with needs ranging from almost nothing to almost daily care. In the following pages you will find lists of plants which may help you in your quest for the right specimen to buy.

House Plants can be bought at any time of the year, but you should take care in winter. Plants stood outside the shop or on a market stall may have been damaged by the cold unless they are hardy varieties — avoid buying delicate plants which are stood in the open as 'bargain' offers.

Now you are ready to buy. If you are picking bulbs, make sure that they are firm and without holes or shoots. When buying indoor plants look for any danger signs — a mass of roots growing out of the drainage holes, a space between the compost and the inside of the pot, floppy leaves etc.

The plant should be wrapped or be in a plastic sleeve to protect it in winter. The danger of cold air on the trip home is obvious — less obvious is the damage that can be caused in the boot of the car in mid-summer. Put the plant in a box on the back seat if you can.

Try to give your new plant a period of acclimatisation. Keep it out of direct sunlight and draughts for a few weeks, and be careful not to overwater. It is normal for a new plant to lose a leaf or two during this period, and do not keep moving it from one place to another as you seek to find a 'proper' home. Just leave it alone in a moderately warm spot away from the sun.

The situation is different with flowering Pot Plants, such as Azalea, Chrysanthemum and Cyclamen, which are purchased in flower in winter. Put them in their permanent quarters immediately and provide as much light as possible.

SHAPES AND SIZES

There are six basic plant shapes and nearly all indoor plants fit into one or other of the groups listed on these two pages. But there are borderline cases, and a few plants change with age from one shape to another. Size is another important consideration when buying a plant. A low-growing variety can look lost against a large bare wall, and a tall tree-like plant will look unsafe on a narrow windowsill. Remember that you may be buying a young plant which may become a child-sized specimen in a few years — check in the A-Z guide if in doubt.

UPRIGHT PLANTS

UPRIGHT PLANTS bear stems with a distinctly vertical growth habit. They vary in height from an inch to the tallest house plants available. Medium-sized upright plants are an essential compo-nent of the Pot Group, providing a feeling of height to offset the horizontal effect created by rosette plants, trailing plants and low bushes. Tall, upright types are often displayed as Stand-alone Plants.

Column Plants have thick vertical stems which are either leaf-less or bear leaves which do not detract from the column effect. Many Cacti and some Succulents have this growth habit.
Examples: Cereus peruvianus
Cleistocactus straussii
Notocactus leninghausii

Trees are an important group, providing Specimen Plants for large displays and the centre-piece in many collections. All trees have the same basic form — a central branched or unbranched stem bearing leaves with small leaf bases. Some are quite small, such as miniature Succulent 'trees' — others are capable of growing to reach the ceiling.
Examples: Aphelandra
Citrus
Codiaeum
Ficus benjamina
Ficus elastica decora
Schefflera

False Palms have stems which are completely clothed by the elongated stem bases when the plant is young. In a mature plant usually only the upper part of the stem is covered by leaves and the characteristically Palm-like effect is created.
Examples: Dieffenbachia
Dracaena
Pandanus
Yucca

BUSHY PLANTS

BUSHY PLANTS are a vast collection of varieties which do not fit into the other groups. The standard pattern is an arrangement of several stems arising out of the compost, with a growth habit which is neither markedly vertical nor horizontal. They may be small and compact like Peperomia or tall and shrubby like Aucuba. Some plants are naturally bushy, others must be pinched out regularly to induce bushiness. The Secrets of Success will tell you if pinching out is necessary.
Examples: Achimenes
Begonia rex
Coleus
Maranta
Peperomia
Pilea

GRASSY PLANTS

GRASSY PLANTS have long narrow leaves and a grass-like growth habit. Very few true grasses are offered as house plants, but there are several grass-like plants with long and extremely narrow leaves. You can, of course, buy a grassy plant from the outdoor plant section at your garden centre — examples which are used include Acorus, Arundinaria, Carex and Ophiopogon.

Broad-leaved Grassy Plants are much more popular — Chlorophytum comosum is widely grown. Several flowering plants have grassy leaves — examples are Billbergia nutans, Vallota, Tillandsia lindenii and Narcissus.

BALL PLANTS

BALL PLANTS are leafless and have a distinctly globular shape. They are nearly all Cacti, and the stem surface may be smooth or covered with hair and spines.
Examples: Echinocactus
Euphorbia obesa
Mammillaria
Notocactus
Rebutia miniscula

ROSETTE PLANTS

ROSETTE PLANTS bear leaves which form a circular cluster around the central growing point. Most rosette plants are low-growing and combine well with bushy and upright plants in Pot Groups and in Indoor Gardens.

Flat Rosette Plants

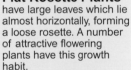

have large leaves which lie almost horizontally, forming a loose rosette. A number of attractive flowering plants have this growth habit.
Examples: Gloxinia
Primula
Saintpaulia

Succulent Rosette Plants

have fleshy leaves borne in several layers and often tightly packed together. This arrangement helps to conserve moisture in the natural habitat.
Examples: Aloe humilis
Aeonium tabulaeforme
Echeveria setosa
Sempervivum tectorum

Funnel Rosette Plants

are common among the Bromeliads. The basal area of the strap-like leaves forms a 'vase' which holds rain-water in the natural tropical habitat.
Examples: Aechmea
Guzmania
Nidularium
Vriesea

CLIMBING & TRAILING PLANTS

CLIMBING & TRAILING PLANTS bear stems which, when mature, are either provided with support to grow upwards or are left to hang downwards on the outside of the container. Many (but not all) varieties can be used in both ways. As climbers they are trained on canes, strings, trellis-work, wire hoops or vertical poles; they can be grown in wall-mounted pots to frame windows or they can be trained up supports to serve as room dividers. As trailers they can be used to spread horizontally or left to trail over the sides of pots.

Climbers are always grown as upright plants. Twining varieties are allowed to twist around the supports provided. Clinging varieties bearing tendrils must be attached to the supports at frequent intervals; if left to grow unattended the stems will soon become tangled together. Varieties bearing aerial roots are best grown on a moss stick (see page 141).

Examples: Passiflora
Philodendron hastatum
Stephanotis

Climbers/Trailers are extremely useful House Plants and many popular varieties belong to this group. When growing them as climbers it is usually advisable not to tie all the stems to a single cane — it is more attractive to spread out the stems on a trellis or on several canes inserted in the pot. When growing them as trailers it is sometimes necessary to pinch out the growing tips.

Examples: Hedera
Philodendron scandens
Scindapsus

Trailers are always grown as pendant plants, with stems hanging downwards, or as creeping plants, with stems growing along the soil surface. Many trailers have striking foliage or attractive flowers and are best grown in hanging baskets or stood on high pedestals.

Examples: Begonia pendula
Campanula isophylla
Columnea
Fittonia
Nertera
Sedum morganianum
Zygocactus

PLANTS FOR THE WINDOWSILL

There is no such thing as a windowsill plant — the correct choice depends on the orientation. A variety which can flourish in a south-facing window will suffer from light shortage in a north-facing location. Ivy will do well in a sunless north window but would do badly in the glare of a south-facing window.

Plants for the south-facing window

ANIGOZANTHOS
BEDDING PLANTS
BOUGAINVILLEA
CACTI
CELOSIA
CEROPEGIA
CHLOROPHYTUM
CITRUS
COLEUS
GERANIUM
GERBERA
GYNURA

HIBISCUS
HIPPEASTRUM
IMPATIENS
IRESINE
JASMINUM
KALANCHOE
NERIUM
PASSIFLORA
ROSA
SANSEVIERIA
SUCCULENTS
ZEBRINA

Mammillaria hahniana

Gerbera jamesonii

Plants for the east- and west-facing window

AECHMEA
AGLAONEMA
ANTHURIUM
APHELANDRA
BEGONIA
BELOPERONE
CALADIUM
CALATHEA
CAPSICUM
CHLOROPHYTUM
CHRYSANTHEMUM
CORDYLINE

CROTON
CUPHEA
GARDENIA
GLOXINIA
GYNURA
HOYA
IMPATIENS
POINSETTIA
SAINTPAULIA
SANSEVIERIA
SPATHIPHYLLUM
TRADESCANTIA

Chrysanthemum morifolium

Caladium hortulanum

Plants for the north-facing window

AGLAONEMA
ANTHURIUM
AZALEA
BEGONIA REX
BROMELIADS
CHLOROPHYTUM
CYCLAMEN
DIEFFENBACHIA
DRACAENA
FUCHSIA

GARDEN BULBS
HEDERA
MARANTA
PHILODENDRON
PILEA
SANSEVIERIA
SCHLUMBERGERA
SCINDAPSUS
SPATHIPHYLLUM
VINES

Pilea cadierei

Tulipa greigii

PLANTS FOR DARK CORNERS

It is a temptation to try to brighten up a dark corner with House Plants, but there is a question to ask before you start — is there enough light to support the plant? It should be possible to read a newspaper in the darkest part in late morning or early afternoon and the plants should cast at least a vague shadow on a bright day.

The test above will reveal whether there is enough light, but you will have to be careful when deciding what to grow. The choice will be limited if the corner is truly shady. In the list below you will find no flowering plants but there are a number of easily-available and attractive foliage ones.

It will help if the surface of the corner is papered or painted in white or a pale colour — a mirrored surface is even more helpful. The list of suitable plants will unfortunately not be enlarged — if you want to have flowers and/or a wider range of foliage plants, it will be necessary to take a different approach. You can use bright-light types for a few weeks and then move them to a bright location to recuperate for a week or two. An alternative route is to buy pots of brightly-coloured flowering types and treat them as a temporary display in the same way as you would treat a vase of cut flowers.

AGLAONEMA	PELLAEA
ASPIDISTRA	PHILODENDRON SCANDENS
ASPLENIUM	SANSEVIERIA
FICUS PUMILA	SCINDAPSUS
HEDERA	SYNGONIUM

CAST-IRON PLANTS

There is a group of plants which will tolerate an amazing range of conditions — dreary and cold corners, bright and stuffy rooms, periods of neglect and so on. Grow some of these plants if you are convinced that everything you touch will die. These plants won't, providing you don't keep the compost saturated and you don't bake them on an unshaded south-facing windowsill in summer. Watering should really be based on the particular needs of each plant, but as a general rule you can water once a week during the growing season and once every two weeks in winter.

ASPARAGUS	FATSIA
ASPIDISTRA	HELXINE
BILLBERGIA	NEANTHE
CHLOROPHYTUM	SANSEVIERIA
CISSUS	SUCCULENTS
FATSHEDERA	TRADESCANTIA

Chapter 5

INDOOR PLANT CARE

Indoor plants must depend on you for their basic needs. Leave them in deep shade or without water and they will die. They will slowly deteriorate without food and virtually all varieties must be kept frost-free.

Warmth, light, water, and nutrients — a list of essentials for all. There is a secondary list of requirements which some, but not all, plants require — increased air humidity, fresh air, freedom from draughts etc. Finally there are techniques which are not life-saving exercises — simple procedures such as trimming, training and cleaning to make the plants look better.

These may seem like long lists, but success with indoor plants calls for neither hard work nor great skill. There are a few basic rules. Do not try to treat all plants the same way — look at the Secrets of Success in the A-Z section. Remember excesses of water, food etc can be fatal, and remember that there is a resting period, usually in winter, when much less water, food and heat are required. Pick off withered leaves and dead flowers, and keep watch for pests and diseases. And spare a thought for the poor outdoor gardener who has to work in the wind and rain, with holes to dig, weeds to hoe and lawns to mow!

Spend a few minutes every few days looking carefully at the leaves, stems and compost. You will soon learn to tell when things are wrong. The appearance and feel of the compost will tell you when water is required. The appearance of the foliage will tell you when the water, temperature, light, food or humidity level is wrong. Some people grow indoor plants for years without ever really looking at them or bothering to learn what the leaves have to tell.

WARMTH

Most indoor plants came to us from the warm regions of the world, and they are raised commercially in glasshouses. This has led to the mistaken belief by many people that higher than normal room temperatures are necessary to ensure success.

In fact few plants will flourish at temperatures which are regularly above 75°F (24°C) in ordinary room conditions. The reason for this is that the amount of light on the leaves and the moisture in the air are much higher in their native home than in your living room, and so their need for high temperatures is correspondingly less.

Nearly all will thrive in the 55°-75°F (13°-24°C) range — some grow quite happily in rooms which are a little too cool for human comfort. There are exceptions to this general rule — many flowering Pot Plants need a maximum temperature of 60°F (16°C) in winter, and some tender varieties require a minimum of 60°F (16°C).

Most plants can tolerate temperatures slightly above or below their preferred range for short periods. The real enemy is excessive temperature fluctuations. For most plants a drop of 5°-10°F (3°-6°C) at night is beneficial, but a sudden cooling down by 20°F (11°C) can be damaging or fatal. It may be necessary to move pots off windowsills in frosty weather. Cacti and Succulents are the exception — wide fluctuations are not a problem because in their desert home they have adapted to hot days and cold nights.

Temperature Guide

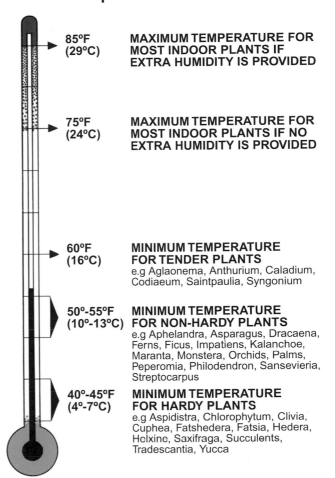

85°F (29°C) — MAXIMUM TEMPERATURE FOR MOST INDOOR PLANTS IF EXTRA HUMIDITY IS PROVIDED

75°F (24°C) — MAXIMUM TEMPERATURE FOR MOST INDOOR PLANTS IF NO EXTRA HUMIDITY IS PROVIDED

60°F (16°C) — MINIMUM TEMPERATURE FOR TENDER PLANTS
e.g Aglaonema, Anthurium, Caladium, Codiaeum, Saintpaulia, Syngonium

50°-55°F (10°-13°C) — MINIMUM TEMPERATURE FOR NON-HARDY PLANTS
e.g Aphelandra, Asparagus, Dracaena, Ferns, Ficus, Impatiens, Kalanchoe, Maranta, Monstera, Orchids, Palms, Peperomia, Philodendron, Sansevieria, Streptocarpus

40°-45°F (4°-7°C) — MINIMUM TEMPERATURE FOR HARDY PLANTS
e.g Aspidistra, Chlorophytum, Clivia, Cuphea, Fatshedera, Fatsia, Hedera, Helxine, Saxifraga, Succulents, Tradescantia, Yucca

Must-have Equipment

On this page and in the A-Z guide you will find the minimum and maximum room temperatures for a wide variety of indoor plants. A standard thermometer is a useful aid, but it will not tell you the lowest night temperature when you are asleep in winter, nor does it record the highest temperature reached when you are away from home in summer.

The answer is to buy a **MAXIMUM-MINIMUM THERMOMETER**. Once the double-bulb model was the only type available, but the digital type is simpler to use.

Danger Signs: Faulty temperature

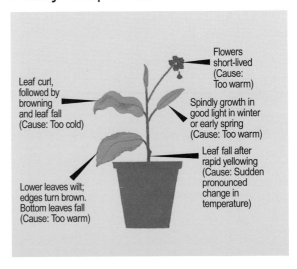

Flowers short-lived (Cause: Too warm)

Leaf curl, followed by browning and leaf fall (Cause: Too cold)

Spindly growth in good light in winter or early spring (Cause: Too warm)

Leaf fall after rapid yellowing (Cause: Sudden pronounced change in temperature)

Lower leaves wilt; edges turn brown. Bottom leaves fall (Cause: Too warm)

WATER

How often will I have to water my plants? This is every beginner's question, and getting the right answer is vital. Plants will suffer if the roots receive too little water — overwatering is the prime cause of death of indoor plants.

Unfortunately there is no simple answer to the beginner's question, but there are a number of guidelines. Never guess your plant's watering requirement is the first rule — look it up in the A-Z guide. There are four basic types of water requirement, and these are set out in the Watering Guide. Unfortunately the correct gap between watering cannot be so easily defined — it can range from a single day to several months. The required frequency of watering depends on the plant, the pot size, compost type, season, room conditions etc. The once-a-week routine may be satisfactory for a limited range of foliage plants, but even here you will have to extend the gap in winter. The real answer is to learn how to tell when the plant needs watering.

Must-have Equipment

An **INDEX FINGER** is the most useful aid for determining when watering of plant pots is necessary.

A **MOISTURE METER** is the most useful aid for determining when watering of large containers is necessary. As an alternative you can make a dip-stick gauge — see page 124.

Watering Guide

◄ **DRY IN WINTER Plants**
Desert Cacti and Succulents should be treated as Moist/Dry Plants during the active growth season from spring to autumn. During the winter the compost should be allowed to dry out almost completely.

◄ **MOIST/DRY Plants**
Most foliage House Plants belong in this group. The standard recommendation is to water thoroughly and frequently between spring and autumn, and to water sparingly in winter, letting the top 1/2 in. (1 cm) of compost dry out each time between watering. This drying out of the surface between watering is especially important during the resting period from late autumn to mid spring.

◄ **MOIST AT ALL TIMES Plants**
Most flowering plants belong in this group. The compost is kept moist, but not wet, at all times. The standard recommendation is to water carefully each time the surface becomes dry, but never frequently enough to keep the compost permanently saturated. There is no rule to tell you which plant belongs in this group — look up individual needs in the A-Z guide.

◄ **WET AT ALL TIMES Plants**
Very few plants belong in this group. Water thoroughly and frequently enough to keep the compost wet, nor merely moist. Examples are Azalea and Cyperus.

The first vital step

Your new plant may suffer or die if you fail to carry out this simple task, yet it is rarely mentioned in books or articles. Look at the pot — it is quite likely that the compost is level or mounded above the rim of the pot. This makes proper watering very difficult. So your first job is to create an adequate watering space. This calls for removing excess compost in order to create a gap between the rim of the pot and the compost surface. This should be about 1/2 in. (1 cm) in a small pot and 1 in. (2-3 cm) in a larger pot.

How to water
Watering can method

Water in the morning — do not water if bright sunlight is shining directly on the pot. The pot should be stood in a drip tray or in a waterproof pot holder. Pour water slowly, using a watering can with a long spout. Put the end of the spout under the leaves and close to the rim — let the water drain through and inspect after about 10 minutes. Water again if no water has come through. Empty any water left in the drip tray or pot holder after about 30 minutes.

Immersion method

A useful technique for hairy-leaved plants and for Cyclamen and other types which do not like water on their crowns. It is also the method to use if the compost has dried out more than usual. Stand the pot in a deep bowl and add water to about one-quarter to three-quarters of the height of the pot. Leave it until the compost surface is wet. Lift out the pot and let it drain.

Watering troubles:
Water not absorbed
Cause: Surface caking
Cure: Prick over the surface with a fork or miniature trowel. Then immerse the pot to compost level in a bucket or bath of water

Water runs straight through
Cause: Shrinkage of compost away from the side of the pot
Cure: Immerse the pot to compost level in a bucket or bath of water

When to water

Inspect the pots every few days in summer and weekly during winter. Measuring water loss by lifting the pot can be useful, but it does require some skill. Lift the pot immediately after watering — remember the weight. Lift the pot again when a need to water has been established by another method — again try to remember the weight. Use the span of these two weights when you lift the pot in future to see if it needs watering. Easy for some people — impossible for others.

•

The best method is to rub the surface with your index finger. If the compost is dry and powdery, water if the plant belongs to the MOIST AT ALL TIMES group.

•

Insert your finger to the full length of the fingernail into the compost close to the edge of the pot. If the surface of your finger is dry after it is withdrawn, water if the plant belongs to the MOIST/DRY group.

•

Plants in large receptacles pose a special problem — the top inch or two may be dry but the compost at the bottom may be waterlogged. A moisture meter is the best way to check on the watering needs in this situation.

Danger Signs:
Too little water

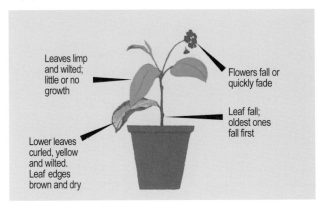

Leaves limp and wilted; little or no growth

Flowers fall or quickly fade

Leaf fall; oldest ones fall first

Lower leaves curled, yellow and wilted. Leaf edges brown and dry

Too much water

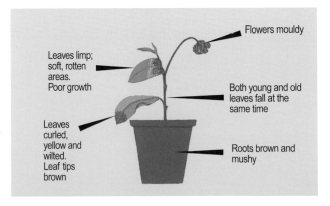

Flowers mouldy

Leaves limp; soft, rotten areas. Poor growth

Both young and old leaves fall at the same time

Leaves curled, yellow and wilted. Leaf tips brown

Roots brown and mushy

LIGHT

There are two distinct aspects of light which control growth. The first one is **duration**, and this aspect is fairly constant for nearly all types. There must be 12-16 hours of natural light or sufficiently strong artificial illumination in order to maintain active growth. Less light will slow down food production, which is why the resting period of foliage plants is not broken by the bright but short-lived sunny days in winter.

The second aspect is **intensity**, and unlike duration its need varies enormously from one plant to another. Some types flourish on a sunny windowsill but quickly deteriorate in a shady corner, others will grow in light shade but cannot survive when exposed to sunlight.

As you move from a sunny window towards a corner of the room you will pass from Full Sun to Shade in about 8 ft (2.5 m). Walking with your back to the window you may notice little change, but the light intensity will have dropped by about 95% over that short distance.

Danger Signs: Too little light

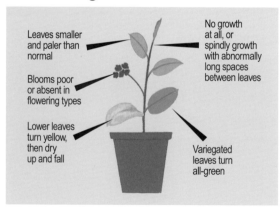

Leaves smaller and paler than normal

No growth at all, or spindly growth with abnormally long spaces between leaves

Blooms poor or absent in flowering types

Lower leaves turn yellow, then dry up and fall

Variegated leaves turn all-green

Too much light

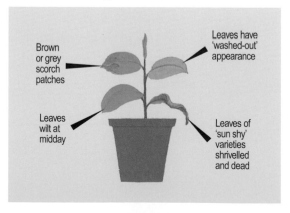

Brown or grey scorch patches

Leaves have 'washed-out' appearance

Leaves wilt at midday

Leaves of 'sun shy' varieties shrivelled and dead

Light Guide

FULL SUN
Area with as much light as possible, within 2 ft (60 cm) of a south-facing window
Very few House Plants can withstand scorching conditions — only the desert Cacti, Succulents and Pelargonium can be expected to flourish.

SOME DIRECT SUN
Brightly-lit area, with some sunlight falling on the leaves during the day
Examples are a west-facing or an east-facing windowsill. This is the ideal site for many flowering and some foliage House Plants.

BRIGHT BUT SUNLESS
Area close to but not in the zone lit by direct sunlight
Many plants grow best when placed about 5 ft (1.5 m) from a window which is sunlit for part of the day.

SEMI-SHADE
Moderately-lit area, within 5-8 ft (1.5-2.5 m) of a sunlit window or close to a sunless window
Very few flowering plants will flourish.

SHADE
Poorly-lit area, but bright enough to allow you to read a newspaper during several hours of the day
See page 149.

DEEP SHADE
Unsuitable for all indoor plants.

Notes on light

- The leaves and stems of a windowsill plant will bend towards the glass. To prevent lop-sided growth it is necessary to turn the pot occasionally — make only a slight turn each time. Do not turn the pot of a flowering plant when it is in bud.

- A flowering plant will suffer if it is moved from the recommended lighting to a shadier spot. The number and quality of the blooms are strictly controlled by both the duration and intensity of the light. Without adequate lighting the foliage may grow perfectly happily but the floral display is bound to disappoint.

- A foliage plant can be suddenly moved from its ideal location to a shadier spot with no ill-effect. It will survive but not flourish — try to move it back to a brighter area for about a week every 1-2 months to allow it to recuperate.

- A plant should not be suddenly moved from a shady spot to a sunny windowsill or the open garden. It should be acclimatised for a few days by moving it to a brighter spot each day.

HUMIDITY

When you turn on a radiator to warm up the cold air in winter, the room becomes comfortable, but the amount of water vapour in the air decreases and is no longer enough to keep it moist. The air becomes 'dry' — in technical terms the Relative Humidity has fallen.

As a general rule indoor plants need less warm air and more moist air than you think. Central heating in the depths of winter can produce air with the Relative Humidity of the Sahara Desert. Very few plants actually thrive in such conditions — many foliage plants and most flowering ones will suffer unless the humidity around the leaves is raised. You can lessen or even avoid the problem by finding a moist home for your plants — the kitchen or bathroom are the usual examples.

You can use a humidifier to increase the Relative Humidity of the whole room. It is, however, much more usual to use a technique which produces a moist microclimate around the plant while the atmosphere in the rest of the room remains as dry as ever.

There are three basic techniques for increasing the air humidity around plants — these are described on this page. For plants which originated in the jungle these techniques may not be enough to ensure active growth in a centrally-heated room — such plants will benefit from the humid atmosphere in a Glass Garden (page 131-134). The Orchidarium is a useful way to keep Moth Orchids in bloom for many months. Place a 2 in. (5 cm) layer of hydroleca (expanded clay pellets) at the base of an ordinary glass fish tank and stand the pots on it. Water to cover the bottom half of the hydroleca layer — do not cover. Water as necessary to make sure that the water level at the bottom of the Orchidarium is kept at about the half-way mark of the hydroleca level.

Humidity Guide

Relative Humidity	
100%	**SATURATED AIR**
90%	
80%	**JUNGLE AIR** Summer greenhouse conditions in temperate regions
70%	
60%	**SUMMER DAY IN TEMPERATE REGIONS** Best range for indoor plants growing in ordinary room conditions
50%	
40%	
30%	
20%	**DESERT AIR** Winter centrally-heated conditions in temperate regions
10%	
0%	**BONE-DRY AIR** Not found in nature

Raising the humidity

Misting

Use tepid water in the morning so that the foliage will be dry before nightfall. Cover all the plant, and do not mist when the foliage is exposed to bright sunlight. Misting does more than provide a temporary increase in humidity. It has a cooling effect on hot sunny days, it discourages red spider mite and it reduces the dust deposit on leaves.

Grouping

Plants grown in Pot Groups and Indoor Gardens have the benefit of increased moisture around the leaves. The best method of raising the humidity is to use a pebble tray — see page 115. Make sure that there is enough space between them to avoid the onset of Botrytis.

Double potting

Use an outer waterproof container and fill the space between the pot and the container with moist compost. Keep this packing material thoroughly and continually moist so that there will always be a surface layer of moisture to evaporate and raise the Relative Humidity.

Danger Signs: Too little humidity

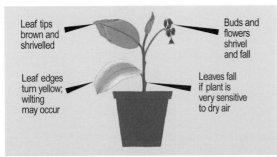

Leaf tips brown and shrivelled

Buds and flowers shrivel and fall

Leaf edges turn yellow; wilting may occur

Leaves fall if plant is very sensitive to dry air

NUTRIENTS

All plants, indoors and out, need an adequate supply of nitrogen, phosphates and potash together with small amounts of trace elements.

In the garden it is usual to apply fertilizers to top up the soil's natural resources, but even in their absence the plant can continue to draw on the soil's supply of nutrients by sending out new roots. Indoors the position is quite different. The compost in the pot contains a limited amount of food, and this is continually depleted by the roots of the plant and by leaching through the drainage holes. Once the nutrient supply is exhausted regular feeding when the plant is actively growing must take place. Cacti can survive for a long time without any feeding, but vigorous foliage plants and flowering plants coming into bloom are seriously affected if not fed.

Composts contain enough plant food for about 2 months after repotting. After this time feeding will be necessary if the plant is not dormant. The time to feed regularly is during the growing and flowering seasons — spring to autumn for foliage and most flowering plants, and during winter for winter-flowering types. Feeding should be reduced during the resting period.

NITROGEN (N)	The *leaf maker* which promotes stem growth and foliage production. Needs to be balanced with some potash for Orchids
PHOSPHATES (P_2O_5)	The *root maker* which stimulates active rooting in the medium. Necessary, but all compound fertilizers have sufficient
POTASH (K_2O)	The *flower maker* which hardens growth so that flowering is encouraged at the expense of leaf growth
TRACE ELEMENTS	Present in some house plant feeds — derived from organic or chemical sources. Shortage can cause leaf discoloration

Danger Signs: Too little fertilizer

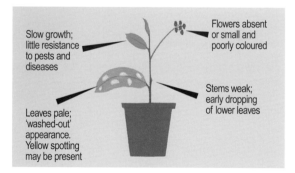

Slow growth; little resistance to pests and diseases

Flowers absent or small and poorly coloured

Stems weak; early dropping of lower leaves

Leaves pale; 'washed-out' appearance. Yellow spotting may be present

Too much fertilizer

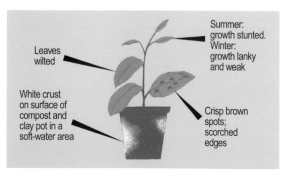

Leaves wilted

Summer: growth stunted. Winter: growth lanky and weak

White crust on surface of compost and clay pot in a soft-water area

Crisp brown spots; scorched edges

What to use

House plant foods are nearly always compound fertilizers containing nitrogen, phosphates and potash. The popular ones are sold as all-purpose products, but for the specialist there are Cactus, Citrus and Fern formulations. Orchids are best fed with a feed specifically recommended for them — the dilution and perhaps ingredients are different.

Liquid feeds

It is generally agreed that the most effective way to feed plants in pots is to use a liquid fertilizer. Watering and feeding are carried out in a single operation — the recommended amount is added to the water, and this is used at watering time. This avoids the danger of overfeeding, and the amount of feed can be reduced or stopped when necessary.

Tablets & Granules

Slow-release tablets and granules are available. They are placed on the surface or pushed into the compost where they slowly release their nutrients over a period of time. Convenient, but the fertilizer supply cannot be regulated to fit in with the season, and distribution in the compost is not even. These problems do not arise with the liquid feed method.

Dropper bottles

These autofeeders have appeared in recent years. The plastic bottle contains diluted fertilizer and the neck of the inverted bottle is inserted into the compost after the tip of its cap has been removed. Novel, but it can be unsightly in a display and as with tablets the distribution of nutrients in the pot is not even.

GROOMING
Cleaning

Dust is an enemy in a number of ways. It spoils the appearance of the foliage and it blocks the leaf pores. It forms a light-reducing screen as well as the possibility of containing plant-damaging chemicals in some industrial areas.

It is therefore necessary to remove dust when it becomes obvious on the foliage. The usual technique is to syringe or sponge the leaves with clean water. Wash plants early in the day so that they will be dry before nightfall. If the foliage is very dirty it should be lightly dusted with a soft cloth before washing — failing to do this may result in a strongly adhesive mud when the water dries. Remember to support the leaf in your hand when washing, and it is better to syringe and not sponge young foliage. Cacti, Succulents and plants with hairy leaves should not be sprayed or washed — use a soft brush to remove dust.

Polishing

Untreated   Treated

Even clean foliage tends to look dull and tired as it ages — the glossy sheen of new leaves is soon lost. Many plant-polishing materials are available, and you should choose with care. Olive oil will produce a shine, but it also collects dust.

The best plan is to buy a product which is specially made for plants — aerosols are simple to use and are the preferred method. Liquid products should be applied by gently wiping the foliage with a piece of cotton wool soaked with the liquid. Wipes are popular.

There are a few rules. Do not polish young leaves and never press down on the leaf surface. Read the label before use — it will have a list of plants which should not be treated.

Pruning

Pinching out is the removal of the growing point of a stem — use finger and thumb or a pair of scissors. **Pruning** is the removal of excessive growth — use secateurs or a pair of scissors. **Trimming** is the removal of dead leaves, damaged parts and faded flowers.

Pinching out is used to induce branching in bushy and trailing plants such as Coleus, Tradescantia and Pilea. Pruning is used with some climbing plants to induce the opposite effect. Here one or more main shoots are selected and trained as required, the weak side shoots being cut out cleanly at their junction with the main stem.

Many plants will soon deteriorate if not regularly pruned and trimmed. For example some climbing plants such as Ivy and Philodendron scandens produce stems in winter with abnormally small and pale leaves — this growth must be cut back in spring. Always cut back over-long branches and old leafless stems. Removing dead flowers may prolong the flowering period of many species.

Prune flowering plants with care — there are no general rules. Some, such as Fuchsia, Geranium and Hydrangea, bear blooms on new growth. Others flower on old wood.

Training

Training is the support given to stems to ensure maximum display. This method of grooming is, of course, essential for climbing plants. It is also necessary for non-climbers with long, weak stems (e.g Fatshedera), heavy flower-heads (e.g Hydrangea) and brittle stems (e.g Impatiens).

Avoid using a single cane wherever possible — use instead a framework of three or four canes. The canes should reach the bottom of the pot. Many other types of support are available — trellises, moss sticks (page 141) and wire hoops for inserting within the pot. There are also climbing frames of wire or wood to use outside the pot.

Do not tie stems too closely to the support. Train new growth before it is long enough to be untidy and difficult to bend. Vines must be trained frequently or the tendrils will tie the stems together.

PROPAGATION

There are four basic reasons for raising indoor plants at home — to have more plants without having to buy them every time, to replace old specimens with vigorous new ones, to have plants which would otherwise be unobtainable and lastly to provide gifts for friends.

Some indoor plants cannot be raised without special equipment — you have to invest in a thermostatically controlled propagator or leave it to the nurseryman. But a number of different types can be propagated quite simply in the kitchen or spare room. It is strange that there are many people who grow their own vegetables and yet are daunted by the idea of raising their own indoor plants.

The basic ways to increase your stock of indoor plants are shown on this page. There are other propagation techniques, but they are either not popular or can be used on only a limited range of plants. Seed Sowing is generally left to commercial growers, and Spore Sowing is just for Ferns. Air Layering is used for thick-stemmed plants which have become leggy, and Layering is for climbers and trailers with long, flexible stems.

Cuttings

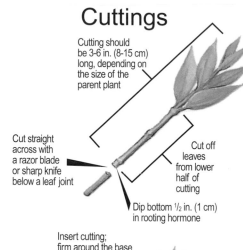

Cutting should be 3-6 in. (8-15 cm) long, depending on the size of the parent plant

Cut straight across with a razor blade or sharp knife below a leaf joint

Cut off leaves from lower half of cutting

Dip bottom ½ in. (1 cm) in rooting hormone

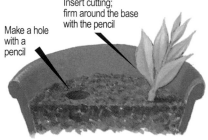

Insert cutting; firm around the base with the pencil

Make a hole with a pencil

Cuttings are by far the most usual way to raise indoor plants at home. As a general rule spring or early summer is the best time, but consult the A-Z guide to make sure. Insert cuttings in the damp compost as soon as they have been prepared, but Cactus and Succulent cuttings are left to dry for several days.

Place four canes in the pot and drape a plastic bag over them — secure with a rubber band. Place the pot in a bright but sunless spot — keep at 65°F (18°C) or more. Water the compost and lift out each cutting when new growth is obvious. Transfer each one into a small pot of Potting Compost. Firm gently and water to settle the compost around the roots.

Plantlets

A few species produce miniature plants at the end of flowering stems (e.g Chlorophytum and Saxifraga sarmentosa) or on mature leaves (e.g Asplenium bulbiferum). Propagation is easy. If no roots are present on the plantlet, peg it down in moist Seed & Cutting Compost. Sever the plantlet from the parent plant when rooting has taken place. If the plantlet bears roots, it can be propagated by removing it from the parent plant and potting up as a rooted cutting.

Offsets

Some plants produce miniature plants as side shoots (e.g Cacti and Bromeliads) or as tiny bulblets next to the parent bulb (e.g Hippeastrum). Stem offsets should be cut off as near the main stem as possible — keep any roots which are attached. Pot up each one in Seed & Cutting Compost and treat as an ordinary stem cutting. Separate bulb offsets from the parent bulb and pot up.

Division

A number of plants form several clumps or daughter rosettes (e.g Ferns, Saintpaulia and Sansevieria). Knock the plant out of its pot in spring or early summer and carefully pull off one or more segments. Do this by gently removing some compost to expose the connection between the clump and the rest of the plant. Sever the join by hand or with a sharp knife. Transplant the segments using Seed & Cutting Compost. Water sparingly until new growth starts.

REPOTTING

Most indoor plants thrive in pots which appear to be too small for the amount of leaf and stem on the plant. It is a mistake to repot into a larger pot or container unless the plant is definitely pot-bound — check in the A-Z guide to see if there is a recommended period between moving from one pot into another. Some plants will only flower when they are pot-bound, and there are others such as Bromeliads which should never need repotting.

There are a few signs to look for if you think that it may be time to move the specimen into a larger pot. Roots start to quickly grow through the drainage hole, and the compost will have started to dry out so that frequent watering is necessary. Perhaps the most obvious symptom is that stem and leaf growth have significantly slowed down in spring and summer despite having been fed regularly.

The final check is to remove the pot as shown in diagram 3 below. If the plant is pot-bound you will see masses of matted roots but not much compost. If it is not pot-bound, simply replace the pot.

For a variety of reasons, especially with large Stand-alone Plants and trained specimens, you may not wish or be able to repot. The pot should then be top-dressed every spring by carefully removing the top 1-2 in. (3-5 cm) and replacing with fresh compost.

The best time is in spring, so that the roots will have plenty of time to become established before the onset of the resting season. Choose a pot which is only slightly larger than the previous one — too large a difference will result in a severe check to growth. Have everything ready before you start — pots, compost, watering can etc. Check in the A–Z guide to see if the plant can be divided up at repotting time.

1 If the pot has been used before, it must be thoroughly scrubbed out. A new clay pot should be soaked in water overnight before use.

2 If a clay pot is used, cover the drainage hole with 'crocks' (broken pieces of pot or brick). Place a shallow layer of compost over the crock layer.

3 Water the plant. One hour later remove it from the pot by spreading the fingers of one hand over the soil surface. Invert, and gently knock the rim on a table. Run a knife around the edge if it is necessary. Remove the pot with the other hand.

4 Take away the old crocks. Carefully tease out some of the matted outside roots. Remove any rotten roots but avoid at all costs causing extensive root damage.

5 Place the plant on top of the compost layer in the new pot and gradually fill around the soil ball with compost, which should be slightly damp.

6 Firm the compost down with the thumbs, adding more until level with the base of the stem. Finally tap the pot on the table several times to settle the compost.

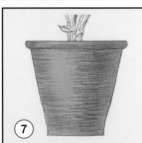

7 Water carefully and place in the shade for about a week, misting the leaves daily to avoid wilting. Then place the plant in its growing quarters and treat normally.

TROUBLES

There is not going to be much satisfaction in growing and displaying indoor plants unless you learn how to avoid plant troubles. Pests and diseases are not usually to blame — in most cases the cause of problems or death is too little or too much of one or more of the essential growth factors — light, water, warmth, humidity and nutrient supply. The first task is to choose plants which can be expected to flourish in the conditions you can provide. Buy healthy specimens, and learn to recognise the symptoms and causes of problems — many plant troubles can be stopped or cured if tackled quickly.

APHID (Greenfly)

Small, sap-sucking insects, usually green but may be black, grey or orange. All plants with soft tissues can be attacked; shoot tips and flower buds are the preferred site. Flowering Pot Plants are especially susceptible. The plant is weakened and sticky honeydew is deposited. Spray with an indoor plant insecticide if necessary.

BOTRYTIS (Grey Mould)

Grey, fluffy mould which can cover leaves, stems, buds and flowers if conditions are cool, humid and still. All soft-leaved plants can be affected — Begonia, Cyclamen and Saintpaulia are particularly susceptible. Cut away all affected parts. With remaining plants reduce watering and misting — improve ventilation.

CROWN & STEM ROT

Part of the stem or crown is soft and rotten. When the diseased area is at the base of the plant it is known as basal rot. The fungus usually kills the plant — the usual course is to throw the plant away. If you have caught the trouble early you can try to save it by cutting away all diseased tissue. In future avoid overwatering, under-ventilating and keeping the plant too cool.

SCALE

Small, brown discs attached to the under-side of leaves. These immobile adults are protected from sprays by the outer waxy shells, but they can be wiped off with a damp cloth or a babycare cotton bud. If a plant is allowed to become badly infested the leaves turn yellow and sticky with honeydew — eradication is difficult or impossible at this stage.

VINE WEEVIL

The adults attack leaves, but it is the 1 in. (3 cm) creamy grubs which do the real damage. They live in the compost and rapidly devour roots and bulbs. The root system will have been seriously damaged by the time the plant has started to wilt. Imidacloprid is used as a preventative by growers, but control is not practical at home.

BROWN TIPS/EDGES

If tips but not edges are brown, the most likely cause is DRY AIR. Another possible reason is BRUISING by people or pets touching the tips. If edges are yellow or brown, the possible causes are many — OVERWATERING, UNDERWATERING, TOO LITTLE LIGHT, TOO MUCH SUN, TOO MUCH HEAT, OVERFEEDING, DRY AIR or DRAUGHTS.

NO FLOWERS

The commonest causes of bud drop are DRY AIR, UNDERWATERING, TOO LITTLE LIGHT, MOVING THE POT and INSECT DAMAGE. Lighting problems (TOO LITTLE LIGHT and WRONG DAY LENGTH) are the most likely cause of blooms failing to appear when the flowering season arrives — other causes include OVERFEEDING and DRY AIR.

POOR GROWTH

In winter this is normal for nearly all plants, so do not force it to grow. In summer the most likely cause is UNDER-FEEDING, OVERWATERING or TOO LITTLE LIGHT. If these factors are not responsible, and the temperature is in the recommended range, then the plant is probably POT-BOUND and needs repotting into a larger pot.

SUDDEN LEAF FALL

Rapid defoliation without a prolonged pre-liminary period of wilting or discoloration is generally due to a SHOCK to the plant's system. There may have been a large drop or rise in temperature, a sudden increase in daytime light intensity or a strong cold draught. DRYNESS at the roots can result in sudden leaf loss with woody specimens.

WILTING LEAVES

An obvious cause is SOIL DRYNESS due to underwatering, but it is not the only reason for wilting leaves. WATER-LOGGING due to impeded drainage or watering too frequently can be the cause, and so can TOO MUCH LIGHT (especially if wilting occurs at midday), DRY AIR, TOO MUCH HEAT, POT-BOUND ROOTS or PEST DAMAGE.

Chapter 6

CUT FLOWERS A–Z

The purpose of this chapter is to give you information on hundreds of different plants which are used by flower arrangers. In theory there is no reason why a part of any plant may not be cut and taken indoors to be used in a flower arrangement. In practice, however, we use the term 'cut flowers' to cover blooms which have been bought, cut from the garden or from indoor plants, together with foliage or stems which are known to be suitable for arranging indoors.

We snip away on our plot and/or we buy a bunch of flowers and then set about making our display. There are scores of books to inspire us with examples of arrangements and to give us general advice on how to prepare and put the material together. It is therefore surprising that so little information is available on individual cut flowers. There are so many A-Z guides on garden flowers and shrubs with descriptions and care instructions, and yet so few A-Z guides on cut flowers for indoor display. Some cut flowers are suitable for drying by hanging them upside down in an airing cupboard. Cut the blooms on a dry day just before they are fully open. Drying will take 1-8 weeks.

On the following pages you will find a list of over 400 florist and garden flowers, shrubs and trees which are known to be suitable for arranging, together with basic information on them for the flower arranger. A key to the information provided is set out below.

CUTTING or BUYING STAGE

Recommended stage for cutting flowers in the garden or when to buy

B Bud Stage. Some colour, not open
O Open Stage. Some flowers open
R Ripe Stage. All flowers open

CONDITIONING METHOD

See page 243 for details. Virtually all require conditioning. Some need pre-conditioning

P1 Woody stem treatment
P2 Milky sap treatment
P3 Spring bulb treatment
P4 Floppy stem treatment
P5 Large leaf treatment
C Condition for 2-8 hours

VASE LIFE

Life expectancy if cut at the right stage and given proper treatment

★ Less than 6 days
★★ 6-10 days
★★★ Over 10 days

Latin name	Common name	Cutting or Buying Stage	Conditioning method	Vase life	Notes
STACHYS	Lamb's Ears	—	C	★★★	This perennial is grown for its attractive evergreen silvery foliage. The pale purple flowers are of little significance
STACHYURUS	Stachyurus	O	P1 then C	★★	A welcome alternative to the ever-popular Witch Hazel and Winter Jasmine as a source of late winter flowers

Latin name	Common name	Cutting or Buying Stage	Conditioning method	Vase life	Notes
ACACIA	Mimosa, Wattle	O	P1 then C	★★	Woody branches with grey, ferny leaves and small clusters of tiny yellow flowers. Dries well
ACANTHUS	Bear's Breeches	O	P2 then C	★★★	A midsummer garden plant with deeply divided leaves and tall spires of hooded purple and white flowers
ACHILLEA	Yarrow	R	P1 then C	★★★	Flat heads of tiny blooms (usually yellow) and feathery foliage appear in summer. A popular dried flower — see page 161
ACONITUM	Monkshood	O	C	★★	Helmet-like blue or violet flowers on long stalks — leaves are deeply cut. All parts are poisonous
AESCULUS	Horse Chestnut	—	P1 then C	★★★	For spring foliage display cut the shoots when the swollen black buds are beginning to open
AGAPANTHUS	African Lily	O	C	★★	Trumpet-shaped blooms in ball-like clusters on top of long stems. White ones are available, but blue is the usual colour
ALCHEMILLA	Lady's Mantle	O	C	★★★	A favourite plant for use as filler material — sprays of greenish-yellow tiny flowers and downy, lobed foliage
ALLIUM	Ornamental Onion	O	C	★★★	Globes of starry flowers — good as a cut flower but not popular. Dry at the seed-head stage — see page 161
ALSTROEMERIA	Peruvian Lily	O	C	★★★	Not common in gardens, but seen in florists everywhere. Trumpets in many colours. Can be dried at the seed-head stage — see page 161
ALTHAEA	Hollyhock	O	C	★★	A good choice when you need tall line material. Floral spikes can be dried — see page 161 for instructions
AMARANTHUS	Love-lies-bleeding	R	C	★★★	A half-hardy annual with long tassels of red tiny blooms in summer — green-flowered variety available
AMARYLLIS	Belladonna Lily	B	C	★	A garden or conservatory plant with trumpet-like blooms on top of thick stalks. Available from florists in autumn
AMMI	Queen Anne's Lace	O	C	★★	A good florist flower with airy heads of small white flowers. Available all year, but hard to find
AMMOBIUM	Winged Everlasting	O	C	★★	Not one for the fresh arrangement — a white Daisy-like flower available as dried material. Keeps its colour well
ANAPHALIS	Pearl Everlasting	O	C	★★	An easy-to-grow perennial with silvery leaves and clusters of starry white flowers. Floral spikes can be dried — see page 161
ANEMONE	Anemone, Windflower	O	C	★	There are several garden types, some long-lasting. The florist one is the Poppy Anemone — not good in floral foam

Achillea

Agapanthus

Alchemilla

Alstroemeria

Latin name	Common name	Cutting or Buying Stage	Conditioning method	Vase life	Notes
ANETHUM	Dill	O	P1 then C	★★	A garden herb — its heads of tiny flowers and feathery foliage look like a yellow version of Queen Anne's Lace
ANIGOZANTHOS	Kangaroo Paw	O	P1 then C	★★★	A conservatory plant with Iris-like leaves and furry flowers-heads. Fresh or dry — not easy to find
ANTHEMIS	Chamomile	O	C	★★	Daisy-like flower cut from the garden for fresh arrangements — more often used as a dyed dried flower
ANTHURIUM	Anthurium	R	C	★★★	A showy conservatory plant with a straight or curled column-like flower-head above a palette-like bract
ANTIRRHINUM	Snapdragon	O	C	★★	An old garden favourite — cut in summer or buy all year round from the florist. Not suitable for drying
AQUILEGIA	Columbine	O	C	★	Colourful spurred blooms appear above the ferny foliage in early summer. Grow the McKana hybrids
ARTEMISIA	Wormwood	—	P1 then C	★★★	An excellent choice if you want grey-leaved line material which has feathery foliage. Suitable for drying — see page 161
ARUM	Cuckoo-pint	—	P5	★★★	The leaves of wild and garden Arums are used as filler material. Grow the variegated A. italicum 'Pictum'
ARUNDINARIA	Bamboo	—	P1 then C	★★★	The cane-like stems with grassy leaves provide line material for tall arrangements — not often used
ASPARAGUS	Asparagus Fern	—	C	★★★	There are several of these 'florist ferns', such as the oval-leaved Smilax and the needle-leaved Emerald Fern
ASTER	Michaelmas Daisy	O	P1 then C	★★	Garden blooms in a wide range of colours — most popular types are varieties of A. novi-belgii or A. novae-angliae
ASTER	September Flower	O	C	★★	A. ericoides is not common in the garden, but a familiar sight at the florist. Large sprays of tiny white flowers
ASTILBE	False Spiraea	O	P1 then C	★	An herbaceous border plant with large feathery plumes in midsummer. Cut for drying at the seed-head stage — see page 161
ASTRANTIA	Masterwort	O	C	★★	A drab cottage garden plant — out of favour with gardeners but quite widely used by flower arrangers
AUCUBA	Spotted Laurel	—	P1 then C	★★★	The leaves of the variegated varieties of Aucuba are brightly splashed with yellow — winter berries are bright red
AVENA	Oat	R	C	★★	Not often used as fresh material, but widely used in the dried state. Cut and dry when heads are green or brown — see page 161

Anthurium

Antirrhinum

Asparagus

Aster ericoides

Latin name	Common name	Cutting or Buying Stage	Conditioning method	Vase life	Notes
BALLOTA	Ballota	—	C	★★★	A garden plant to grow for its long stems clothed with silvery furry leaves. Can be dried for winter use — see page 161
BANKSIA	Giant Bottlebrush	O	P1 then C	★★★	Hard-to-buy fresh material but freely available as a dried flower. Cone-like flower-head is large and upright
BERBERIS	Barberry	O	P1 then C	★★	A useful green- or purple-leaved shrub for line material. Cut in spring for floral display — in autumn for berries. Remove thorns
BERGENIA	Elephant Ear	—	P5	★★★	The leathery leaves are excellent filler material for a large display. Available from the garden all year round
BETULA	Birch	—	P1 then C	★★★	Good line material for modern displays — can be used when bare, when coming into leaf and when bearing catkins
BOUVARDIA	Bouvardia	O	P1 then C	★★	A house plant available all year round from the florist. Large clusters of tubular flowers — white, pink, orange and red
BRIZA	Quaking Grass	O	—	★★★	An excellent ornamental grass with nodding heads on fine stalks. Use fresh when green or dry when ripe
BUDDLEIA	Butterfly Bush	O	P2 then C	★★	Well-known garden shrub with tiny flowers in tall cones or round globes. Use as line material in summer arrangements
BUPLEURUM	Bupleurum	O	P1 then C	★★	There is just one species (B. fruticosum) for garden use — florist types are tender. Available as dried material
BUXUS	Box	—	P1 then C	★★★	A small-leaved hedging plant — foliage all-green or variegated. Good line material, suitable for small arrangements
CALENDULA	Pot Marigold	O	C	★★	Orange-flowered cottage garden annual — modern varieties available in colours ranging from pale cream to deep orange
CALLICARPA	Beauty Berry	—	P1 then C	★★★	In winter the bare stems of this garden shrub are clothed with violet or bright purple berries
CALLISTEPHUS	China Aster	O	C	★★★	A popular bedding plant with single or double Chrysanthemum-like flowers. There are many different shapes and colours
CALLUNA	Scotch Heather	O	P1 then C	★★	White or pink bell-shaped flowers in summer or autumn. Many types have coloured foliage
CAMASSIA	Quamash	O	C	★	A bulb for heavy soil and partial shade. Flowering stems appear in summer — 2–3 ft (60 cm-1 m) high with starry blooms
CAMELLIA	Camellia	O	P1 then C	★★	Foliage is oval and glossy — the showy blooms are 2–5 in. (5–12 cm) across. Excellent for floating in a shallow dish

Bouvardia

Buxus

Calendula

Callistephus

Latin name	Common name	Cutting or Buying Stage	Conditioning method	Vase life	Notes
CAMPANULA	Bellflower	O	P2 then C	★★★	Star- or bell-shaped blooms in white, blue or lavender. Flowers outdoors in June-August, but can be bought in spring
CANNA	Indian Shot	—	P5	★★	This bulb is grown as a bedding plant for its showy blooms, but arrangers use the large bronze or purple leaves
CARTHAMUS	Safflower	O	C	★★	Orange flowers above clustered leaves on tall stems. Rare as a fresh florist flower — popular as a dried flower
CATANANCHE	Cupid's Dart	O	C	★★★	A good choice for the flower arranger's garden. The Cornflower-like flowers appear above the greyish grassy leaves in summer
CATTLEYA	Corsage Orchid	R	C	★★★	Waxy, beautiful Orchids in wide range of colours. Best ones are sold with cut ends in water tubes — do not remove
CEANOTHUS	Californian Lilac	O	P1 then C	★★	Deciduous and evergreen shrubs which bear heads of tiny fluffy flowers in summer or autumn. Blue is the usual colour
CELOSIA	Celosia	R	P2 then C	★★★	The large and brightly-coloured flower-heads are crested ('cockscomb') or plumed. Available as a florist flower
CENTAUREA	Cornflower	R	C	★	A colourful annual for fresh and dried displays. Wiry stems bear sprays of flowers — blue, white, pink, purple or red
CHAENOMELES	Japonica	B or O	P1 then C	★★	Red, pink or white blooms appear on this popular garden shrub in spring. For a long display cut at the bud stage
CHEIRANTHUS	Wallflower	O	P1 then C	★★★	Grow the ordinary Wallflower for April displays or the Siberian Wallflower for May blooms. The flowers are fragrant
CHELONE	Chelone	O	C	★★	An easy-to-grow but unusual perennial for the flower arranger. Penstemon-like pink or purple blooms appears in summer
CHIMONANTHUS	Winter Sweet	O	P1 then C	★★	The small flowers borne on the leafless stems are not particularly eye-catching but they are very fragrant
CHOISYA	Mexican Orange	O	P1 then C	★★	Cut for its glossy foliage all year round or for its waxy fragrant blooms in spring and again in autumn
CHRYSANTHEMUM CARINATUM	Annual Chrysanthemum	O	C	★★★	The blooms of this bedding plant are often boldly zoned in bright colours with a dark central disc. Double varieties are available
CHRYSANTHEMUM FRUTESCENS	Marguerite	O	P1 then C	★	An evergreen with divided leaves and multi-flowered stems. Usual type has white florets around a central yellow disc
CHRYSANTHEMUM MAXIMUM	Shasta Daisy	O	P1 then C	★	An old favourite in the herbaceous border with flowers borne singly. Usual type has white florets around a central yellow disc

Campanula

Cattleya

Centaurea

Chrysanthemum frutescens

Latin name	Common name	Cutting or Buying Stage	Conditioning method	Vase life	Notes
CHRYSANTHEMUM X MORIFOLIUM	Florist's Chrysanthemum	O	P1 then C	★★★	One of the most popular of all florist flowers — available all year round in a variety of shapes, sizes and colours
CIMICIFUGA	Bugbane	O	P2 then C	★★	A large perennial sometimes recommended for flower arranging, but its smell is unpleasant
CIRSIUM	Plumed Thistle	O	P2 then C	★★	Several species are offered to gardeners — the florist Cirsium is C. japonicum. Pink powder-puff flowers
CLARKIA	Clarkia	O	C	★★★	This hardy annual bears semi-double or double blooms on upright stems in summer. Red, pink, white or purple
CLEMATIS	Clematis	O	P2 then C	★	A deciduous or evergreen climber. Attractive trailer for displays, but blooms are short-lived
COBAEA	Cathedral Bell	O	C	★	Cobaea is an annual climber, bearing bell-like purple flowers. A useful trailer for the arranger but not easy to grow
CONVALLARIA	Lily of the Valley	O	C	★★	An old favourite for indoor display. Small white bells hang from the stems — used to add fragrance to spring displays
CONVOLVULUS	Shrubby Bindweed	—	C	★★	The shrub C. cneorum is useful for the flower arranger. It provides a year-round supply of silvery foliage
COREOPSIS	Tickseed	R	C	★★	Both the annual and perennial forms of Coreopsis are good for cutting. Flowers are yellow with or without red or brown
CORNUS	Dogwood	O	P1 then C	★★	Many uses. There are varieties with coloured bark, variegated leaves, attractive flowers and berries
CORTADERIA	Pampas Grass	R	C	★★★	The largest of the grasses — excellent line material for a grand display. Wear gloves when handling the leaves
CORYLUS	Hazel	R	P1 then C	★★	A most useful tree to grow — best is C. avellana 'Contorta' with its twisted branches. Cut and use at the catkin stage
COSMOS	Cosmea	O	C	★★	An annual with delicate ferny foliage and large flowers which look like single Dahlias. White, pink and red are the usual colours
COTINUS	Smoke Bush	—	P1 then C	★★	A red- or purple-leaved variety of the Smoke Bush provides attractive foliage material
COTONEASTER	Cotoneaster	—	P1 then C	★★★	Many evergreen and deciduous varieties are offered. Cut in autumn for masses of berries and rich foliage colours
CRATAEGUS	Hawthorn	B or O	P1 then C	★	Available from garden and hedgerow. White, pink or red flowers in May or June. For forcing indoors cut at the bud stage

Chrysanthemum x morifolium

Cortaderia

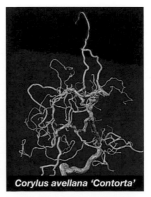
Corylus avellana 'Contorta'

Cotinus

Latin name	Common name	Cutting or Buying Stage	Conditioning method	Vase life	Notes
CROCOSMIA	Montbretia	O	C	★★	Red, orange and yellow blooms on arching stems in late summer. Sword-like leaves are useful as line material
CROCUS	Crocus	B or O	C	★	Not a good cut flower unless brought in at the bud stage — the vase-life is brief. Autumn-flowering types are available
CUPRESSUS	Conifer	—	P1 then C	★★★	A term loosely applied by flower arrangers to sprigs of any feathery conifer. Conifer cones are quite widely used
CYCLAMEN	Cyclamen	O	C	★★★	An excellent but rarely used cut flower to grow in the garden. There are varieties with marbled and silver-zoned leaves
CYMBIDIUM	Cymbidium	R	C	★★★	A popular florist Orchid. The usual form is a long flower-head bearing 10-25 blooms. There are miniature varieties
CYNARA	Cardoon, Artichoke	B, O or R	C	★★★	This plant is used in several ways. The shiny grey leaves are good foliage material — the seed-heads are used fresh or dried
CYTISUS	Broom	O or R	P2 then C	★★	Whippy branches, tiny leaves and Pea-like flowers. Good line material where a curved shape is required — e.g Inverted crescent
DAHLIA	Dahlia	O	P2 then C	★★	Very popular as a garden plant — much less so as a florist flower. Pompon varieties have longest vase-life and dry best
DAPHNE	Daphne	O	P1 then C	★	D. mezereum bears masses of fragrant starry flowers on stiff branches in February. Colour is deep pink or white
DELPHINIUM CONSOLIDA	Larkspur	O	C	★★	Larkspur looks like a miniature Delphinium with ferny foliage. This garden annual is a popular source of line material
DELPHINIUM ELATUM	Delphinium	O	C	★★	This perennial produces bold spikes clothed with large flowers in a wide range of colours
DENDROBIUM	Singapore Orchid	R	C	★★★	Each flower-head bears about 10 blooms — many hybrids are available. Usually sold with the cut end in a small water tube
DEUTZIA	Deutzia	O	P1 then C	★★	This easy-to-grow garden shrub provides leafy branches with open bells in white, pink, red or mauve in spring or summer
DIANTHUS BARBATUS	Sweet William	O	C	★★★	Densely-packed flattened heads of flowers in midsummer — the blooms are single-coloured or distinctly-eyed
DIANTHUS CARYOPHYLLUS	Carnation	O	C	★★★	Stems with a single large bloom are 'Standards' — 'Sprays' bear several smaller blooms. Cut stem just above a node
DIANTHUS SPP	Pink	O	C	★★	More delicate stems, narrower leaves and smaller flowers than Carnations. Types are Annual, Old-fashioned and Modern

Crocosmia

Dahlia

Delphinium elatum

Dianthus caryophyllus

Latin name	Common name	Cutting or Buying Stage	Conditioning method	Vase life	Notes
DICENTRA	Bleeding Heart	O	C	★★★	An easy-to-grow old favourite — very useful where arching flower stems are needed. D. formosa has feathery foliage
DICTAMNUS	Burning Bush	O	C	★★	An unusual border perennial which provides tall spikes of fragrant spidery flowers in midsummer
DIGITALIS	Foxglove	O	P2 then C	★★	Well-known garden plant with spires of bell-shaped flowers. Grow 'Foxy' if space is short. Can be dried at the seed-pod stage
DORONICUM	Leopard's Bane	O	P2 then C	★★	Bright yellow Daisy-like flowers in spring. It is one of the first border perennial plants to bloom — worth growing
ECHINACEA	Purple Coneflower	O	P2 then C	★★	Closely related to Rudbeckia — there is the same prominent cone-like disc, but the petals are pink or purple
ECHINOPS	Globe Thistle	O or R	P1 then C	★★★	Round Thistle-like heads on tall stalks — excellent for use fresh or dried. Blue is the usual colour
ELAEAGNUS	Elaeagnus	—	P1 then C	★★★	This foliage shrub is a must for the flower arranger's garden. Choose one or more of the varieties with yellow-splashed leaves
EREMURUS	Foxtail Lily	O	P1 then C	★★	A garden and florist flower widely used as line material in large arrangements. White, yellow or pink flowers on tall spikes
ERICA	Heather	O	P1 then C	★★	Choose carefully and you can have a Heather bed in bloom all year round in white, pink, red or mauve
ERYNGIUM	Sea Holly	O or R	C	★★★	A very spiny Thistle-like plant with a metallic blue sheen. Use as fresh or preserved material — see page 161
ESCALLONIA	Escallonia	O	P1 then C	★★	The stems of this evergreen are clothed with shiny leaves. The small white, pink or red flowers appear in summer
EUCALYPTUS	Eucalyptus	—	P1 then C	★★★	Excellent grey or silvery line material. Maintain supply of juvenile leaves by cutting shrub back each spring
EUONYMUS	Euonymus	—	P1 then C	★★★	Deciduous type (Spindle) cut for berries, but evergreen types are much more widely used as year-round variegated foliage
EUPHORBIA	Spurge	O	P2 then C	★★	There are a number of garden perennial Spurges which are useful. Stems are leafy — flower-like bracts are red or yellow
EUPHORBIA FULGENS	Scarlet Plume	O	P2 then C	★★	A house plant available as a florist flower. The long arching stems are clothed with red, white or yellow 'flowers'
EUPHORBIA MARGINATA	Snow in Summer	—	P2 then C	★★★	A half-hardy annual for the garden. It is grown for its attractive white-margined foliage and the white 'flowers' in summer

Elaeagnus

Eremurus

Eucalyptus

Euphorbia fulgens

Latin name	Common name	Cutting or Buying Stage	Conditioning method	Vase life	Notes
EUSTOMA	Prairie Gentian	O	C	★★★	A house plant available as a florist flower. It deserves to be more popular — the blooms appear in clusters
FAGUS	Beech	—	P1 then C	★★★	Fresh or preserved leafy branches. Choose from green (Common Beech) or purple (Copper Beech)
FATSIA	Fatsia	—	P5	★★★	Grow this one in the garden as a source of really large leaves, deeply lobed and shiny. A variegated Fatsia is available
FERNS	Fern	—	P2 then C	★★	Numerous types are used in flower arranging, ranging from filmy Maidenhair to the tough Leather Leaf
FOENICULUM	Fennel	O	C	★★	This one is cut from the herb garden rather than the border. Use it for its ferny foliage and tiny yellow flowers
FORSYTHIA	Golden Bell Bush	B or O	P1 then C	★★★	Popular garden shrub, flowering in March and April before the leaves appear. Cut earlier for winter blooms indoors
FREESIA	Freesia	O	C	★★	A very popular florist flower, available all year round in a wide range of colours. The bell-shaped flowers are single and fragrant
FRITILLARIA IMPERIALIS	Crown Imperial	O	P3 then C	★	A centrepiece for a spring arrangement — a group of pendant blooms hang from the leafy crown on the tall stem
FUCHSIA	Fuchsia	O	P1 then C	★	Choose a hardy variety for growing in the border — half-hardy ones are bedded out in late spring. Beautiful bell-shaped flowers
GAILLARDIA	Blanket Flower	O	C	★★★	A familiar sight in the herbaceous border — large Daisy-like flowers with red or orange petals tipped with yellow
GARDENIA	Gardenia	O	P1 then C	★	A house plant available as a florist flower. Beautiful and fragrant, but vase-life is short. Sometimes floated in a shallow dish
GARRYA	Silk Tassel Bush	O	P1 then C	★★★	Long and slender catkins drape the bush in January and February. Cut and arrange fresh in winter or dry for later use
GENISTA	Broom	O	P1 then C	★★	These shrubs have wiry stems, tiny leaves and a mass of yellow, Pea-like flowers in summer. Useful line material
GERBERA	Transvaal Daisy	O	P1 then C	★★★	A very popular florist flower, available all year round. The Daisy-like heads are brightly coloured and large or very large
GEUM	Avens	O	C	★	An old garden favourite and sometimes used in arrangements, but the blooms hang their heads and vase-life is short
GLADIOLUS	Sword Lily	O	C	★★	An excellent cut flower. Remove the top bud. Pick off faded flowers and re-cut stems to prolong vase-life

Freesia

Garrya

Gerbera

Gladiolus

Latin name	Common name	Cutting or Buying Stage	Conditioning method	Vase life	Notes
GLORIOSA	Glory Lily	O	C	★★	A house plant available as a florist flower. The Lily-like flowers are yellow and red with swept-back petals
GODETIA	Godetia	O	C	★★	This hardy annual is free-flowering and easy to grow. The gaily-coloured funnel-shaped flowers close up in the dark
GOMPHRENA	Globe Amaranth	O or R	P1 then C	★★	Globular 'everlasting' type — available as a florist flower but best known as dried material. Available in several colours
GRASSES	Grass	O	C	★★★	A number of grasses are used by flower arrangers and some (e.g Briza, Cortaderia and Avena) have individual entries
GYPSOPHILA	Baby's Breath	O	C	★★	Very widely used as filler material — loose clusters of tiny white or pale pink flowers on wiry stems. Easy to dry — see page 161
HAMAMELIS	Witch Hazel	B or O	P1 then C	★	Showy, spidery flowers appear on leafless branches between December and late February. The blooms are yellow or orange
HEBE	Woody Veronica	O	P1 then C	★★	These evergreen shrubs provide filler material. Some are used for their floral spikes — others for their unusual foliage
HEDERA	Ivy	—	P1 then C	★★★	Trailing material cut from the garden or hedgerow. When planting, choose varieties with unusual or variegated leaves
HELENIUM	Sneezewort	O	P1 then C	★★★	Easy-to-grow perennials — each Daisy-like bloom has a prominent central disc. Flower colours are yellow, red and brown
HELIANTHUS	Sunflower	O	P1 then C	★★	For giant heads grow the annual type — the perennials have smaller blooms. Dry at the seed-head stage — see page 161
HELICHRYSUM ANGUSTIFOLIUM	Curry Plant	—	C	★★★	Quite different from the popular Straw Flower described below. This one provides grey and feathery foliage material
HELICHRYSUM BRACTEATUM	Straw Flower	O	C	★★★	The most popular of the 'everlasting' flowers — they look like double Daisies with strawy petals
HELICONIA	Lobster Claw	O	C	★★	A house plant available as a florist flower. Spectacular blooms in yellow, red or orange — the large bracts are claw-like
HELIPTERUM	Everlasting Flower	O	C	★★★	This annual is often listed as Acroclinum in the seed catalogues. Similar to but less popular than Helichrysum
HELLEBORUS	Hellebore	O	P1 then C	★★	Included here are the Christmas Rose and Lenten Rose — pink, purple or white in winter or spring. Not good in floral foam
HEMEROCALLIS	Day Lily	O	C	★★	Pick or buy when only one or two flowers are open. Each bloom only lasts a single day, so display changes with time

Gypsophila

Hedera

Helianthus

Heliconia

Latin name	Common name	Cutting or Buying Stage	Conditioning method	Vase life	Notes
HEUCHERA	Coral Flower	O	C	★★	Slender stems in summer, bearing dense clusters of tiny bell-shaped flowers. White, coral, pink and red are available
HIBISCUS	Rose of China	B or O	P1 then C	★	A house plant occasionally offered as a florist flower. Each bloom lasts for only a day — buds continue to open
HIPPEASTRUM	Amaryllis	O	C	★	Large, trumpet-shaped flower. Fill hollow stem with water and plug with cotton wool before arranging
HOSTA	Plantain Lily	O	P5	★★★	Pretty flowers, but used mainly as foliage material. Many leaf types available — cream, green, bluish grey and white-edged
HYACINTHUS	Hyacinth	O	P3 then C	★	Very fragrant and attractive spring bulbs, but better grown in bowls than cut for flower arrangements
HYDRANGEA	Hydrangea	O	P1 then C	★★	Large heads of white, pink or blue florets. 'Mophead' and 'Lacecap' varieties available — see The Flowering Shrub Expert
HYPERICUM	St John's Wort	O	P1 then C	★★	Popular garden shrub with large Buttercup-like flowers — some with attractive fruits in autumn
IBERIS	Candytuft	O	C	★★	Annual and perennial types are grown as garden plants. Clusters of white, pink or red flowers. Dry at seed-head stage
ILEX	Holly	—	P1 then C	★★★	A great favourite at Christmas, of course, but good line material all year round. Choose variegated types for extra colour
IRIS	Iris	O	C	★	Many varieties, ranging from tiny rockery ones to the tall florist Irises available throughout the year. Popular line material
IXIA	Corn Lily	O	C	★★	Garden bulb or florist flower with six petalled stars on wiry stems. Centre is usually dark red or brown
JASMINUM	Jasmine	O	C	★★	There are summer-flowering ones, but it is the Winter Jasmine which is popular. Arching leafless stems and yellow flowers
KALANCHOE	Flaming Katy	O	C	★★	A house plant available as a florist flower. Each flower-head is made up of tubular blooms. Many colours available
KALMIA	Kalmia	O	P1 then C	★★	Large heads of pink bowl-shaped flowers above Rhododendron-like leaves. Takes several years to reach flowering stage
KERRIA	Jew's Mallow	O	P1 then C	★★	Single or double yellow flowers on arching stems. An invasive shrub, so regular cutting for arranging will not harm it
KNIPHOFIA	Red Hot Poker	O	P1 then C	★★	Familiar herbaceous perennial which adds brightness and height to summer displays. Red, yellow and orange/red

Hosta

Hydrangea

Ilex

Iris

Latin name	Common name	Cutting or Buying Stage	Conditioning method	Vase life	Notes
LABURNUM	Golden Rain	O	P1 then C	★	Long sprays of yellow Pea-like flowers. Sometimes recommended, but remember all parts are poisonous
LAGURUS	Hare's Tail Grass	O	C	★★★	One of the Ornamental Grasses for the arranger's garden. Grow as an annual for the cream-coloured flower-heads
LATHYRUS	Sweet Pea	O	C	★★	Lovely flowers on long stems — some but not all varieties are fragrant. Condition in shallow water and keep cool
LAURUS	Bay Laurel	—	P1 then C	★★★	Foliage material — the evergreen leaves are oval, glossy and wavy-edged. Often scorched by frost and cold winds
LAVANDULA	Lavender	O	P1 then C	★★★	Used for centuries as a fragrant fresh or dried cut flower. Grey leaves — pale purple, dark purple or white blooms
LAVATERA	Mallow	B or O	C	★★★	Annual or perennial garden plant — flower looks like a miniature Hibiscus. Annuals have brighter colours than perennials
LEPTOSPERMUM	New Zealand Tea Tree	O	P1 then C	★★	A florist flower and rather tender garden shrub. The branches bear masses of white, pink or red open flowers in summer
LEUCADENDRON	Silver Tree	O	P1 then C	★★★	Unusual line material — the stems bear silvery foliage and the cone-like flower-heads are yellow, pink or red
LEUCOSPERMUM	Pincushion	O	P1 then C	★★★	This Protea relative bears round flower clusters which have a spiny look — hence the common name
LIATRIS	Gayfeather	O	C	★★	Erect spikes densely clothed with pink or pale purple small fluffy flowers. Flowers open from the tip downwards
LIGUSTRUM	Privet	—	P1 then C	★★★	Readily available line material. For added colour choose a variegated or yellow-leaved variety. White flowers in summer
LILIUM	Lily	O	C	★★★	Very popular as line or dominant material. Beautiful shapes and beautiful colours. Remove anthers to avoid staining
LIMONIUM	Statice	O or R	C	★★★	Small flowers in a variety of colours — widely used both as fresh and dried material. Very easy to dry
LONICERA	Honeysuckle	O	C	★	Colourful, tubular flowers appear over a long period — fragrant but short-lived. Attractive foliage types are available
LUNARIA	Honesty	O	C	★	Sometimes used as fresh material, but much more often dried at the mature seed-head stage. Pods are disc-like
LUPINUS	Lupin	O	P4 then C	★★	Stately spires of Pea-like flowers in many colours. Fill hollow stem with water and plug with cotton wool before arranging

Lathyrus

Liatris

Lilium

Limonium

Latin name	Common name	Cutting or Buying Stage	Conditioning method	Vase life	Notes
LYSIMACHIA	Loosestrife	O	C	★★	Herbaceous perennial or florist flower with tiny yellow or white starry blooms above lance-shaped leaves
MAGNOLIA	Magnolia	B or O	P1 then C	★	Shrub or tree with beautiful flowers. Use either the starry blooms of M. stellata or the goblet-shaped flowers of M. soulangiana
MAHONIA	Mahonia	O	P1 then C	★★	A dual-purpose shrub grown for its attractive spiny leaves and heads of fragrant yellow flowers in winter or spring
MALUS	Apple	B or O	P1 then C	★★	Branches bearing Apple blossom are useful as line material in spring. For forcing, cut at the bud stage
MATTHIOLA	Stock	O	P1 then C	★★	Annual or biennial garden plant with small spikes of single or double flowers in white, pink, red, purple or yellow. Good fragrance
MOLUCCELLA	Bells of Ireland	O or R	P2 then C	★★★	Rather colourless in the garden but a joy for the flower arranger. Large green floral bells are borne on graceful stems
MONARDA	Bergamot	O	C	★★★	A border perennial for damp soil. The white, pink or red flower-heads are made up of whorls of blooms on upright stems
MUSCARI	Grape Hyacinth	O	P3 then C	★★	An excellent choice for Miniature arrangements — the bell-like blooms are clustered at the top of each flower spike
MYOSOTIS	Forget-me-not	O	C	★	A popular spring-flowering annual — blue, white or pink varieties are available. Easy to grow, but vase-life is short
NARCISSUS	Daffodil, Narcissus	B, O or R	P3 then C	★	Very popular cut flowers. Cutting time depends on type — large singles in bud, doubles when they are fully open
NELUMBO	Lotus	B	C	★	An exotic florist flower with large Water-lily blooms and decorative leaves. Cut seed-pods are sold as dried material
NEPETA	Catmint	O	C	★★	Sprays of tubular blue or violet flowers are borne above the grey-green leaves. Crushed foliage is aromatic
NERINE	Guernsey Lily	O	C	★★★	A cluster of pink spidery-petalled flowers is carried on top of each leafless stalk. Needs a sheltered spot in the garden
NICOTIANA	Tobacco Plant	O	C	★★	Annuals with tall stems and fragrant tubular flowers. Buy a variety which does not close during the day
NIGELLA	Love-in-a Mist	O	C	★★	Multi-petalled flowers half-hidden in finely cut foliage. Fresh and dried seed-pods more widely used than flowers
OENOTHERA	Evening Primrose	O	P1 then C	★★★	Good for cutting – the buds continue to open to give a long flowering period. Poppy-like blooms are large and yellow

Matthiola

Moluccella

Narcissus

Nigella

Latin name	Common name	Cutting or Buying Stage	Conditioning method	Vase life	Notes
ONCIDIUM	Dancing Lady Orchid	R	C	★★★	Small or tiny flowers are borne on long stems which may be erect or arching. Available in many colours
ORIGANUM	Marjoram	O	C	★★★	One from the herb garden rather than the flower border. White, pink or mauve flowers and fragrant small leaves
ORNITHOGALUM	Star of Bethlehem	O	P3 then C	★★	Also known as Chincherinchee. Starry white flowers are borne in sprays, ball-like heads or spikes
PAEONIA	Paeony	O	P1 then C	★★	Large bowls of petals — single, semi-double or double in a wide range of colours. Perennial or deciduous shrub
PAPAVER	Poppy	B or O	P2 then C	★	Cut these papery-bloom plants when the buds are showing colour. Main use of Poppies is as dried seed-heads
PAPHIOPEDILUM	Slipper Orchid	R	C	★★★	Waxy, beautiful Orchid borne singly on the stem. Best ones sold with cut ends in water tubes — do not remove
PELARGONIUM	Geranium	O	C	★	Cut from the garden when the first flowers are opening. Highly-coloured Zonal Geranium leaves are useful filler material
PENSTEMON	Penstemon	O	P1 then C	★	Attractive tubular flowers are clustered on erect stems — the leaves are glossy. Too short-lived for general use
PHALAENOPSIS	Moth Orchid	R	C	★★★	Numerous flat-faced Orchids are borne on each arching stem. Best ones sold with cut ends in water tubes
PHILADELPHUS	Mock Orange	O	P1 then C	★★	White or creamy-white flowers appear in great profusion on these popular garden shrubs in summer
PHLOMIS	Jerusalem Sage	O	P1 then C	★	An unusual plant — the stalkless hooded blooms are bright yellow, and are arranged in whorls along the woolly-leaved stems
PHLOX	Phlox	O	P1 then C	★★	The varieties of Phlox bear flat-faced blooms in rounded clusters or tall columns. Many different colours are available
PHORMIUM	New Zealand Flax	—	P5	★★★	A perennial grown for its sword-like leaves. This foliage may be self-coloured (green, bronze, purple etc) or striped
PHOTINIA	Photinia	—	P5	★★★	Hardy shrubs grown for their oval foliage which is bronze or coppery red when young. The best known is 'Red Robin'
PHYSALIS	Chinese Lantern	R	C	★★★	Flowers are insignificant — this plant is grown for its large lantern-like orange seed-pods
PHYSOCARPUS	Nine Bark	O	P1 then C	★★	An unusual shrub for the arranger's garden. The three-lobed leaves are golden, and the flower-heads are dome-shaped

Ornithogalum

Phalaenopsis

Phormium

Physalis

Latin name	Common name	Cutting or Buying Stage	Conditioning method	Vase life	Notes
PHYSOSTEGIA	Obedient Plant	O	C	★★	Tubular flowers on upright spikes. These blooms stay in position if moved — hence the common name
PIERIS	Pieris	O	P1 then C	★★	A dual-purpose shrub which has become popular. In spring there are bright red new leaves and sprays of white flowers
PITTOSPORUM	Pittosporum	—	P1 then C	★★★	This evergreen shrub provides good line material — the black twigs bear shiny leaves with wavy edges
PLATYCODON	Balloon Flower	B or O	P2 then C	★★	The buds swell into large, angular balloons before opening out to produce saucer-shaped flowers. Blue is the usual colour
POLIANTHES	Tuberose	O	C	★★★	Bulbous plant with grassy leaves and fragrant flowers. The white flowers are trumpet-shaped. Remove the top bud
POLYGONATUM	Solomon's Seal	O	C	★★★	Both the oval leaves and the green-tipped white blooms are decorative. These flowers are borne on arching stems
PRIMULA	Polyanthus, Primrose etc	O	C	★★	There are many types — see The Flower Expert for details. As a general rule they thrive best in partial shade
PROTEA	Protea	O	P1 then C	★★★	An exotic flower, renowned for its large size and extended vase-life. Usually bought as dried material
PRUNUS	Flowering Cherry	O	P1 then C	★★	White or pink blossom appears in spring. The branches may be twiggy or straight, the leaves green or purple
PULMONARIA	Lungwort	O	C	★★	An old favourite in the flower border — white-spotted leaves and pale purple flowers. Modern varieties are brighter
PYRACANTHA	Firethorn	—	P1 then C	★★★	A large bush or wall shrub which has small glossy leaves on its thorny branches and masses of red or orange berries in autumn
PYRETHRUM	Pyrethrum	O	C	★★	A popular plant in the arranger's garden. Large Daisy-like flowers are borne singly on long stalks above feathery foliage
PYRUS	Pear	B or O	P1 then C	★★	White blossom in spring. Most interesting foliage type is P. salicifolia pendula with silvery, Willow-like leaves
QUERCUS	Oak	—	P1 then C	★★★	Branches of the Common Oak may be used, but the florist forms have deeply-cut leaves and red or brown colouring
RANUNCULUS	Turban Buttercup	O	P2 then C	★★★	Brightly-coloured florist flowers which last for a long time in water. Available in a wide range of colours
RESEDA	Mignonette	O or R	C	★★	Tiny yellowish flowers are borne in cone-like trusses. This plant is used for its fragrance rather than the floral display

Platycodon

Primula

Protea

Pyrethrum

Latin name	Common name	Cutting or Buying Stage	Conditioning method	Vase life	Notes
RHEUM	Rhubarb	—	P5	★★	Young stalks of Rhubarb are sometimes used in arrangements. The curled red foliage is decorative, but also poisonous
RHODODENDRON	Azalea, Rhododendron	B or O	P1 then C	★★	Azaleas are cut for their flower-heads — Rhododendrons for their flowers and large glossy leaves
RIBES	Flowering Currant	B or O	P1 then C	★★	Popular shrub which bears drooping clusters of pink or red flowers in spring. Cut at the bud stage for forcing
ROSA	Rose	O	P1 then C	★★	The range of garden Roses is vast — the choice of florist Roses is more limited. Cut when buds are just opening
ROSMARINUS	Rosemary	O	P1 then C	★★	Useful line material — the long stems bear aromatic grey-green leaves and clusters of blue or white flowers
RUDBECKIA	Coneflower	O	P2 then C	★★★	One of the Daisy-like flowers found in the herbaceous border. It is late-flowering — the petals are red, yellow or brown
RUMOHRA	Leather Leaf	—	C	★★★	A strange latin name, yet the Leather Leaf fern is one of the basic foliage materials used by many florists
RUSCUS	Butcher's Broom	—	C	★★★	Another foliage plant which is popular with florists. The sharp-pointed leaves are really flattened stems. Red or yellow berries
RUTA	Rue	—	P1 then C	★★★	A recommended foliage plant for use as filler material. The ferny leaves are grey-green — a blue-green variety is available
SALIX	Willow	O	P1 then C	★★★	A large genus of trees and shrubs used by flower arrangers for the catkins borne by a number of varieties
SALPIGLOSSIS	Painted Tongue	O	C	★	The flowers of this bedding plant are eye-catching — each velvety, funnel-shaped bloom is prominently veined
SALVIA	Sage	O	C	★★	All the Salvias can be used as cut flowers — the red annuals, the biennial Clary and the blue perennial S. superba
SAMBUCUS	Elder	—	P5	★★★	The foliage of the Common Elder is too plain — choose instead one of the yellow-, purple- or ferny-leaved varieties
SANTOLINA	Lavender Cotton	—	P1 then C	★★★	A good choice if you want silvery plant material with narrow finely-divided leaves. Flowers have little display value
SAPONARIA	Soapwort	O	C	★★	A cottage-garden plant occasionally sold by florists. Erect stems bear lance-shaped leaves and pink or white flowers in sprays
SARCOCOCCA	Christmas Box	O	P1 then C	★★★	This evergreen shrub is of interest in late winter when the stems are clothed with white-petalled flowers. Strong fragrance

Rosa

Rosmarinus

Rumohra

Ruscus

Latin name	Common name	Cutting or Buying Stage	Conditioning method	Vase life	Notes
SARRACENIA	Pitcher Plant	R	C	★★	Search for or order this one for 'Jungle' arrangements — it is an insect-eater with water-filled 'pitchers'. Truly exotic
SCABIOSA	Scabious	O	P1 then C	★★	Flat-faced single or double flowers with ruffled petals. Colour is usually blue but white, lavender and red are available
SCHIZANTHUS	Poor Man's Orchid	O	P2 then C	★	This bedding plant bears miniature Orchid-like flowers above ferny leaves. Should be more widely grown and used
SCHIZOSTYLIS	Kaffir Lily	O	P2 then C	★★	Rising above the grassy foliage are the flowering spikes which look like miniature Gladioli — pink and red varieties available
SCILLA	Bluebell, Squill	O	P3 then C	★	Upright stems above strap-like leaves bear drooping flowers — bells or stars in blue, white, mauve or pink
SEDUM	Stonecrop	O	C	★★★	A succulent plant with fleshy leaves and flat heads of tiny flowers. Red and pink are the usual colours. Lasts well in water
SELAGINELLA	Creeping Moss	—	P5	★★★	The small ferny leaves of this Victorian favourite are useful in Miniature arrangements
SENECIO	Senecio	—	P1 then C	★★	Grow S. greyi for its densely-felted silvery foliage — the yellow Daisy-like flowers are a bonus. Other species are rather tender
SISYRINCHIUM	Pigroot	O	C	★★★	S. striatum is a hardy perennial. The leaves are grassy and cream trumpet-shaped flowers are borne in slender spikes
SKIMMIA	Skimmia	O	P1 then C	★★★	In spring there are clusters of tiny white flowers — in autumn the glossy red berries appear and last all winter
SOLIDAGO	Golden Rod	O	C	★★★	Feathery plume-like flower-heads stand above the narrow leaves. Colours range from cream to dark yellow
SOLIDASTER	Solidaster	O	C	★★★	This Solidago x Aster hybrid has tiny yellow Aster-like flowers grouped in plumes like Solidago flower-heads
SORBUS	Mountain Ash	O	P1 then C	★★	This tree has several uses — creamy flower clusters in spring, attractive foliage and bright berries in autumn
SPARAXIS	Harlequin Flower	O	C	★★	A rather tender bulbous plant which produces starry blooms on wiry stems. Wide range of petal colours
SPATHIPHYLLUM	Peace Lily	R	P1 then C	★★★	A house plant available as a florist flower. White Arum-like blooms above large lance-shaped leaves. Miniature varieties available
SPIRAEA	Spiraea	O	P1 then C	★★	A large and varied group of popular garden shrubs. White, pink or red flowers are borne in round clusters or long spikes

Schizanthus

Solidago

Solidaster

Spathiphyllum

Latin name	Common name	Cutting or Buying Stage	Conditioning method	Vase life	Notes
STACHYS	Lamb's Ears	—	C	★★★	This perennial is grown for its attractive evergreen silvery foliage. The pale purple flowers are of little significance
STACHYURUS	Stachyurus	O	P1 then C	★★	A welcome alternative to the ever-popular Witch Hazel and Winter Jasmine as a source of late winter flowers
STAPHYLEA	Bladder Nut	—	P1 then C	★★★	An interesting rarity. This shrub produces long bladder-like fruits in late summer and autumn. Not difficult to grow
STEPHANANDRA	Stephanandra	—	P1 then C	★★	The zig-zagging shoots of this shrub are recommended as foliage line material. The leaves are deeply lobed
STEPHANOTIS	Wax Flower	O	P2 then C	★	A house plant available as a florist flower. Heavily-scented white waxy blooms usually associated with bridal bouquets
STOKESIA	Stokes' Aster	O	P2 then C	★★	An unusual one for the arranger — blue or white Cornflower-like blooms appear from midsummer to late autumn
STRANVAESIA	Stranvaesia	—	P2 then C	★★	Branches are cut in autumn or winter for the bunches of bright red or yellow berries and red-tinged foliage
STRELITZIA	Bird of Paradise	O	C	★★	Large and dramatic flower in green, blue and orange — looking rather like the head of a crested bird. Difficult to preserve
SYMPHORICARPOS	Snowberry	—	P1 then C	★★★	Useful trailing material for winter displays. The long slender stems bear marble-like white, pink or purple berries
SYRINGA	Lilac	O	P1 then C	★	Masses of tiny flowers are borne in crowded conical spires in colours ranging from white to deepest purple
TAGETES	Marigold, Tagetes	O	C	★★★	African Marigold, French Marigold and Tagetes are very popular annuals which last well in water
TANACETUM	Tansy	O	P1 then C	★★★	The foliage is ferny and the flowers are tightly packed buttons which look like miniature Chrysanthemums
TELLIMA	Tellima	—	C	★★	An uncommon hardy ground cover used as foliage material. T. grandiflora has bronze- and purple-leaved varieties
TELOPEA	Waratah	O	P1 then C	★★	This large and exotic flower is sometimes used by floral decorators for showy displays. The globe-shaped bloom is red
THALICTRUM	Meadow Rue	O	C	★★	The stems are slender and the dainty leaflets are ferny. The foliage is used and so are the large heads of tiny flowers
THYMUS	Thyme	O	C	★★	A small-leaved herb with green or variegated foliage. Flowers range from white to red — used as filler material

Stephanotis

Strelitzia

Symphoricarpos

Syringa

Latin name	Common name	Cutting or Buying Stage	Conditioning method	Vase life	Notes
TIARELLA	Foam Flower	O	C	★★	A dainty ground cover. The tiny flowers are white and star-like, and the large lobed leaves turn bronze in winter
TILIA	Lime	O	P1 then C	★★	Stems of this tree are cut when the ball-like clusters of greenish-yellow flowers appear in midsummer
TILLANDSIA	Air Plant	—	—	★★★	The Air Plant most commonly used by arrangers is Spanish Moss. Grey strands used at the base of dried displays
TOLMIEA	Piggyback Plant	—	C	★★	A house plant which is fully hardy outdoors. Good trailing material — small plantlets appear at the base of mature leaves
TRACHELIUM	Throatwort	O	C	★★★	A florist flower bearing large heads of tiny blooms. The colours available are blue, white and pink. Leaves are oval
TRADESCANTIA	Spiderwort	O	C	★★	The herbaceous perennial and not the popular house plant. The silky flowers last for only a day, but buds continue to open
TRICYRTIS	Toad Lily	O	C	★★★	An excellent cut flower which is rarely seen. The bell-shaped blooms have dark spots and are borne above grassy leaves
TRITELEIA	Triteleia	O	C	★	This blue-flowering bulb is offered by some florists in spring and summer. The flower-head looks like a miniature Agapanthus
TRITICUM	Wheat	R	C	★★★	Not often used fresh, but widely used in the dry state. A good choice where stiff and straight line material is required
TROLLIUS	Globe Flower	O	P2 then C	★★	Globular flowers which look like giant Buttercups appear on top of erect stems. Colours range from cream to orange
TROPAEOLUM	Nasturtium	O	P2 then C	★★	Widely grown bedding plant which produces masses of yellow, orange or red flowers all summer long
TULIPA	Tulip	B or O	P3, P4 then C	★★	Very popular florist flower — cut or buy when buds are showing colour. Longer lasting in water than in floral foam
TYPHA	Reed Mace	R	C	★★	The well-known 'Bulrush' — harvest when the poker-like seed-heads have started to turn brown. Good material for a tall display
VALLOTA	Scarborough Lily	O	C	★	A house plant occasionally seen as a florist flower. The red or white bell-like flowers are borne above the sword-like foliage
VANDA	Lei Orchid	R	C	★★★	Each horizontal flower-stalk bears 5-10 flat-faced flowers which are waxy and fragrant. Many colours available
VENIDIUM	Monarch of the Veldt	O	C	★★★	A half-hardy annual which deserves to be better known. The Sunflower-like blooms have a large black disc

Tolmiea

Tropaeolum

Tulipa

Typha

Latin name	Common name	Cutting or Buying Stage	Conditioning method	Vase life	Notes
VERBASCUM	Mullein	O	P1 then C	★★★	The tall and stately Mullein provides good line material. The branched spires bear saucer-shaped flowers
VERBENA	Verbena	O	C	★★★	A bedding plant which should be more widely used. Small Primrose-like flowers are borne in clusters on top of the stems
VERONICA	Veronica	O	C	★★	A florist flower which is available all year round. The narrow pointed spikes bear blue (occasionally white) flowers
VIBURNUM	Viburnum	O	P1 then C	★★	A wide range of shrubs grown for their flowers and their berries. The winter or spring flower-heads are usually white
VINCA	Periwinkle	O	C	★★	Good trailing material from the garden — both green and variegated foliage varieties are available. Blue, mauve or white flowers
VIOLA	Viola, Pansy	O	C	★	Well-known bedding plants which have been used as cut flowers for generations. Enormous colour range
VITIS	Ornamental Vine	—	C	★★	This climber is grown for its lobed foliage which turns golden and then crimson in autumn. Good trailing foliage material
WATSONIA	Watsonia	O	C	★★	A florist flower rarity, occasionally seen in floral decorator arrangements. Flower-stalk bears small tubular flowers in two rows
WEIGELA	Weigela	O	P1 then C	★★	A popular deciduous garden shrub with green or variegated leaves. Clusters of white, pink or red flowers in late spring
WISTERIA	Wistaria	B or O	P1 then C	★	The twining stems are covered with hanging chains of Pea-like flowers. Colours are white, blue, mauve or purple
XERANTHEMUM	Common Immortelle	O or R	C	★★★	One of the 'everlasting' group of annuals. The petals of the Daisy-like flowers are strawy and crisp
XEROPHYLLUM	Bear Grass	—	C	★★★	This modest member of the Lily family is hardly ever mentioned in plant lists, but its grassy leaves are often used by florists
YUCCA	Yucca	—	P5	★★	Sword-like leaves sometimes used in Free-style and Abstract arrangements — be careful with the sharp edges and tips
ZANTEDESCHIA	Calla Lily	O	C	★★	Upturned trumpets on long stems — upright central column is yellow and the 'petal' colour is white, yellow or pink
ZEA	Maize, Sweet Corn	O	C	★★	Tall grassy plant with swollen seed-heads topped by tassels of silky threads. Ripe fruits (cobs) sometimes used in displays
ZINNIA	Zinnia	O or R	P2 then C	★★	The globular or Daisy-like flowers may be single, semi-double or double in white, yellow, orange, red, purple and green

Verbascum

Veronica

Xerophyllum

Zantedeschia

Chapter 7

FLOWER ARRANGING

If you buy a bunch of flowers and put them in a water-filled vase, you will have made a flower arrangement. It will have brought the beauty of living colour into the house. Of course some of the plant material may not have been properly prepared by you, the colours may not be right for the location and the display may quickly die, but it is an arrangement.

The purpose of this section is to show you how to do better. It will help you to choose the right plants, it will tell you how to prepare the plants before making an arrangement, and how to care for them to ensure that they stay fresh as long as possible. There are a few things to buy and various clear-cut techniques to learn — this is the craft side of flower arranging.

There is also the artistic side of flower arranging, and here there are no clear-cut rules. From the artistic viewpoint the arrangement has to please you and others by having a 'professional' look. It will have style, but which style? Many arrangers belong to the Natural school which believes that the flowers, stems, leaves etc should be grouped informally to give a 'straight-from-the-garden' look. No rule books for these arrangers.

The Formal school sees things differently — for them the arrangement should be a stylised affair — the Inverted Crescent, Symmetrical Triangle, the Hogarth Curve etc. Finally there is the Modern School, which seeks to create shapes that are neither as Nature intended nor is there any attempt to create a formal arrangement.

So what are you to do? Should you become a 'natural' flower arranger or follow the rules of the formal styles to create arrangements such as the Line-mass arrangement which is to be seen in hotel foyers everywhere?

The best plan is to get to know the basic design features such as colour, proportion, balance etc described on later pages, and then study the section on Styles. Begin with the Formal ones such as Mass, Line etc where there are guidelines to follow, and then try some Modern arrangements to see if that is the style which really appeals to you.

All this will let you satisfy the first purpose of making an arrangement — to satisfy your creativity by producing a 'professional' arrangement. But there may be a second purpose. To win a prize at the local show? To impress your friends? These are worthwhile aims, but in this book we shall dwell on the role of using a flower arrangement to improve the decor of the room instead of serving merely as an attractive ornament.

THE TEN STEP GUIDE TO FLOWER ARRANGING

STEP 1 : Read the BASICS OF GOOD DESIGN

STEP 2 : Collect the necessary EQUIPMENT

STEP 3 : Buy the required MECHANICS

STEP 4 : Collect suitable CONTAINERS

STEP 5 : Collect suitable BASES & ACCESSORIES

STEP 6 : Decide on the LOCATION

STEP 7 : Choose a STYLE

STEP 8 : Obtain the PLANT MATERIAL

STEP 9 : Make the ARRANGEMENT

STEP 10 : Care for the ARRANGEMENT

STEP 1 : Read the BASICS OF GOOD DESIGN

There will have been many times in the past when you have looked at a floral display and have known at once that it had been created by a skilled flower arranger. You may have been impressed by the size or the presence of exotic flowers, but the arrangement which arouses instant admiration has something more — it has **Harmony**.

Harmony is a design term used to describe a display in which the individual parts blend together to produce an attractive whole. To achieve this, most or all of the basic features of good design will be present — there will be a variety of **Texture**, the ingredients will be in **Proportion**, there will be a feeling of **Movement** and there will be the proper use of **Colour**. All these design features concern the beauty of the arrangement in its container, but in this book we must also include the **Background**, which takes on an extra dimension when one of the main purposes of the display is to improve the decor of the room and not merely serve as an ornament. In this section you will find information on all of these features of good design.

There is an additional design requirement. This is the need to use a **Style** which fits in with your skill, artistic temperament, location for the display, etc — see page 217-239 for information on the various Styles used in flower arranging.

That leaves one fundamental question which needs to be answered — must you slavishly follow all these rules about shape, colour, proportion and so on in order to be a good flower arranger? After all, most of these principles and elements are shared with other forms of artistic endeavour, yet Picasso and Rembrandt couldn't have followed the same rules!

In fact Picasso did learn the rules and styles of classical painting and he applied them at the start of his career — it was later that he evolved his own styles and techniques. Apply this principle as your approach to flower arranging — learn and practice the classical features of good floral design, and then depart from one or more if you are indeed a budding Picasso. But do this on the basis of knowing full well that you are departing from the traditional rules and principles which are well-known to you and not merely doing your own thing out of ignorance.

Colour

Colour is one of the first things you notice when looking at an arrangement, and so some understanding of colour is useful. This does not mean that you have to learn and then slavishly follow a lot of rules. Some of the so-called rules are suspect and far too much has been written about what goes with what and how to avoid colour clashes — "never put pink next to dark crimson" and so on. Colour is a matter of personal taste.

The basis of Colour Theory is the Colour Wheel which is shown on page 93 — you will see that it is made up of numerous pure hues from which shades and tints are derived. There are basically three ways of putting these colours together so that the viewer will feel that they 'go together'. The boldest way is to use contrasting colours which face each other across the wheel, the most restful way is to use analogous colours which are situated next to each other, and the most subtle way is to use the tints and shades of a single hue.

If you are arranging flowers for home display rather than for the flower show then you can ignore the colour wheel and its associated schemes if you like. In this case you should try to get a clear understanding of the properties of warm and cool colours (see page 93) and to ensure that the colours chosen are right for the room, the lighting, the season, the container and the design needs of the arrangement.

Choosing a Colour Scheme

WHAT IS THE ROOM LIKE? Look at the colour of the walls, furnishings etc — try to pick up one of the important ones in the plant material you choose. The background is important — see page 187. A dark-coloured display will stand out well against a pale wall but will be dimmed by a dark oak panel or maroon curtains. On the other hand a pale or warm-coloured arrangement is enhanced by a dark background.

HOW IS THE ROOM LIT? Beware the dark corner. Blue or violet flowers may glisten in sunlight, but in a dimly-lit site may disappear from view. At night the colours are affected by the source of artificial lighting. Ordinary light bulbs may dull cool colours and brighten warm ones, whereas fluorescent tubes brighten the cool colours and dull down the warm colours. The effect of candlelight is to darken cool colours and give a yellowish look to warm ones.

WHAT IS THE SEASON OF THE YEAR? In Japan the season is all-important — in the Western world it is just an optional consideration. Spring is a time for yellows and blues, summer for a polychromatic medley (page 185), autumn calls for browns with oranges and yellows, and Christmas is the time for white and bright red.

WHAT CONTAINER WILL BE USED? A common mistake is to have a container which is colourful enough to detract from the arrangement. If you do plan to use a bright or strongly-patterned vase or bowl then it should link up with the colour in the arrangement, or else the container will become an over-prominent focal point. White can be important here — always use some white flowers in an arrangement made in a colourful container.

HOW CAN THE COLOURS ENHANCE THE ARRANGEMENT? Do not use equal amounts of different colours in your scheme — let one dominate and be enriched by the others. Do not spread the various colours evenly over the display or you will end up with a 'spotted dog' effect — group some of the colours together. Be careful with hues — they tend to be dominant. The classic recommendation is to use hues in small amounts and to rely mainly on tints and shades. Tints are easier than shades to fit in to most schemes as they combine well with each other.

Colour Schemes

MONOCHROMATIC

In a monochromatic scheme the various tints and shades of a single hue are used.

This is the easiest way to ensure that you will capture the mood you are trying to create — choose red for a dramatic effect, yellow for brightness, blue for a restful effect and so on. Do use a wide range of the basic colour if you can, varying from pale tints to the darkest shades. Stems and/or leaves are available in tints and shades of green, brown or white, so a 'true' monochromatic scheme is only available in these colours. The limited variation of colour means that the physical form of the display is more noticeable — aim for an assortment of shapes, sizes, textures etc.

ANALOGOUS

In an analogous scheme the two, three or four hues are all neighbours on the wheel.

Such an arrangement has some of the subdued charm of the monochromatic scheme but there is a much larger range of plants from which to make your choice. There is no need to keep to the hues — tints and shades are very important here and will add to the interest of the display. An analogous scheme can be muted and restrained by working with just blues and mauves or it can be exciting with reds and purples. Do not use each colour in equal amounts — let one dominate. In the illustrated example the yellow hues and shades are dominated by the oranges and browns.

CONTRASTING

In a contrasting scheme the chosen colours are directly across from each other on the wheel.

With a modern Line arrangement the aim is often to create maximum impact with flower colour and so hues are used — blue Iris with orange Gerbera, yellow Rose with violet Lisianthus and so on. Contrasting schemes are always lively but they need not be over-bright. The secret is to use tints of the colours involved to produce a pastel arrangement — pink with powder blues, buffs alongside lilac-coloured blooms etc. In this way a contrasting scheme can be as subdued as an analogous one. Another approach is to use the tint of one colour and a shade of the contrasting one.

POLYCHROMATIC

In a polychromatic scheme colours from all or scattered parts of the wheel are used.

In summertime flowers are sometimes collected from all over the garden and then arranged to give a display which is a multicoloured mixture spanning the spectrum. Reds and violets, yellows and blues, oranges and purples — the result can be pleasing but all too often it is not. First of all, the effect may be just too bright, and it is usually wise to look for tints of the various hues. Next, the effect may be too spotty — avoid using all the colours in equal amounts. Let just a few colours dominate the display and use the others as restrained filler material.

Balance

Physical balance is vital — if the arrangement is markedly asymmetrical it may tip over. The mechanics must always be securely fixed and the container should always be heavy enough to support the plant material. Add sand, gravel etc if necessary. Visual balance is not the same thing — this calls for the arrangement to look stable even if it is clearly one-sided. There are various ways to increase the visual weight of the lighter side — dark flowers look heavier than pale ones, and round flowers look heavier than trumpet-shaped ones. There is also top-to-bottom balance. Large flowers placed centrally and close to the bottom of the arrangement give a feeling of good balance — incorrect placement can make the display look unbalanced, as shown below.

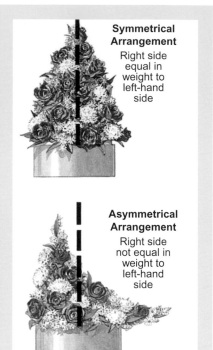

Symmetrical Arrangement
Right side equal in weight to left-hand side

Asymmetrical Arrangement
Right side not equal in weight to left-hand side

Top heavy

Bottom heavy

Movement

Movement involves using techniques and materials which move the eye from one part of the display to another — this movement is due to rhythm being present in the design. Without rhythm (for example, a bunch of Roses in full flower stuck in a vase) the arrangement looks static and monotonous. There are various ways of producing movement and five of them are illustrated on this page.

With many facing Line-mass displays and with most Free-style arrangements another design principle is incorporated — dominance. This involves having one or more areas to which the eye is drawn and rests there for a short time — this area is known as a focal point. The usual method is to include a small group of bold flowers — described in this book as dominant material. There are other ways of creating focal points — an unusual container, striking foliage and so on. The golden rule is that you must never overdo it — no item should be so dominant as to detract the eye for a long time from the rest of the display.

Hide all or part of tall, straight stems

Have an irregular line of various-sized blooms

Use foliage of various sizes and contrasting shapes

Have flowers at various stages of development

Place flowers 'in' and 'out' in the arrangement

PROPORTION

A flower arrangement is made up of several elements which may be visible — container, plant material and possibly a base and accessories. Good proportion means the size of elements should be in scale so as to give a pleasing effect. As stated on page 237 it is with the Landscape, Petite and Miniature arrangements that poor proportion is most likely to be seen, with over-sized flowers and accessories as the main culprits. But out-of-scale arrangements can occur with any style, and the most common fault is to have a container which is the wrong size for the plant material. For centuries the Golden Ratio illustrated on the right has been used as the yard-stick for perfect proportion. It will certainly satisfy the show judges and look 'right' in the home, but it is often ignored.

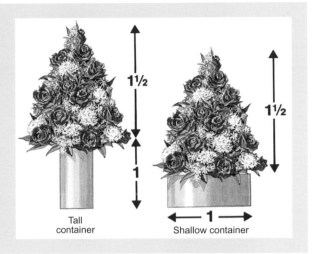

$1\frac{1}{2}$

1

$1\frac{1}{2}$

1

Tall container

Shallow container

BACKGROUND

The arrangement may be perfectly in proportion but it can be quite wrong for the background or setting in which it has been placed. To avoid a problem there are several aspects to consider. First of all there is the style of the room — obviously an Abstract arrangement would look out of place in a chintzy cottage setting. The size of the room is equally important — a Petite arrangement in a large and lofty hall can look pathetic. The type of wall surface is important — see the illustrations. There are also practical problems to avoid — dining table arrangements which obstruct conversation and hall arrangements which obstruct free passage are examples.

TEXTURE

Plant material comes in all sorts of textures — glossy, velvety, downy, dull, prickly etc. A glossy flower appears brighter when placed next to matt foliage, and shiny leaves will make the arrangement sparkle in strong lighting. The role of a variety of textures is to increase the attractiveness of the arrangement by avoiding monotony. It is most important when there is little variation in the colour of the flowers, and when only a small amount of plant material is used in a Free-style arrangement.

STEP 2 : Collect the necessary EQUIPMENT

It is important if you are a beginner not to get the wrong impression from the large array of tools and other equipment illustrated and described on these two pages. Only a few (bucket, scissors, knife and watering can) are essential items for the beginner — the rest are optional extras. Do keep the sharp things such as scissors and knives well away from children and try to store all the items together in a box. When arranging flowers place a large plastic sheet over the work surface.

Bucket MUST HAVE ITEM

A water-filled bucket is a vital piece of equipment for collecting flowers from the garden and for conditioning the blooms before making an arrangement. Choose the type with side handles as the standard free-swinging handle can damage flowers during transport. Do not use the kitchen pail — keep a bucket just for flower arranging.

Cut flower preservative

Several brands are available in powder or liquid form. A cut flower preservative is basically a bacteriocide to prevent slime and smells from developing in the vase-water, plus sugar to prolong the life of fresh flowers. It is worthwhile to use one of these products at the conditioning stage.

Knife MUST HAVE ITEM

Buy a craft knife with a sharp blade — it will have all sorts of uses. You will need it for scraping stems, removing leaves and stripping away thorns. It is also employed for preparing stem ends by making a sloping cut and occasionally a vertical slit. There is also floral foam to cut and excess clay to remove.

Watering can MUST HAVE ITEM

Vital, of course, for topping up the water supply in the container or floral foam holding a fresh flower arrangement. Buy a plastic one and look for two important features — the spout should be long and narrow, and it should arise from the base of the can.

Secateurs

Never try to cut through thick and woody stems with ordinary scissors — use instead a pair of secateurs. You can buy the ordinary garden type, but there are narrow ones made specially for the flower arranger.

Mister

A hand sprayer capable of producing a fine mist of water droplets is an aid to keeping an arrangement looking fresh in warm weather. Apply the mist slightly above the top of the display — do this once the arrangement is finished and repeat daily if you can.

Cocktail sticks

(Other name : Toothpicks)

Not in all the textbooks, but a handy multi-purpose aid. Use a cocktail stick to create a hole in floral foam for a soft stem or use one to attach a fruit to the foam holding a flower display. Several sticks are sometimes taped around the base of a candle to secure it in a table arrangement.

Floral scissors

MUST HAVE ITEM

Most ordinary scissors are not suitable for cutting stems — they tend to crush the tissues. Choose a floral pair — the blades are short and one is serrated. At the base there may be a notch — use this for cutting thin wire, but not for woody stems.

Wire

Use wire to bind clumps of cut flowers together. There are basically three types of wire. The strongest is **Stub wire**, **Rose wire** is thinner, and **Reel wire** is the finest and is wound on a bobbin — it is extensively used by florists for binding plant material.

Paints & Finishes

Aerosol paints can be used at any time of the year but it is at Christmas that they really come into their own — arrangements with gold or silver pine-cones, berries, leaves and flowers can be seen everywhere. Paints are widely used, of course, on containers, mechanics, bases etc as well as on plant material.

STEP 3 : Buy the required MECHANICS

Placing flowers in a vase or jug of water is an age-old way of creating a floral display, but for nearly all modern-day arrangements it is necessary to use materials which keep the foliage and flowers in place within the container. These materials and their associated aids are known as mechanics. They must be fixed securely and should be hidden from view. Only a few (floral foam, adhesive clay, chicken wire and frogs) are essential items — the rest are optional extras.

Floral foam `MUST HAVE ITEM`
(Other name : 'Oasis')

Usually referred to by its most popular brand name, this cellular plastic material was invented in the 1940s and has become the leading mechanic for the home flower arrangement. There are two types — green foam which is soaked in water and then used for fresh plant material, and brown or grey foam which is used only for dry and artificial displays. The green foam can be bought in various shapes — 'blocks' and 'rounds' are the most popular. It is extremely light, but the weight increases by over 30 times when saturated. This green foam should never be allowed to dry out once it has been soaked — if you wrap it in foil or plastic film after use it should be suitable for several more arrangements. The great advantage of foam is that stems can be held at any angle in both shallow and deep containers, and the problem of smelly water is removed. Just a few draw-backs — extra support with chicken wire is necessary for a large display and a few plants (e.g Daffodils and Tulips) find water uptake difficult. See page 246 for details on how to use floral foam.

Adhesive tape
(Other name : 'Oasis Tape')

This strong sticky tape is available in both wide and narrow forms. The wide tape is mainly used to secure floral foam or crumpled chicken wire to the container. Narrow tape is occasionally stretched across the top of a shallow wide-mouthed container in criss-cross fashion to form a plant holding grid.

Frog `MUST HAVE ITEM`

This is the simplest type of foam anchor. It is a small plastic disc with 4 vertical prongs — the base is attached to the container with adhesive clay and the block or round of floral foam is pressed down on to the prongs. More than one may be required if a large block of floral foam is used.

Adhesive clay MUST HAVE ITEM
(Other name : 'Oasis Fix')

A non-setting sticky clay in strip form which holds dry surfaces together. It is widely used for securing a frog, pinholder or candle cup (see page 193) to the container — brown and green types are available. **Plasticine** can be used as a substitute.

Florist cone
(Other names : Flower tube, Flower funnel)

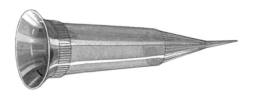

This miniature vase is used in large arrangements where foliage or flowers need to be placed above their stem height. The usual type of cone is about 1 ft (30 cm) long and the pointed end is generally tied to a cane which is then pushed into the floral foam or chicken wire. Fill the cone with water before inserting the stems.

Marbles

Small pebbles, round marbles and flattened glass nuggets have long been used to hold the stems of cut flowers. When inserting the stems there will be some slight movement of the arrangement.

Pinholder
(Other name : Kenzan)

A series of sharply-pointed pins are firmly held in a solid base which may be circular or rectangular. Its main advantage is that it will hold thick and heavy stems securely — the pinholder may be used on its own in a shallow dish or with other mechanics for a large display in a deep container. Choose a model with a heavy base and a large number of sharp brass pins. The drawback with this mechanic is that it is expensive — if you can have only one then choose the 3 in. (8 cm) round size. Stick it to the base of the container with adhesive clay. With the **Well Pinholder** there is no need for a container as the metal dish holds water.

Chicken wire MUST HAVE ITEM
(Other names: Wire mesh, Wire netting)

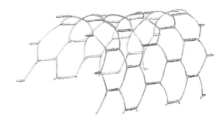

The grade to buy is fine gauge 2 in. (5 cm) mesh. Cut off the firm edge, roll into a tube, crumple into a ball and fit into the container — see page 248 for details. Chicken wire is the preferred mechanic for an arrangement with a large number of tall or heavy stems. The 1 in. (3 cm) mesh grade is often used to cover a floral foam block if a large display is planned. Some (but not all) experts prefer galvanised wire to the plastic-coated variety — be careful not to scratch the sides of a valuable container. Wash and dry after use — it can be used again and again.

STEP 4 : Collect suitable CONTAINERS

The range of containers is vast. They come in all sorts of shapes, sizes and materials — glass, pottery, metal, wood, plastic, cane, terracotta and so on. The container, plants and the surroundings must all be right for each other — a rustic-style container in a chintzy room, a muted coloured vase against a pastel background, a tall cylinder for a stylised modern arrangement, and so on. You will need a large selection — charity shops, bring-and-buy sales etc are excellent sources.

Vase & Jug

There is no precise definition of a vase, but it is generally taken to mean a container which is at least as tall as it is wide, and is often quite narrow with a restricted mouth. It remains the favourite container for cut flowers and the choice is immense. The glass vase continues to be popular, although underwater stems can look unattractive. A **Bud vase** is a tall and thin vase which holds a single specimen of Rose, Tulip or Orchid. Metal vases were once popular, but the Victorian **Silver trumpet vase** is out of favour.

The vase should be in keeping with the type of display and the furnishings of the room in which it is to stand. Tall spikes of flowers generally call for a vase with near-vertical sides, and very bright surfaces or showy patterns are rarely successful. **Jugs** are lipped containers with a single handle which are useful for arrangements in a period room.

Wall hanger

The **Pew end** or **Hanging frame** is a handled wire or plastic frame in which a block of moist or dry foam is inserted and then used for making a fresh or dried arrangement.

Wreath

Wreaths bedecked with flowers, berries and foliage are favourite features for the Christmas table. A moss-filled frame is sometimes used, but a floral foam ring is the more usual choice these days.

Floral foam container

A plastic container which has internal projections designed to hold a block or round of floral foam. This type of container is cheap but it is purely functional. This means that it should be either hidden by plant material or be placed in an attractive outer container.

Basket

For fresh flower arrangements it will be necessary to have a waterproof container within — this can be either a plastic bowl or a sheet of polythene stapled to the inner rim.

Miscellaneous objects

The list of suitable household items is almost endless — jelly moulds, wine glasses, decanters, kettles, saucepans, old aerosol tops, coffee pots etc. Other objects which can serve as containers include shells and driftwood. Hollowed-out vegetable marrow and melon are eye-catching, but the gas emitted shortens the life of cut flowers.

Candle cup

The candle cup is a shallow dish of plastic or metal which holds a block or round of floral foam, and which has a short stem at the base. Fix this stem into a candlestick or bottle with adhesive clay and tape the piece of foam in place.

Rose bowl

Once a favourite container for table decoration but no longer popular. The low cylindrical base of pottery or glass holds water, and the plant-holding lid consists of either a criss-cross of thick silvered wires or a series of round holes for the stems.

Bowl & Tray

These are the shallow group of containers. The **Cup** and **Dish** are shallower than the **Fish bowl** type, and are widely used for table arrangements. A **Tazza** is a cup borne on a relatively tall and narrow stem — an **Urn** is a more robust cup in pottery, stone or plastic borne on a short and stout stem and often with handles and a square base. Even more shallow is the **Tray** — a flat container with raised sides used for Line arrangements.

STEP 5 : Collect suitable BASES & ACCESSORIES

A base is an object placed between the container and the support on which it stands. It is an optional extra, used to protect the polished surface from water splashes and condensation. A base can be employed to improve both the visual appeal and sense of balance. It is, however, a common mistake to overdo it and have a base which is so large and/or bright that the eye is diverted away from the floral display.

An accessory is an item of non-plant material which is included with or alongside the arrangement. Its purpose is generally purely decorative although candles which are lit serve a practical function. Some flower arrangers never use accessories except at Christmas, when bells, ribbons, candles etc are key features of table arrangements. Accessories can add interest, but restraint is essential. Fruit, moss and driftwood are sometimes added to an arrangement, but these are items of plant material and not true accessories.

Wood base

Rectangles or rounds made out of plywood, blockboard, chipboard or fibreboard can all be used, but the most popular by far is the cork base.

Oriental base

This base will heighten the 'oriental' appearance of a decorated Chinese vase with an exotic arrangement.

Stone base

Pieces of marble, slate, alabaster, limestone etc make excellent decorative bases in the right setting. Stone gives a feeling of solidity, and a section which has a hollow designed to hold a small container is especially useful.

Covered base

Plain rounds of wood are sometimes covered with felt or stretch nylon to make them more suitable as bases. The cloth is either cut and glued on to the board or tailored as an elasticated slipcover in which the board is placed.

Table mat

A straw, bamboo or plastic-faced table mat is the most popular base for an arrangement which is to be displayed in the home. Be careful which one you choose if it will be visible — avoid shiny and highly decorated surfaces. In most cases the table mat is not meant to add to the decorative effect, so use the smallest practical size.

Tree section

The crosscut of a tree trunk with or without bark makes an excellent decorative base for some but not all arrangements. An oval section is a favourite for holding containers with Landscape exhibits or Line arrangements (see page 237) — the container is usually set at one side rather than in the middle of the base. The tree section can be left untreated or stained with a wood dye, and is often coated with furniture wax or varnish.

Candle

Candles are an important accessory for the dining table arrangement. When unlit, climbers such as Ivy can be wound around each candle and flowers can clothe the base. When lit they provide a fire hazard if you are careless. Make sure that each candle is firmly fixed in the arrangement. One way is to tape four cocktail sticks to the base and then push the points firmly into the foam — make sure that there is no plant material touching the wax surface.

Figurine

You will either love or hate the idea of figures in wood, metal, pottery, glass etc as part of your flower arrangement. For some the presence of such an accessory provides extra interest and a way to underline the theme of the display — biblical figures next to a Christmas arrangement, a Chinese fisherman alongside an Ikebana display etc. For others such distractions are regarded as unnecessary or downright bad taste.

Ribbon

Bows and trailing ribbons usually belong to the world of floristry rather than the realm of the flower arranger, but there are times when this accessory can add to the appeal of a display. A few hints — buy polypropylene ribbon from a florist rather than satin ribbon from the haberdashery department of a store. Next, always trim the ends with a sloping cut — curl these ends by drawing them firmly and quickly over the back of a knife. As with other accessories you must be careful not to overdo ribbon decoration. It is generally a welcome addition to Christmas decorations and some church displays, but it is usually out of place with ordinary living room arrangements.

STEP 6 : Decide on the LOCATION

We enjoy the plants and flowers in the garden, parks and countryside and we want them in our home. There are two basic ways to do so — you can have pots of indoor plants or displays of cut flowers. This is not an either/or situation — most of us choose to have both at various times and ways in one or more rooms in the place where we live.

You have decided to make a flower arrangement. The bunch of flowers you have bought may have up to now been simply put in a vase to add a splash of living colour in the living room or kitchen. There is nothing wrong with that. But now you want to make an arrangement which will be attractive enough to serve as a focal point in the area around it.

So far you have been guided through a number of preliminary steps with information on things you need to know before you get started. In the next section there are the exciting parts — the various styles of floral displays, and the way to choose and prepare the plant material for arranging.

Before that stage we must look at an all-important step — the decision where the arrangement is to go. There are six areas where you may find a display of cut flowers in the home, and the role of an arrangement in these sites is described in detail on the following pages. The importance of the role they play varies widely. It would be unusual to find a living room which did not have flowers on show for at least part of the year — it would be equally unusual to find a bathroom with a floral display. The role of the arrangement also varies widely from one room to another. In the hall or living room it may have to be eye-catching enough to serve as a centre of attention for the visitor. In the kitchen or bedroom its job may be to provide a touch of living colour for the family or just for you.

A few guidelines. Firstly, an arrangement is most satisfying when the container, plant material and style are all in keeping with the character and decor of the room. Masses of cottage garden flowers in jugs or earthenware bowls will add colour and charm to a chintzy living room, but the stark and simple lines of a modern living room call for a much more contemporary arrangement such as Line or Informal Line-mass which you will read about later. Next, from the design point of view it is better to have one major display and then one or more subsidiary linked ones than to have a number of similar-sized displays. Finally, don't overdo it. Your home is not a florist shop — flower displays all over the place will diminish the impact of a really good arrangement.

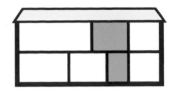

The Hall/Landing

The entrance hall is an excellent site for a flower arrangement. It is here that the visitors gain their first impression of your home, and there are few things which can match the ability of a collection of flowers to transform the hall from a dark and uninviting place into a lively and welcoming one. You can use flowering pot plants or a floral arrangement for this display, and do think about the conditions before making your choice. Poor light and cold nights severely limit the house plants you can use, but they are not a problem for a flower arrangement.

Nobody stands for long in the hall, so the display should be eye-catching enough to make an immediate impression. Unfortunately most halls are long, cramped and narrow, which means that you probably cannot create this eye-catching effect with grandeur. You must rely instead on bold colour or a distinctive shape to make a wall, windowsill or side table display interesting. A couple of precautions. Firstly, make sure that the container is heavy or low enough and the plant material restricted enough to prevent the display from being knocked over by running children or clumsy visitors. Secondly, remember that a large display in a small hall will make it look smaller.

Of course these restrictions do not apply if you have a spacious hall. Here is the place for the pedestal or polished table bearing a really expansive and colourful display to welcome the visitor. The landing needs a different approach. It is generally a place for a dried or artificial arrangement rather than fresh flowers.

HALL
PICTURE GALLERY

Everything in this hall, apart from a small group of polished stones, fits in with the white, black, cream and brown colour scheme. An all-white arrangement has been chosen to be part of this scheme.

▽

△
Here the arranger wanted something different. The flowers set out to make a statement. A multicoloured collection of spring flowers to serve as a contrast to the plain background.

The arranger set out to add colour to a hall with pale walls and staircase. The choice of a few large pink and mauve pom-pom type flower-heads in a tall and narrow vase is quite dramatic. ▷

◁ *The task here was to provide a colourful display against a dark background. Carnations, Chrysanthemums, Freesias and Pinks have been used to provide a kaleidoscope of colour, shapes and textures*

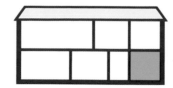

The Kitchen

The kitchen is second only to the living room as the most popular place for indoor plants — more than half have at least one on the windowsill or by a work surface. Most of these pot-grown specimens appreciate the moist air, and water for keeping the compost damp is readily to hand. Flower arrangements are much less of a feature in the kitchen — there is often not the space for the type of display we create for the living room. The kitchen is often regarded as a work area, and however irrational it may be we want a living area for the display we have created, and so the first choice is the living or dining room. In the same way we hang our pictures in these rooms rather than the kitchen.

However, much of the day is often spent in the kitchen, and flowers help to bring the garden indoors. The house plant display is so often one of green leaves rather than bright blooms, and so one should consider the kitchen for a flower arrangement even if space is limited. This is the place for a compact and casual seasonal arrangement — Daffodils in spring, Roses in summer and berries plus coloured leaves in autumn. Nothing too grand — a tied bunch in a vase (page 245) is excellent. The experts advise that the container should be in keeping with the food/kitchen image — an enamel pot, old kettle, earthenware jug etc. This is right for the traditional kitchen but a little out of place in a modern stainless-steel one.

KITCHEN
PICTURE GALLERY

The standard kitchen display — a bunch of flowers from the garden stuck in a vase. It may add nothing to the decor, but it is a reminder of our work outdoors. ▷

◁ *A different approach here. The purely linear flower-heads of Liatris have been chosen to complement the straight line decor of a modern kitchen.*

Brightly-coloured arrangements are usually found in the living room and hall rather than the kitchen, but the householder here has put together an eye-catching red, white and green display to liven up the work surface. ▷

◁ *A vase of Daffodils can be seen in millions of kitchens in the spring — a reminder that the gardening season has begun. Note how the use of foliage has turned a simple bunch into a design feature.*

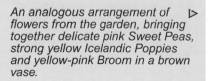

An analogous arrangement of flowers from the garden, bringing together delicate pink Sweet Peas, strong yellow Icelandic Poppies and yellow-pink Broom in a brown vase. ▷

Red Gerberas, green ears of Barley and green leaves in a glass vase. An unusual collection — even more unusual is the use of a red food dye to colour the water. ▷

◁ *In contrast to the colourful display above, this all-white arrangement in silver plated jugs provides a restful point of interest. The plants are a collection of daisy-like plants in a wide range of sizes — Dahlias, China Asters, Asters and Masterworts.*

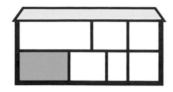

The Living Room

It is not surprising that the living room is chosen as the prime site for the showiest flower displays. Making an arrangement is extremely satisfying, but it is equally important to enjoy the display once it has been created. This means putting it in a place where we can relax and look at our handiwork, and the living room is the one spot in the home where we do have time to sit and look around. It is also the room where the family gathers and friends sit with their coffee cups, and so displays here get more than a casual glance. This means that it has to be a place for our best work — mechanics must be completely hidden and later on arrangements must be broken up before the flowers droop.

The living room consists of a number of recommended plant stations which can be used to house floral displays. The open fireplace between spring and autumn is a key focal point. Windows are also important — a windowsill arrangement links the garden with the room, but unfortunately a sunny window is not a plant-friendly spot. A bare corner is an excellent site for a floor standing or table-borne display. At the other end of the scale are the side table displays — here the object is to create attractive arrangements which are compact enough not to get in the way. A final word of caution — don't try to fill every potential plant station with floral arrangements. House plants will undoubtedly be a good choice for one or more places in this room and will provide a permanent and living green backcloth to complement your colourful floral creations. These temporary focal points can be either flower arrangements or pot plants which reflect the season.

LIVING ROOM
PICTURE GALLERY

Nothing more than a piece of drift-wood, a few Moth Orchids and a touch of Polypodium Fern. Muted perhaps, but the effect is still eye-catching. ▷

◁ *In contrast to the arrangement above, this one is imposing. The key point here is the way the Gladioli and container blend in with the colour of the chairs, cushions and candles. An object lesson in looking at the location before deciding what to buy.*

GROUPING

Here the tall Symmetrical triangle arrangement brings together the two blue and white vases and the carved console table. ▷

◁ The paired formal arrangements in decorative vases bring together the portrait and the fireplace, thereby creating a single design unit.

PICTURE FRAMING

The garland arrangement in a Neo-classical vase groups together the portrait and the other antiques into a harmonious whole — an excellent example of using cut flowers to create an eye-catching feature. ▷

◁ *A fine oil painting with an unusual arrangement of flowers, vegetables and fruit in front of it. Both are admirable, but which one is the focal point?*

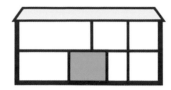

The Dining Room

The dining room is an area which is often chosen for displaying a flower arrangement. The central feature, the dining table, is not in use for much of the day or for days on end, and looks quite bare without some form of central decoration. There is a wide choice — a pair of candlesticks, a bowl of fruit and so forth, but the favourite choice in countless homes is a floral display. Height and width of the display are usually governed by the size of the room and table — a small Biedermeier arrangement in the modest room or a silver-housed lavish arrangement in the grand home. There is an additional fact to consider when deciding on the size of a dining table arrangement — you will have to keep it fairly compact and light if it is to be removed from the table when a meal is served.

Flowers on the table reduce the bare look associated with many dining rooms, and so does a display on the sideboard. There should be some plant material link between the two but they should not be identical, as their location is quite different. The table display will usually be seen from every angle and here an all-round arrangement (see page 217) is necessary, whereas a facing arrangement is chosen for space-saving reasons for the sideboard. If the table is small enough to allow conversation across its width then the arrangement must be low enough to allow the talkers to see each other — 1 ft (30 cm) is the recommended maximum height. Make sure that the displays are pest-free.

The remarks so far have concerned the dining room when used for the family. It is, however, a place which is widely used for entertaining (and impressing) friends, and when so employed it offers scope for more eye-catching arrangements.

DINING ROOM PICTURE GALLERY

An attractive table display — multi-containered but monochromatic. An interesting feature is that it is the candles and not the flowers which are dominant. ▷

◁ *Something very different to the table displays in this picture gallery. The modern lines of the room called for a Free-style design. Monstera leaves are the dominant feature, but the most interesting point is the use of the stems in the vase as a key element of the design.*

CENTREPIECES

◁ A Biedermeier arrangement of yellow and golden flowers. Very simple, of course, but such displays bring a bright splash of colour to the centre of the table.

Just a few Anemone flowers floating in a bowl of water — surely one of the simplest of all flower arrangements. However, using spectacular flowers such as Orchids or Anthurium in this way will attract the attention of your guests. ▷

◁ A formal arrangement of yellow and pink/orange Roses on a table set for lunch. The container has been wrapped in yellow fabric to tone with the soft furnishings in the room.

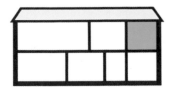

The Bathroom

A display of cut flowers in the bathroom is much more likely to be seen in a magazine than in the home — its lack of popular appeal as a place for floral arrangements is due to two basic features which are shared with the kitchen. The bathroom is generally considered as a utility area so that much thought goes into the functional furnishing (bath, vanity unit, mirrors etc) but much less into purely decorative items. Furthermore the moist atmosphere makes it a poor home for many dried flowers — large blooms with papery petals tend to rot under such conditions.

Despite all this, few others areas in the home need the colours and variety of shapes of a flower arrangement more than the typical bathroom — often a somewhat colourless place dominated by geometric shapes and hard surfaces. Although a couple of features are shared with the kitchen, as stated above, the approach to the display should be different. The casual arrangement belongs in the kitchen — here you can be more dramatic. The bathroom is a place where you can afford to be experimental and have displays which might not appeal to everyone — Abstract, Free-style and the rest. Interior decorators recommend eye-catching containers — silvery metal or shining glass.

As always fresh flower arrangements are best, with an artificial flower display if you want permanence. Dried flowers can be used, but you should choose the ones which do not mind moisture in the air as long as there are periods of dryness in between. The best known examples are Statice, Lavender and Helichrysum.

BATHROOM PICTURE GALLERY

△
This designer bathroom called for an arrangement which was equally eye-catching. This Line arrangement of Dahlias, Corylus avellana contorta and Miscanthus Herman Mussel satisfied the need perfectly.

Green is the dominant colour here, with tall Cyperus flower stalks serving as the main feature. A touch of white is provided by a few Gladiolus flower-heads. ▷

◁ A Mass arrangement of pastel shades at the side of the wash basin. This could well provide both a patch of living colour and fragrance to the rather stark decor of the average bathroom.

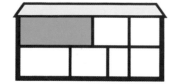

The Bedroom

As with any other room in the house, flowers will brighten up a bedroom. However, it seems that our attitude to having floral arrangements in the bedrooms is somewhat complex. In the family bedrooms the displays tend to be made with dried or artificial material rather than fresh blooms, and there is no general agreement why this should be. Some interior decorators feel that bedrooms are in use for too short a time during the waking hours to make a display lasting for only a week worthwhile. Also when the children are still at home having to top up the containers in several rooms just prolongs the time spent on housework. Finally, there are people who still believe the old wives' tale that flowers are unhealthy in a bedroom.

Things are different with the guest bedroom. When people come to stay it is quite common practice to place a simple arrangement of fresh flowers on the dressing table or bedside table. It is always regarded as a thoughtful touch, and perhaps we like the idea of our visitors admiring our handiwork. Avoid heavily-scented flowers such as Hyacinth and Jasmine. For most people the bedroom is a place for a restful arrangement. Delicate blooms are chosen — Sweet Peas rather than Peonies, Pinks rather than large Roses. To enhance this restful effect blues, mauves and creams are the favoured colours. However, the arrangement does not have to be restful — cheery colours to brighten the room are quite acceptable as the visitor gets ready for bed, and when the lights are off a gaily-coloured arrangement cannot keep him or her awake.

BEDROOM PICTURE GALLERY

The ever-popular Gypsophila/Rose bedroom combination. A little of the garden brought indoors to make a pastel and perhaps fragrant arrangement. ▷

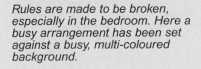

◁ *Pink against pink seems to break the background rule on page 100, but the pink background is patterned, and the pink Dahlias have a deep green leafy fringe. Not for every room, but a restful arrangement for a bedroom.*

Rules are made to be broken, especially in the bedroom. Here a busy arrangement has been set against a busy, multi-coloured background. ▷

A quite different approach to the arrangement below. Here a colourful selection of individual blooms has been put together to contrast with the decor of the room. ▷

◁ *The object here was to provide an arrangement which would blend with the colour scheme of the bedroom. No attempt has been made to make it an eye-catching feature.*

STEP 7 : Choose a STYLE

There are hundreds of different types of flower arrangements and it is not possible to fit all of them into neat pigeon-holes with clear-cut definitions. Some groupings are possible, however, to help you in your quest to find a style which will suit your skill, artistic temperament, materials available and the location where it will be placed.

First of all, you can decide between an all-round and a facing arrangement, as described below. Then there is the split between the informal and formal arrangement. Little pre-planning goes into the informal display — strict geometric shapes (triangles, crescents, fans etc) are avoided and instead a free-flowing natural effect is sought. With the formal display there are guidelines to follow and the placing of the plant material is planned beforehand. The shapes are generally (but not always) geometric. Surprisingly, creating a really successful informal arrangement calls for at least as much artistic talent as making an 'impressive' formal one.

All-round and facing, informal and formal — these concepts are needed in order to decide the visual effect of the finished display. They do not, however, help you to put a name to an arrangement you may see in a magazine or in a friend's house. Set out on page 219 is a classification adopted by some (but not all!) flower arrangers. See page 240 if the terms *line material, dominant material* and *filler material* are new to you.

Most arrangements in the Western world are traditionally made in either the Mass or Line-mass style, and for many years the formal geometric shape was dominant. But things have changed — the trend is now towards less stylised displays which have an informal shape. So do try your hand at a 'modern art' arrangement and see if it appeals to you.

THE ALL-ROUND ARRANGEMENT

The all-round arrangement is designed to be seen from all sides, and is therefore chosen for a table or room centrepiece display. When seen from above it is usually circular, but may be broadly oval or square.

THE FACING ARRANGEMENT

The facing (or flat-back) arrangement is designed to be seen only from the front and perhaps the sides, and is therefore chosen for a shelf or sideboard display. Do not place too close to the wall.

MASS
style

Little or no open space is enclosed within the boundary of the arrangement — any space present is not a basic requirement of the style

page 220-223

LINE
style

Open space within the boundary of the arrangement is a key feature — much or all of the display is line material described on page 240

page 224-229

LINE-MASS
style

Some open space is present within the boundary of the arrangement — only part of the area between the framework of line material is filled with leaves and/or flowers

page 230-235

MISCELLANEOUS
style

An arrangement which does not belong to any of the basic styles (Mass, Line or Line-mass), or an arrangement including two or three of these styles

page 236-239

MASS style

Little or no open space is enclosed within the boundary of the arrangement — any space present is not a basic requirement of the style. The Mass style originated in Europe, beginning according to tradition with the Renaissance and first glorified in the paintings of the Dutch Masters in the 17th century. The style came into full flower in the late Victorian era — silver trumpets packed with flowers and foliage, roughly oval in outline and often a kaleidoscope of colour. The 20th century was a period of modification — the triangle became the most popular shape and arrangements became much looser and less formal. This trend has continued into the 21st century.

The Mass style has several basic features. Generally the arrangement is an all-round one, and line material is used to create a skeleton of an upright axis and several horizontal laterals. This framework is then more or less completely covered with flowers and/or other plant material. There is usually no attempt to make any particular part a distinct focal point and transition is considered important. Transition means that changes within the arrangement are gradual rather than abrupt — colours, shapes etc of neighbouring blooms tend to blend together rather than stand out in sharp contrast. In the 1980s the Natural approach became popular — plant material is massed together "like flowers in the garden, with enough space for the butterflies".

BUNCH IN A VASE

◁ This is the simplest arrangement, and also the only one for millions of people. The stem bases of a shop-bought or florist-delivered bunch are cut and then the flowers put in a vase which is half-filled with water. In summer a variety of blooms are taken from the garden and treated in a similar way. All too often the effect is stiff and the display is short-lived, so a few hints may be useful. Condition the flowers before you start (see page 243) and most floral arrangements can be improved by adding some foliage from the garden. Cut the stems to different lengths to give the display a roughly triangular shape. For a more natural and free-flowing effect make a **tied bunch** — see page 245 for details.

BIEDERMEIER

This arrangement is a flat or domed mass floral display in a round and shallow container. In the true Biedermeier the blooms are arranged to give concentric circles of different colours and there is an outer collar of foliage. The term, however, is used nowadays for any circular low arrangement where the stems are almost completely hidden. The Biedermeier has long been used as a table arrangement and continues to be popular. A single flower type or a medley of different blooms can be used — a good way to display spring flowers or Roses. Other names include **posy** and **domed display** — mechanics may or may not be used.

▷

TRADITIONAL MASS

◁ Traditional is the usual term for the classic massed arrangement which is held in place by floral foam or crumpled chicken wire. The use of these mechanics allows displays of various shapes to be created — oval, fan etc. The most popular outline these days is the triangle, but this shape was surprisingly rare before World War II. The Traditional arrangement is to be seen everywhere in sizes ranging from table centrepieces to ceiling-high displays. In all cases the first step should be to create a central upright axis with line material and then the dominant flowers should be inserted. The final step is to use filler material to cover all or nearly all of the line material.

BYZANTINE CONE

This ancient-style arrangement is not recommended for the display of fresh flowers — it is difficult to keep moist, the effect is extremely formal and a lot of plant material is required. The mechanic is traditionally a moss-filled wire frame but these days a floral foam cone is used. A modern Byzantine cone can be created for a grand or formal setting where it can be impressive, or in the home it can provide an addition to Christmas decorations. However, it uses artificial or dried material and not fresh flowers. The surface of the brown floral foam is first covered with leafy sprigs and then a variety of short-stemmed blooms, fruits, berries, accessories etc are added to provide interest and colour.

▷

MASS PICTURE GALLERY

This simple display shows how eye-catching a Contrasting colour arrangement (see page 185) can be. ▷

A Traditional Mass display which seems to have stepped out of an old Dutch painting. It appears to have been thrown together, but a good deal of skill is required to create the vibrance associated with this type of arrangement. ◁

This all-white Modern Mass display of Lilies and Gerberas with a dark leafy background shows how effective a Monochromatic arrangement can be. ▷

◁ *The Analogous colour scheme and the unusual wooden container come together in this simple Modern Mass arrangement to create an attention-grabbing feature.*

This Mass arrangement is to be seen almost everywhere in spring — a bunch of Daffodils placed in a vase. No attempt to be particularly creative perhaps, but the stems have been skilfully cut to different lengths to create an impressive display. ▷

◁ *This combination of tiny pink Roses and white Gypsophila makes an airy and pastel arrangement, with the dark vase providing colour contrast.*

LINE style

Open space within the boundary of the arrangement is a key feature — much or all of the display is line material as described on page 240. The Line style is the opposite of the Mass design in nearly every way. Origin, mechanics and the choice and use of plant material are all quite different. The Line concept originated in the East and rules were laid down in China more than 1000 years ago — the Mass style is a product of the West and began much later. The basic feature of a Line design is limited use of plant material with support often provided by a pinholder — in the Mass style the flowers and foliage are in water, or supported by floral foam or crumpled chicken wire.

These are perhaps details — the fundamental feature of the Line style is that each element of the design is important in its own right and the air space contained within the framing line material is vital to the overall effect of the display. As the name indicates, it is the lines and not the mass which are the main source of appeal. Another key difference is that transition (page 220) is not important — in fact it is positively undesirable with many Line arrangements. We do not know just when the Line style was adopted in the West — Ikebana aroused much interest when exhibited at the first Chelsea Flower Show in 1912, but it was in the U.S between 1955 and 1975 that the Western Line style really took hold.

VERTICAL

The Vertical arrangement is the only type of Line style which is formal, geometric and defined by clear-cut rules. The all-important feature is bold line material which is set vertically to form a central axis. The simplest form is a single stem bearing showy flowers along its axis — Calla Lily is a good example (see page 228). The more usual form is a leafy stem or a flowering stem such as Rose or Liatris with a single or small group of dominant flowers placed along the axis or close to the base. Short wings of foliage are used to cover the mechanics at the bottom of the arrangement — typical examples are variegated Hosta, feathery Fern and leathery Rhododendron.

IKEBANA

Ikebana or Japanese-style flower arranging has been practised for many hundreds of years, but it remains a mystery to the Western mind. The 'two sticks and a flower' slur shows how little we understand the wealth of symbolism behind the deceptively simple arrangements — Ikebana ('making flowers live') is a path to self-enlightenment and not just a way of doing the flowers for millions of Japanese. It is not possible, of course, to describe even the fundamental principles in a few words, but you can create a simple design by following the magical rule of three. Arrange three pieces of line material with three different heights or centres of interest — highest is Heaven, Man is central and Earth is lowest. See page 250 for more details.

FREE-STYLE

During the 1960s a new style appeared — asymmetrical, irregular in outline and sparse. The important feature is that the line material is left mainly uncovered by flowers and/or foliage, and any additional plant material is generally bold and eye-catching. Contrasting colours are now no longer feared and there is little or no attempt to cover spaces within the design with filler material. The container is generally fully exposed, which means that it must be chosen with care as it will be part of the design. No tedious rules, a display to fit in with today's life-style. This Western Line arrangement has been given a variety of names, including **Modern**, **Contemporary** and **Free-line**.

ABSTRACT

In the progression from the formal Mass style to the informal Line designs of today, this is the final stop. It takes Free-style a stage further. This is not really a flower arrangement — it is a piece of art in which living and/or dead plant material is used as the decorative medium. The line plant material is replaced by a metal and/or wooden sculpture, and the plant material may be painted or sliced. The definition may seem straightforward, but in practice there is no clear-cut line between the Free-style and Abstract designs. This style has been around for many years, but it was not until the 1980s that the public started to take notice.

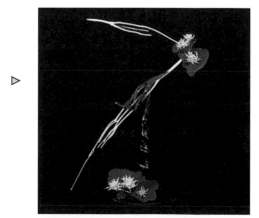

LINE
PICTURE GALLERY

" *This buffet table arrangement was designed in one of my favourite containers, a Val Spicer candelabra. The three containers were filled with soaked floral foam which was taped down to take the weight of the foliage, fruit and flowers. A colour scheme of peach, apricot, red and burgundy was chosen to complement the cuisine. The foliage included Ivy, Fatsia, dried Strelitzia and Pineapple tops. The fruit (Lychees, Plums, black Grapes, Apples and Pomegranates) complemented the flowers — Anigozanthos, dark red Tulips, miniature Cymbidiums, Anthuriums, Genista and miniature Gerberas. The design was unified by the use of swirling Bear Grass.* " Betty Jones

IKEBANA

The Nageire style dates originally from the 12th century. It is a classical arrangement in a tall cylindrical vase — the effect is flowing and natural. In this slanting version the long horizontal stem is the Heaven line. ▷

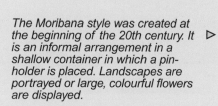

◁ *The Shoka (Seika) style began in the 18th century. It is a formal arrangement with strict rules governing the lengths and angles of the stems. It is basically a triangular and usually stiff style in which all the stems arise from a single point.*

The Moribana style was created at the beginning of the 20th century. It is an informal arrangement in a shallow container in which a pin-holder is placed. Landscapes are portrayed or large, colourful flowers are displayed. ▷

*Extremely simple, but effective.
Three tied bunches of Daffodils
with Arum italicum and Corylus
avellana contorta as
companions* ▷

◁ *The simplest of all Line
arrangements — a single stalk
bearing bold flowers with the
minimum of filler material below.
The Calla Lily in the illustration is a
good choice. An excellent focal
point in the right setting.*

A Modern arrangement by Marian Aaronson, full of movement and contrast. The five Strelitzia flowers circle within the clipped Palm leaves and the loops of Phormium foliage. ▷

◁ A stylish modern Line arrangement — five flower stalks in a twig-wrapped vase with raffia as filler material. Sure to be admired, but only in the right location.

LINE-MASS style

Some open space is present within the boundary of the arrangement — only part of the area between the framework of line material is filled with leaves and/or flowers. The period between 1950 and 1965 was an exciting time for flower arranging. The pioneering work by people like Constance Spry and Julia Clements continued to popularise the idea that making a flower arrangement could be an artistically-satisfying experience and not just a way of bringing garden flowers indoors. Equally important was the appearance of floral foam which made possible for everyone the creation of impressive displays. In light of this rapidly-growing interest in arranging flowers, the marriage of the Western Mass style and the Line style from the East was inevitable.

Line-mass became an important concept — a style in which the skeleton formed by line material was clothed but not covered by other flowers and/or foliage. The early teachers set out guidelines but unfortunately these were regarded as rules, and so for many years geometric patterns were carefully reproduced. Dominant material was dutifully grouped at the base and filler material was used to ensure a neat transition between the various elements. Things have now loosened up — irregular designs are now popular. This style is excellent for natural arrangements ... after all, the garden with its twiggy shrubs above the massed flowers in the border is really a Line-mass arrangement!

SYMMETRICAL TRIANGLE

◁ For about sixty years the Symmetrical triangle has remained the most popular Line-mass arrangement. In the beginning strict formality was the rule, with the two horizontal ribs at the base being composed of the same line materials and the two sides of the triangle being almost identical to each other. This somewhat stiff arrangement is sometimes sneeringly referred to as the 'florist' design but it persists because of its popular appeal. There is a feeling of solidity and perfect balance, but these days a looser and less formal approach is generally preferred by the home flower arranger. A wider variety of line material is used and the outline is flowing and uneven.

ASYMMETRICAL TRIANGLE

The Asymmetrical triangle is even less formal and often more eye-catching than the modern version of its more popular symmetrical sister. The lateral ribs are markedly different in ▷ length so that the arrangement has a distinctly off-centred or L-shaped look and the basal flowers and/or leaves often drape gracefully over the edge of the container. With a bold centre of interest and an interesting range of filler material this design is a good choice for the show bench. It also fits in well with modern decor, but in more traditional surroundings a pair of arrangements which are mirror images of each other are sometimes placed side by side to create a more balanced feel.

CRESCENT

An attractive arrangement for a foam-filled shallow dish — not much material is required but it must be chosen with care. The ◁ usual approach is to use bare, leafy or flowering woody stems from the garden to create the curved outline and then to add either home-grown or shop-bought flowers and foliage at the centre. You may be fortunate enough to find suitably arched woody shoots, but it is usually necessary to bend them after cutting — see Hogarth curve below. These curved stems are pushed into the ends of the block with one side appreciably higher than the other — the secret of success is to create the impression that the crescent is made from a group of uncut stems. Hide the mechanics with dominant and filler material.

HOGARTH CURVE

The elongated S was the 'line of beauty' described by the painter William Hogarth. The Hogarth curve design is based on this shape and it is showy and full of movement. But it is also highly formal, and its popularity has declined with the trend ▷ away from geometric arrangements. In order to create the S outline you will need two sets of matched curved stems for placing in the foam block at the top of a tall container. Long and pliable shoots are used — examples include Broom, Flowering Currant, Winter Jasmine and Rosemary. Soak the stems in water, tie the ends together with string to create a curved shape and leave to dry for several hours. Hide the mechanics with dominant and filler material.

◁

INVERTED CRESCENT

A popular arrangement for the centre of the dining room table where candles are to be included — a candle cup (see page 193) together with a candle holder are used. The display will have to be an all-round one with the line material at the base forming a circle or an oval, depending on the shape of the table. The Inverted crescent may also be used as a facing display in a tall container or in a vase or urn on a pedestal. Here the vertical line material is short-stemmed and the horizontal line material is naturally pendant. This drooping effect is heightened by using lengths of soft-stemmed filler material such as Ivy and Alchemilla around the base.

HORIZONTAL

A popular arrangement for the centre of the dining room table where candles are not to be included and an unobstructed view of people around the table is required. A low rectangular container is generally used and either fresh or dried material can be employed. The basic difference compared with the Inverted crescent is that the basal line material is stiff rather than drooping. Many plants are suitable — Gladiolus, long-stemmed Rose, Box, spray Carnation etc depending on the size of the arrangement. Of course the design is not truly horizontal — at some point a short vertical axis is placed which is usually a centre of interest (focal point) but need not be in the middle of the display.

▷

◁

FAN

In some ways the Fan is the opposite of the Horizontal display — the upright ribs or axes are spreading and showy, and the arrangement is at its best when it is large. Use the Fan to cover the fireplace in summer or in the hall as a prominent display on a pedestal. Five, seven or nine stems of line material are set like spokes in the mechanics. Flowering material is often used — examples include Liatris, Lily, Gladiolus, long-stemmed Rose and Iris. This framework should then be partly filled in with dominant and filler material. Dried flowers make excellent Fan arrangements — suitable line materials for the spokes include Wheat, Reed Mace, Chinese Lantern, Banksia and long-stemmed Rose.

INFORMAL

It is easy to understand the basic principles of an Informal arrangement. It is a Line-mass style with the ribs formed from line material which is partly but not entirely covered by the dominant and filler material, and with an overall outline which is irregular. The artistic ability of the arranger is given free rein as there is no need to create a geometric pattern, and both the symmetry and placing of centres of interest are completely up to you. A few words of warning — the tight rules concerning shape are abandoned but forgetting the principles of colour, proportion, background and movement can result in a mess. Secondly, it is easier to create a pleasing formal rather than an informal arrangement if you are not artistic.

▷

LINE-MASS
PICTURE GALLERY

"*I am a gardener and my greatest joy is arranging flowers from my own garden. This large display was created for a garden party to make a link between a special occasion and the gifts available from the beds and borders around one's home. The container is a stone statue and is filled with a wide range of the beautiful foliage and flowers available for picking in summer. The foliage display is made up of Jasmine, evergreen Honeysuckle, Escallonia and Stephanandra. A profusion of flower colour is provided by Foxglove, blue Delphinium, Campanula, Alchemilla, Astrantia, Peony, Gypsophila and a selection of Roses.*" Edna Johnson

CONTRAST or UNITY?

Both contrast and unity are design approaches used by interior decorators. Here contrast has been used as the dominant feature — flower-heads of widely differing shapes and colours held together by a lichen-encrusted branch. ▷

◁ *Unity is the basic feature of this arrangement. It is a — monochromatic display — the Chrysanthemums, Gladioli, Roses and Carnations are all tints and shades of pink. No hint of contrast here.*

◁ The Inverted Crescent was very popular before the introduction of modern styles such as Parallel, Free-style etc. Its geometric nature is considered old-fashioned by some, but here it has been given an up-to-date treatment with colours in distinct blocks.

This type of Rose arrangement can be seen in homes throughout the country in summer, but it is not easy to classify. The tall blooms form the distinct and partially uncovered ribs associated with Line-mass, but it is Rose foliage and not added plants which provide the filler material. ▷

◁ In this Line-mass arrangement the traditional Holly/Ivy/Conifer collection serves as a muted background to a group of single Chrysanthemums. The bright blooms look like glowing lights on a miniature Christmas tree.

MISCELLANEOUS style

An arrangement which does not belong to any of the basic styles (Mass, Line or Line-mass), or an arrangement including two or three of these styles. The Miscellaneous style is a hotch-potch of arrangements which do not fit neatly into any of the types described on the previous pages. Firstly, there are the arrangements such as the diminutive Miniatures and Petites. With the second set of Miscellaneous arrangements the key feature is that the plant material does not appear to radiate from a single point — Landscape and European arrangements belong here. The third set are uncommon arrangements of massed flowers — the Wreath is described on page 237, but others such as the Swag and Garland are usually made with artificial or dried flowers and are very rarely used in Roomscaping. Another exclusion is the Pot-et-fleur which brings together house plants and cut flowers. This arrangement is really an Indoor Garden — see page 126.

The arrangements in the Miscellaneous style can be expected to change over the years. The popularity of some will decline while others will become more popular. In addition we can expect new ways of putting plant material together which do not fit into any of the other styles.

EUROPEAN

During the 1980s a revolutionary new style spread from Holland — the **Parallel** or European style. In these arrangements the mechanic is generally a rectangular block of floral foam set in a shallow dish, and from it arises the key feature — groups of stems which stand vertically. This line material is not covered up by other plants, although the foam is hidden by a horizontal groundwork of flowers, foliage, fruits, stems etc. There is no transition (see page 220) — blocks of contrasting shapes and colours are placed next to each other, and the vertical lines emerge directly from the horizontal mass. The overall design may be Line or Line-mass, and often (but not always) a 'natural' look is aimed for.

LANDSCAPE

The Landscape arrangement is more at home on the show bench than in the living room or hall — it is an interpretive style. The goal is to create a representation of a tiny piece of the environment — a meadow, wood, beach etc. The result can look a mess unless a few well-established rules are followed. Use a container and base which are in keeping with the theme and do not overdo it — use restrained hints to picture the scene rather than to make a fully-clothed miniature garden. A well-shaped branch can indicate a tree, a few pebbles for the shore, and so on. Next, scale is important — make sure the flowers around your 'tree' are small. Finally, limit the size and number of accessories — they should not dominate the scene.

MINIATURE and PETITE

The small-scale flower arrangement calls for not much material but a good deal of skill. The problem is that a small error which may not be noticed in a standard-sized arrangement can appear to be a glaring error when the whole thing is only a few inches high. In Britain (but not all countries) the size of a Miniature arrangement is a maximum of 4 in. (10 cm) high, wide and deep — a Petite should not exceed 9 in. (23 cm) high, wide and deep. There is, of course, some latitude when it is for the home, but these styles are not often used in Roomscaping. Keeping things in scale is the main challenge — container, plant material and accessories must all be in proportion. You can use fresh or preserved material.

WREATH

In Britain Wreaths are usually associated with either funerals or Christmas, but these circular arrangements are excellent for table display. There are several types of mechanics and containers for Wreaths — the best starting point is a ring of floral foam. Choose a green ring if you plan to use fresh plant material — a dried arrangement requires a brown ring. The first stage is to cover the foam with short lengths of leafy sprigs and then add flowers, fruits, seed-heads etc. The final step is to attach accessories (ribbons, baubles etc) if required. At Christmas, wreath frames covered with natural or artificial leafy material are available for covering with flowers, ribbons and seasonal ornaments.

MISCELLANEOUS PICTURE GALLERY

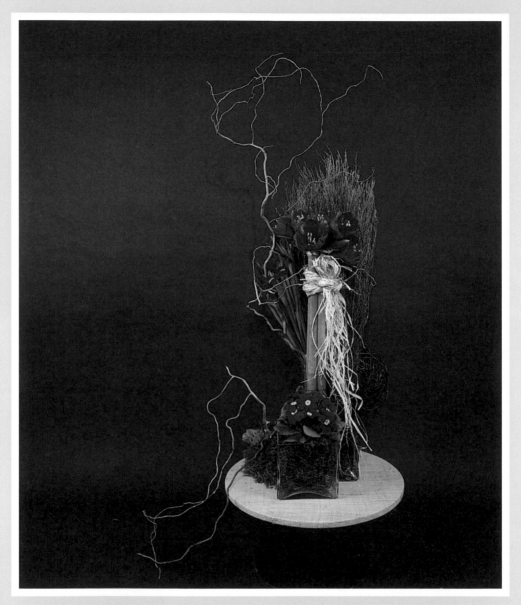

66 *In this piece I have assembled together components chosen for both their individual character and the way in which they work with each other. Smooth glass contrasts with the rough texture of the Broom. Bold splashes of brilliant red are balanced with touches of cool, deep blue. I wanted to make a composition with a strongly vertical feel; the parallel groupings of glass containers, Broom, Amaryllis and Iris helped me to achieve this. The inclusion of softer lines, provided by the raffia, further emphasises the overall severity of shape. Contorted Willow introduces vigorous movement and alleviates the austerity while defining the limits of the design.* 99 Carol Firmstone

A Parallel arrangement of garden flowers and house plants. This is the Open version with the upright line material widely spaced above the 'meadow' of groundwork plants. In the Closed version the vertical stems are much closer together and give a near-Mass effect. ▷

◁ Three Gerbera blooms in a vase does not sound like much of an arrangement, but the clear contrast between blooms and background turns this display into an eye-catching feature.

This formalised spring Landscape arrangement has been made in the traditional style for such displays. A piece of Contorted Willow provides the tree and a variety of spring flowers form the meadow — Daffodils, Grape Hyacinth, Viburnum, Polyanthus etc. No accessories have been used. ▷

STEP 8 : Obtain the PLANT MATERIAL

There are three basic sources for fresh plant material. An important source is the garden, where you can cut blooms which are fresh and at the right stage for arranging indoors. In addition there is a plentiful supply of stems and leaves which are so vital for nearly all displays. The main problem is that there are times when the supply of garden blooms is limited or when you wish to make a display which calls for bigger and brighter flowers than your garden can offer. So you have to turn to an alternative source of supply. There is the countryside — free material again, but there is a Code of Conduct. You can pick flowers apart from a few rare ones which are protected. There are a number of restrictions — the plants must be wild and not planted, they must not be on private land and they must not be dug up. For year-round supplies of bold flowers we must go to the third source — the flower seller. This may be a garden centre or florist, a market stall or the largest supplier of all — a supermarket. The blooms will have been picked some time ago, so do follow the advice on the next page. There are three basic types of plant material — these are described below.

LINE MATERIAL

Other name : Outline material

Line material consists of tall stems, flowering spikes or bold leaves which are used to create the basic framework or skeleton. This line material may be straight or curved, and it sets the height and width of the finished arrangement.
Examples: Box, Privet, Gladiolus, long-stemmed Rose, Eucalyptus, Winter Jasmine, Broom, Forsythia, Delphinium.

DOMINANT MATERIAL

Other names : Focal material, Point material

Dominant material consists of bold flowers or clusters of showy smaller blooms — eye-catching foliage is occasionally used. This dominant material provides a centre or centres of interest.
Examples: Gerbera, Chrysanthemum, Anthurium, Lily, Paeony, Tulip, Poppy, Rose, Hydrangea, Dahlia, Daffodil, Geranium.

FILLER MATERIAL

Other name : Secondary material

Filler material consists of smaller flowers or all sorts of leaves which are used to cover the mechanics and edges of the container, and also provide added interest and colour to the display. Unwanted bare areas are filled.
Examples: Scabious, Geum, Hebe, Holly, Alstroemeria, Aster, Gypsophila, Solidago, Freesia, Ivy, Euonymus, spray Carnation.

BUYING FLOWERS

A long-established florist or a nation-wide super-market chain obviously has a reputation to maintain, but you cannot rely on one supplier always being superior to the others. The only way to judge quality is to look at the stock. If you want out-of-the-ordinary flowers it will be necessary to place an order with a local supplier who can obtain them from the whole-sale market.

Look at the flower buckets first — they should be out of direct sunlight and the water should not be smelly. The foliage should be firm and the cut ends should be immersed. As a general rule choose blooms at the **Open Stage** for a long-lasting display. At this stage multi-flowered stems have a few open blooms and plenty of coloured buds. The **Bud Stage** is too early — tight green buds do not often open indoors. The problem with the **Ripe Stage** is that all the flowers are fully open and so the display will be short-lived. Of course this is not a problem if the display is for a special occasion on the next day. With single Daisy-like blooms the Open Stage is when the petals are fully open but the central disc is free from a dusting of yellow pollen. These are general rules — see below for specific guidance.

Get the flowers home as quickly as possible — do not put them in the boot of the car on a warm day. Condition the blooms (page 243) before using them to make an arrangement.

PLANT	STAGE OF DEVELOPMENT FOR MAXIMUM VASE-LIFE
ALSTROEMERIA	A few flowers open — buds showing colour
ANEMONE	Most flowers open — centres still tight. Buds showing colour
CARNATION — SPRAY	About half flowers open — buds plump and firm
CARNATION — STANDARD	Flowers open — no white threads. Leaves firm and fresh
CHRYSANTHEMUM — SINGLE	Most flowers open. Central discs greenish — no pollen present
CHRYSANTHEMUM — DOUBLE	Flowers open — centres tight and outer petals firm
DAFFODIL — SINGLE	Buds showing colour and beginning to open
DAFFODIL — DOUBLE	Flowers fully open
FREESIA	A few flowers open — buds showing colour
GERBERA	Flowers open. Central discs greenish — no pollen present
GLADIOLUS	A few flowers open — buds showing colour
GYPSOPHILA	Nearly all flowers open
IRIS	A few flowers open — buds showing colour
LILY	A few flowers open — buds showing colour
ORCHID	Flowers fully open
RANUNCULUS	Most flowers open — centres still tight. Buds showing colour
ROSE	Open buds or tight-centred flowers. Some leaves on stems
STATICE	Nearly all flowers open
TULIP	Buds showing colour — leaves not limp

GATHERING GARDEN FLOWERS

Go into the garden in the morning or evening with a bucket half-filled with tepid water. Choose flowers which are at the open stage as described on page 241 — see the table below for additional guidance. Be careful not to cut too many stems from recently-planted specimens. There are three rules concerning cutting — the knife, scissors or secateurs must be clean to avoid bacterial infection, the blades must be sharp to ensure a clean cut, and this cut must be a sloping one so that a large area of water-absorbing surface is exposed. Quickly remove the lower leaves which would be submerged in the arrangement — it is especially important that grey or downy leaves are not left in water. It is essential that the cut ends are not allowed to dry out — get the stems into the bucket as quickly as possible and keep it out of full sun.

Take the bucket indoors when cutting is finished. The plants are not yet ready for arranging — the process of conditioning is required. With some flowers and leaves it will be necessary to undertake a pre-conditioning stage. All of this may seem a lot of trouble, but little effort is required and it avoids the frustration of seeing all the work go to waste after a few days.

From spring to autumn the garden provides cut flowers, but it is also the source for the leaves and stems which are an integral part of many styles.

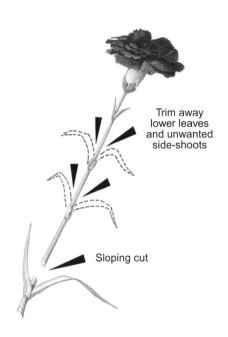

Trim away lower leaves and unwanted side-shoots

Sloping cut

PLANT	STAGE OF DEVELOPMENT FOR MAXIMUM VASE-LIFE
FLORIST FLOWERS	See page 241 — same stages apply to garden-grown material
ACHILLEA	Flowers fully open
ANTIRRHINUM	Bottom half of spike in flower
CORNFLOWER	Flowers fully open
DAHLIA	Most flowers open. Central discs greenish — no pollen present
DELPHINIUM	Most of spike in flower
FORSYTHIA	Buds beginning to open
FOXGLOVE	Bottom half of spike in flower
LILAC	Most of cluster still in bud
LILY-OF-THE-VALLEY	Nearly all flowers open
LUPIN	Bottom half of spike in flower
MICHAELMAS DAISY	Nearly all flowers open
MOLUCCELLA	Flowers fully open
PELARGONIUM	Buds in cluster beginning to open
POPPY	Buds beginning to open
RHODODENDRON	Most of cluster still in bud
SCABIOUS	Buds beginning to open
SWEET PEA	A few flowers open — buds showing colour

CONDITIONING

Some preparation is necessary before you can arrange the plant material. The purpose of this preparation is to ensure that there is no callus at the bottom of the stems nor any air blocks along their length which would shorten vase-life. This process is known as **conditioning**. For some plant material there is a **pre-conditioning** stage — see below.

Before beginning the pre-conditioning stage there is a job to do if the plants have been left out of water for some time. Remove about 1 in. (3 cm) from the bottom of each stem — make a sloping cut.

Pre-conditioning

WOODY STEM TREATMENT

The bottom of woody stems require more than a sloping cut to ensure adequate exposure to water before conditioning. Scrape the bark from the bottom 1-2 in. (3-5 cm) with a knife and then make a 1 in. (3 cm) slit with scissors or knife. Do not hammer the ends as this can lead to bacterial infection.

SPRING BULB TREATMENT

Tulips, Hyacinths and Daffodils need special treatment. Cut away the white part of the stem and make a sloping cut on the green part of the stem. Some spring-flowering bulbs have sap which shortens the life of other flowers — stand them in a bucket of water overnight before conditioning.

WILTED FLOWER TREATMENT

Use the hot-water treatment as a pick-me-up for wilted plant material — Roses and many woody plants respond dramatically to this technique. Cover blooms with a paper bag and immerse the bottom inch of the stems in near-boiling water for 1 minute. An additional benefit is the destruction of bacteria.

MILKY SAP TREATMENT

Several flowering and foliage plants have sap which oozes out to form a waterproof seal. Singeing is the way to tackle this problem — hold a flame (cigarette lighter, match or candle) to the cut end until it is blackened. Treat milky-sap plants such as Poppy, Euphorbia, Ferns, Dahlia and Zinnia.

FLOPPY STEM TREATMENT

A number of flowering plants (e.g Tulips and Lupins) have floppy stems. The usual treatment is to wrap the stems in damp newspaper and then stand the bundle upright in water overnight. Despite treatment Tulips may quickly flop — the answer is floral wire pushed up through the stem. Prick a hole below each flower.

LARGE LEAF TREATMENT

First wash the leaves in tepid water to remove dust and surface deposits. Then immerse in a bowl of tepid water for several hours. Wilted flowers can sometimes be revived in this way. Lift out small leaves after an hour and do not use this technique for grey or downy foliage.

Conditioning

A simple task — the stems are immersed in tepid water in a bucket which is stood in a cool and dark place for 2-8 hours. It is often helpful to add a cut flower preservative (see page 188). For most plants deep immersion is recommended. Spring-flowering bulbs are an exception — condition Tulips, Daffodils etc in shallow water. Don't leave the conditioned plants on the table — go straight from the bucket into the moist floral foam or water-filled container.

STEP 9 : Make the ARRANGEMENT

This is not a recipe book. The following pages do not contain a collection of arrangements with instructions on which plants you have to use and where they have to be placed to produce the display in the photograph. Instead there are step-by-step guides to show you how to put together the various ingredients to produce each of the basic styles.

It is now time to make an arrangement. The method will depend on three basic factors — the style you have chosen to follow, the amount and type of plant material you have assembled, and the mechanics you have decided to use. This means that the amount and sort of work you have to do varies quite widely from one arrangement to another, but there are a few principles which apply to all arrangements — the Ten Golden Rules.

- Keep all your flower arranging bits and pieces together rather than scattering them around the house in various drawers and cupboards. The best plan is to have one or more boxes containing mechanics and equipment in a cupboard which stores a range of containers.

- Before you begin lay a piece of waterproof sheeting over the work surface and have all the things you will need around you.

- Decide on the style of the arrangement and have a rough idea of its size before choosing the container and plant material.

- Choose the container with care — make sure it is waterproof if you are using fresh flowers. The commonest mistake is to choose a vase, dish or bowl which is either too big or bright for the arrangement.

- Choose the plants with care. You will need one or more types of line, dominant and filler plant material, depending upon the style you have chosen to create — see page 240. See page 241-242 and Chapter 6 for information on the recommended time to buy or cut — in nearly all cases the flowers are past their best if they are all fully open and yellow pollen is present.

- The general rule is to put in the line material first to form the basic skeleton, and then to place the dominant plant material with care. Filler material is added last of all to provide extra interest and a cover for the mechanics.

- With Triangular and Fan arrangements the stems should be inserted so that they appear to arise from a point within the mechanics. With Crescent arrangements the line material should appear to pass through the mechanics.

- Avoid dullness and monotony. Stems should be different lengths, dark flowers should be set deeper in the arrangement than pale-coloured ones and not all the flowers should face directly forward.

- Stand back occasionally to check on progress — remember that the viewer will see the finished work when more than an arm's length away.

- Clean throughly and dry all equipment when you have finished. Remember that good aftercare of the arrangement is necessary for satisfactory vase-life — see page 251.

The MASS style — Tied Bunch in a vase

① CHOOSE A CONTAINER
Pick a clean vase or jug which is taller than it is wide. Half fill it with water containing a cut flower preservative (page 188).

② START TO MAKE THE TIED BUNCH
Conditioned flowers and foliage can be inserted directly into the water in the vase without any hand grouping beforehand (see below) but preparing a tied (or hand) bunch will often give a more pleasing effect. For best results the stems should be reasonably long and roughly the same thickness — all foliage which will be in water must be removed. You will need about 20 stems. Hold one of the longest ones between your thumb and forefinger — this will be the central pivot and the point of tying.

③ COMPLETE THE TIED BUNCH
Add further stems with each one at a slight angle — twist the bunch as you go. The heights of the flower-heads and foliage should decrease steadily as you progress, holding the tying point in your closed hand. Do not grip too tightly and the end result will be an all-round domed bunch. Tie at the central point with raffia or string.

④ PLACE THE BUNCH IN THE CONTAINER
Trim the stem bases to the same level and insert in the vase or jug. If you have done the job correctly then the arrangement will fall open slightly to give a natural look. Fill with water to 1-2 in. (3-5 cm) below the rim.

Non-tied Bunch

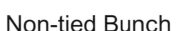

The tied bunch is not for every situation. Soft-stemmed plants like Tulips and Daffodils can be damaged and an arrangement with woody stems and flowers is better created directly in the vase. To help hold the stems in place it is a good idea to add glass marbles or nuggets — in a glass vase they have a decorative effect and also hide the stem bases. Place the tallest stem first to form the central axis — other stems should be progressively shorter and appear to radiate from a point within the container. Use filler material to hide the edge of the vase.

The LINE-MASS style — Crescent

① CHOOSE A CONTAINER

Floral foam allows you to choose from a wide range of containers — a shallow dish is suitable and so is a deep vase or urn. The basic provisos are that the vessel must be waterproof and that the top of the floral foam should be about 1 in. (3 cm) above the rim when it has been fixed in position. The most convenient type is the floral foam container which is designed to hold a rectangular or cylindrical block. This shallow plastic dish (page 193) calls for no additional support for the floral foam, and neither does a container in which a piece of foam has been cut and tightly wedged into the opening. In most cases however, a container is chosen which is rather larger than the piece of floral foam and so is capable of acting as a water reservoir. This dish or bowl may be inserted into or taped onto a larger and more decorative container.

② PREPARE THE FLORAL FOAM

The block of floral foam has usually to be cut to the required size — most people prefer to do this when the material is dry. Thorough wetting in water or dilute cut flower preservative solution is now necessary. A precise time for this operation cannot be given — it may take a minute or up to half an hour depending on the size of the block, water temperature etc. The best procedure is to lower the foam gently into a deep bowl of water and let go — do not push it down. It is ready when the top of the block has sunk to the water surface — take it out promptly as oversoaking leads to a loss of strength. Some arrangers cut ('chamfer') the edges of the block before creating an all-round arrangement.

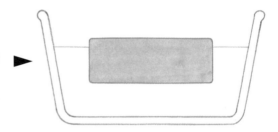

③ PREPARE THE CONTAINER

This is easy with a floral foam container and a block cut to fit — simply push the foam into position. With other containers you will have to secure the block within the container, and using a frog (page 190) is the usual method. The container, frog and your hands must all be clean and dry — put 3 small knobs of kneaded adhesive clay ('fix') on the bottom of the frog and press it on to the base of the dish, bowl etc. Then push the floral foam on to the prongs until it is firmly held. This technique is not always practical — the inner surface of the container may be too shiny or else too valuable to spoil with adhesive clay. The answer here is to put a piece of damp tissue between the floral foam and the bottom of the container before strapping the block with adhesive tape, as shown in the illustration. Making a large arrangement calls for a modification of these instructions. You will need one big piece or several smaller blocks of foam taped together — 2 or more frogs will be required. Tape the blocks into the container and cover the surface with chicken wire which is then tucked into or strapped onto the rim.

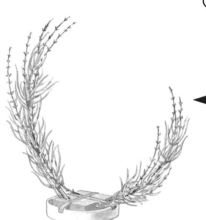

④ INSERT LINE MATERIAL

A Crescent is an easy and effective arrangement to make. As noted on page 231 it does not call for a large amount of plant material, but the stems and flowers must be carefully chosen. The bold outline is provided by curved line material, and you will have to look for this in the garden or countryside. A smooth and regular arc is not essential — in fact many flowers arrangers consider it undesirable. Look for naturally bent twigs on Forsythia, Quince, Ornamental Cherry, Pussy Willow, Dogwood etc. A number of whippy straight stems (Broom, Winter Jasmine, Rosemary and so on) can be curved by following the technique described for the Hogarth curve on page 231. Insert a long branch of line material in the top of the floral foam as shown — do not push stems more than 1 in. (3 cm) into the block. Balance this with a piece of stem in the side of the block at the other end. Repeat the process until a strong skewed crescent is formed. It is advisable to use more than one sort of line material — in the illustration there are Broom and Rosemary.

⑤ INSERT DOMINANT MATERIAL

The arrangement so far has a firm and flowing shape but little interest. To provide a focal point it is necessary to add some dominant material which is usually a small group of eye-catching blooms — Rose, Paeony, Lily, Anthurium, Chrysanthemum, Gerbera, Orchid, Standard Carnation and Dahlia are examples. A pleasing effect is obtained by first grouping the largest dominant flowers close to the base of the arrangement. Then use some of the stems of this dominant material which bears opening flower buds — insert these stems so that they lie part way up the high curve, as shown in the illustration.

⑥ INSERT FILLER MATERIAL

The arrangement now has bold lines and a focal point, but two problems still remain. First of all, there is no softening between the line and dominant material, which is too 'modern' for many arrangers. Secondly, part of the mechanics and the container edges are exposed. The solution for these problems is to add some filler material — examples include leaves of Ivy, Hosta, Eucalyptus, Pittosporum, Conifer, Smoke Bush and small-bloomed flowers such as Gypsophila, Freesia and Alstroemeria. Soft and narrow stems are difficult to push into the foam — use a knitting needle or cocktail stick to make a hole for them. The arrangement is now finished, but look at it carefully before moving it to its chosen spot. A common mistake is to add excessive filler material which may obscure too much of the line material or detract from the focal point. Cut away any filler material which is making the display over-fussy, and consider using a base so as to improve the visual balance.

The MASS style — Traditional Mass

① CHOOSE A CONTAINER

The interest in chicken wire (wire netting) for holding plant stems in a flower arrangement declined sharply with the introduction of floral foam, and it has never recovered. There are, however, several situations where chicken wire remains the preferred mechanic — spring bulbs which find it difficult to take up water from foam, heavy stems and branches which require the support of rigid netting, and some tall plants such as Gladioli which prefer deep water to wet floral foam. For many floral decorators there are two additional virtues. Firstly, stems can be pulled out and reinserted at will until the desired result is obtained. In addition there is some plant movement as the arrangement is being created and this leads to a less stiff effect. The chosen container must be waterproof and the vase, jug or urn should be reasonably wide at the top.

② PREPARE THE CHICKEN WIRE

Preparing a good chicken wire support is not as easy as it sounds — it calls for skill and experience. The basic features are firmness (you should be able to raise the container by lifting up the netting), good stem support (each shoot should pass through 3-4 layers of wire) and a fairly open centre (where most of the stems will be congregated). Use 2 in. (5 cm) mesh and cut a piece which is about twice the width and twice the depth of the container. Remove the thick edge and roll the netting into a loose ball. You are now ready to make the wire support within the container.

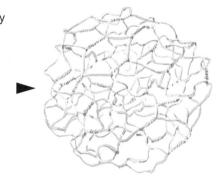

③ PREPARE THE CONTAINER

Push part of the wire ball gently into the container — on no account should it be squashed down. Ease the ball down until the bottom touches the base of the vase or urn. Next, give the top a push so that a layer is formed near the base. Don't be heavy handed, and repeat the process until all the ball is within the container except for a dome of matted wire standing above the rim. If you have been successful then the crumpled meshes will still be large enough for you to be able to push a pencil through several layers — try it. Next, the chicken wire ball should be firm — it should not pull out if lifted. The final stage is to secure it with florist wire, rubber bands or tape. A satisfactory way is to weave adhesive tape through the top wire layer and then secure it to the sides of the container, as shown. Alternatively you may be able to secure the mechanics by bending the chicken wire edges over the rim of the pot. For a large and heavy arrangement some floral decorators place floral foam or a pinholder under the wire ball in the container. Now everything is in position and you are ready to start the arrangement.

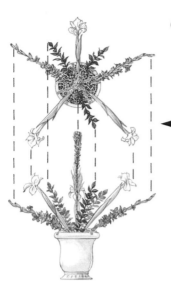

④ INSERT LINE MATERIAL

Before you begin make sure that the leaves that would be in the container have all been removed, and half fill the vase or urn with dilute cut flower preservative solution. The first task is to establish the vertical axis — for this you will need one or more upright stems which are pushed down to the bottom of the container. The choice is large and it is up to you. There are leafy or coloured stems such as Dogwood, Beech, Privet, Elaeagnus, Butcher's Broom and Box. The choice with flowering stems is even greater — a few of the popular ones are Escallonia, Lily, Lilac, Forsythia, Camellia, Kniphofia, Rose, Quince, Foxtail Lily and Delphinium. The laterals forming the base of the display should be inserted after the vertical axis. Their length is usually about ²/₃ of the vertical line material and 5 are used for a modest-sized arrangement — use 7 for a large display. These laterals can all be the same or different material — it's a matter of choice. Whatever you use, do make sure that the ends will be below the water surface. Finally, push in 3 stems of line material which will form the middle ribs of the display, as shown.

⑤ INSERT DOMINANT MATERIAL

The basic skeleton has been created and both the height and width of the display are now fixed. Within this boundary you have to place dominant flowers at intervals all round the arrangement — and that's where the skill comes in. A few hints. Don't just have one of anything — place several examples within the display. Next, group some of the flowers together rather than setting them all out singly. Cut the stems of the largest blooms so that the flowers will be set back in the arrangement and not standing on the outside, and place some of the dominant blooms near the top to ensure centres of interest at several levels.

⑥ INSERT FILLER MATERIAL

The arrangement is now spotted with a collection of eye-catching blooms which are separated by foliage or empty spaces. The final step is to reduce the contrasts by the use of filler material and this once again is a skilful task. Foliage is often important here, especially for covering the chicken wire, fastenings and the rim of the container. This foliage need not be plain green — you can use grey-leaved Senecio or Helichrysum, or variegated leaves such as Aucuba, Ivy and Euonymus. The choice of filler flowers from the florist, garden and countryside is vast — old favourites include Solidago, Statice, Lady's Mantle, Hebe, Santolina, Mimosa, Gypsophila and Freesia. Don't forget the berried plants in winter — Skimmia, Holly, Pernettya, Snowberry etc. Finally, a few hints. Begin from the top and work downwards. Turn the arrangement as you work rather than trying to peer round the side, and remove some of the filler flowers and leaves if the arrangement looks overcrowded. The last task is to ensure that the water level is 1-2 in. (3-5 cm) below the rim.

The LINE style — Ikebana

① CHOOSE A CONTAINER

A pinholder is an excellent way of securing heavy stems in a Line arrangement — it is of little use where a large number of thin stems are to be supported. The usual container is a shallow waterproof dish. If a tall container is to be used, partly fill with sand and then add a layer of melted candle wax. Push a shallow dish firmly into the wax and when set fix the pinholder as described below.

② FIX THE PINHOLDER

The pinholder has to be fixed securely to the bottom of the dish. Place 3 small knobs of kneaded adhesive clay ('fix') to the bottom of the pinholder and press it down on to the dish. Pinholder, hands and dish must be clean and dry — protect your hands with a cloth or gloves if necessary. Position is a matter of personal choice — for Oriental arrangements it is often set off-centre. Half fill the dish with dilute cut flower preservative solution.

③ INSERT LINE MATERIAL

Gladiolus is featured in this example, but many other plants can be used such as Nandina, Forsythia, Flowering Cherry, Lily, Rosemary, Bamboo, Conifer, Heliconia and Rose. Woody stems should be cut at a sharp angle — cut soft stems straight across. Next, push the stem vertically on to or between the spikes. If the stem is to be set at an angle, hold the top of the stem with one hand and apply gentle but steady pressure with the other hand held just above the spikes. Push away from the sloping face, as shown. In this Moribana arrangement the taller stem (the Heaven line) is inserted first and then the shorter one (the Man line).

④ FINISH THE ARRANGEMENT

The final step is to insert the Earth line — in this case a small group of Spider Chrysanthemums and Camellia leaves. Thin stems may need a 'shoe' (a small piece of thick stem into which the narrow shoot is inserted) before being pushed on to the spikes — alternatively you can wire several thin stems together. The pinholder can be covered with gravel if it is visible. Add sufficient cut flower preservative solution to ensure that all the stem bases are fully immersed.

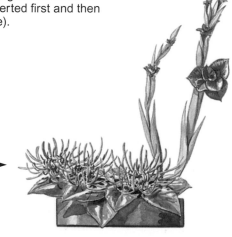

STEP 10 : Care for the ARRANGEMENT

● TOP UP REGULARLY

Water is taken up at a surprisingly high rate, so it is usually necessary to top up the vase or dampen the floral foam every day. Use a long-spouted watering can and add water slowly and gently where space is restricted or foam is being moistened. Use drinking water or rainwater — do not use water which has been chemically softened. The water in the vase should not be changed unless it has become cloudy and evil-smelling.

● USE A CUT FLOWER PRESERVATIVE

Buy a packet or bottle of cut flower preservative — see page 188. It will help to kill the bacteria which contaminate the water and attack the cut ends of the stems. Proprietary preservatives generally contain a cut flower food (cane sugar) as well as a bacteriocide.

● PROTECT FROM HEAT & DRAUGHTS

Draughts cause excessive moisture loss, but are not as harmful as overheating. Keep your arrangement away from direct sunlight, radiators and open fires. The top of a TV set is not a good place for a floral display.

● KEEP AWAY FROM FRUIT

Do not place your arrangement close to a bowl of fruit. Apples, pears etc emit ethylene — a gas which shortens the life of flowers.

● MIST OCCASIONALLY

Apply a mist-like spray above and around the arrangement once it has been placed in position. You can buy a trigger-operated mister at any garden centre, and it should be used regularly if the air is hot and dry. Do not spray close to delicate petals which may be damaged by water droplets.

● DEAD-HEAD WHEN NECESSARY

The vase-life of one flower may be quite different from another species. Remove dead blooms promptly so that the display can continue to look attractive for several more days.

● REVIVE WILTED FLOWERS

If some blooms have wilted it is often possible to revive them by cutting off an inch of stem under water and then using the 'wilted flower treatment' described on page 243. Once revived, return the stems to the arrangement as soon as possible.

● STORE CONTAINER & MECHANICS

When the display is over both the container and metal mechanics (pinholder or chicken wire) should be washed thoroughly in soap and water before drying and storing. Keep moist floral foam wrapped in polythene.

| | AFTER 0 DAYS | AFTER 3 DAYS | AFTER 8 DAYS |

GOOD AFTERCARE

Flower preservative added to vase water. Plants protected from draughts. Fine mist applied to blooms.

POOR AFTERCARE

Flower preservative not added to vase water. Plants not protected from draughts. Mist not applied to blooms.

Chapter 8

PLANT INDEX

Acknowledgements

The author wishes to thank Gill Jackson and Ian Harris for their painstaking work which did so much to transform the words, designs and illustrations into this book. Grateful acknowledgement is also made for the help and images received from Tyrone and Linda McGlinchey (Garden World Images).

There were many others who provided both time and expertise — MD Larry Finlay, Gareth Pottle, Phil Evans, Michelle Signore, Janine Giovanni and Claire Evans of Transworld Publishers; Stuart Booker of Spot On; together with Liz Whiting, Georgia and Mark Whitman, and Darren Clark. To all these people and organisations I owe a great debt of gratitude.

The photographs in this book were drawn from many sources. Acknowledgement is made as follows for images used for the first time: Photographer/Photograph owner or agent (*l* = left, *r* = right, *t* = top, *m* = middle, *b* = bottom) Steve Gosling/Flowerphotos 239 *ml*; Carol Sharp/Flowerphotos 129*br*, 222*br*; Derek Harris/The Garden Collection 199*bl*; Flora Press/The Garden Collection 203*bl*; Neil Sutherland/The Garden Collection 200, 213*tr*, 213*bl*, 214; Georgianna Lane/GWI 198*tr*; Garden World Images 202*ml*, 204, 205*tr*, 205*bl*, 210*tl*, 210*mr*, 212, 215*ml*, 216*tr*, 220, 222*tr*, 223*tl*, 223*mr*, 228*bl*; Dave Logan/istockphoto 4; Clover/Photoshot 223*bl*; Lived In Images/Photoshot 206*bl*; Red Cover/Photoshot 199*tr*, 209*bl*, 215*tr*, 215*br*; Tommy Candler/Elizabeth Whiting 198*bl*; Quentin Harriott/Elizabeth Whiting 203*tr*; Rodney Hyett/Elizabeth Whiting 211; Tim Imrie/Elizabeth Whiting 207*bl*; Lu Jeffery/Elizabeth Whiting 201*tr*, 201*bl*; Di Lewis/Elizabeth Whiting 197, 202*tr*, 202*br*, 206*tr*, 229*bl*, 234*tr*; David Lloyd/Elizabeth Whiting 182, 207*tr*, 218, 228*tr*, 234*bl*; Gwenan Murphy/Elizabeth Whiting 216*bl*; Steve Russell/Elizabeth Whiting 210*bl*; Elizabeth Whiting 222*ml*.